The Transmanaut Chronicles

The Transmanaut Chronicles

A Coming of Age Story from 1977

Chris Pittard

Olympiad Publishing
San Antonio, Texas

OLYMPIAD PUBLISHING COMPANY
1777 N.E. LOOP 410, SUITE 600
San Antonio, Texas 78217

ISBN: 978-0-578-48495-2

Second Printing, April 2019

Cover Art: Dr. Melissa Duvall
Inside Text: Design Mark Blizard

Printed in the United States of America

To my parents without whom I have no car; and to the other Transmanauts, Hector, Tony, and Dana—thanks guys, the story has finally been told.

Remember—L'audace, l'audace, toujours l'audace.

Who dares, wins.

Acknowledgements

"Acknowledgments" sounds rather harsh. Therefore, rather than acknowledging anyone, I would like to thank several people for their contributions to this book. First, I'd like to thank my brother Dana for inspiring me to write this book after his dramatic reunion with someone we met during the 1977 Road Trip. After that, it was a matter of resuscitating memories from the summer of 1977 to give the book the authenticity it deserved. I leaned heavily on those who lived it, for their memories, perceptions, stories and dialogue to bring the book to life, and to make the story as fun and accurate as possible. Thank you Hector, Tony, and everyone else who contributed; you know who you are. I would also like to thank Frederick Williams of Prosperity Publications for his guidance and help in making this book a readable, and hopefully enjoyable, product. Thanks Fred. Finally, I must thank my wife Karen for her support and input as the story took shape, and her encouragement when it looked as if the book would never get done. Thank you, dear.

Contents

Prologue

1977. A different time in America, a simpler time. The Vietnam War had recently concluded, we had a new President in the White House, and the world seemed a fairly tranquil place. Hector, Tony, my brother Dana, and I, were all good friends in 1977. We weren't grown up yet, and the world was still a playground to us. This was a time for us to have fun before going on to the more serious pursuits in life. The laws for drinking were different then – you could drink at 18. I was 20, and they were all 18, so we were all legal to drink in the summer of 1977.

The sexual revolution and the Disco era were in full swing. You know, as red-blooded American males, the thought of sex and girls was never far from our minds. We lived in a time when sex was fairly casual, thanks to the Pill; and there was only the threat of gonorrhea, or syphilis, or maybe herpes. The worst case scenario was if you got a girl pregnant.

In 1977 we were just getting started with our lives; the three of them going off to college, and me off to law school. We didn't do drugs, had never been arrested, had no illegitimate children, and had no involvement in any gang activities. Instead, we had dreams of doing important things in our future and were looking for one last opportunity to have fun, a last fling together before we went our separate ways in life, never knowing if we would ever see one another again.

And when you're from Texas, what better destination than California for a last-fling road trip. California beckoned to us with the promise of beautiful girls, beaches, Hollywood, partying, and unknown adventures in the Land of Sunshine. That makes for a volatile combination – raging hormones, drinking and a road trip. It doesn't get any better than that!

So, in June 1977, we four young Black guys take off on the adventure of our lives; on a road trip to Cali to see what's on the other side. What could possibly go wrong…

Caged

What the fuck am I doing here, and how the hell did I get here? My thoughts raged for the hundredth time as I looked around the inside of the Van Nuys police station. It was two o'clock in the morning, and all the images of the previous few hours ran through my mind like a kaleidoscope – racing down Van Nuys Boulevard; the arrest, the ride to the police station, the booking, and finally, the ultimate degradation – being chained to a bench like some dangerous animal.

Yeah, my ass was chained...yeah, chained...to a damned bench, between a fuckin' drug dealer and a mother fuckin' pimp. This was a dismal place. Bleak gray walls stared back at me from across the corridor. They were encrusted with a dark grime of the dirt and residue from years of bodily fluids of suspects and criminals smeared against them. The bare-bulbed light above me was encased in a metal grating and showed the walls in all their nasty glory and the years of neglect. Damn, even the light bulb was in a cage.

Down the hall, the holding cells were full of suspects and criminals. The air reeked of the sharp, sour smells of urine, and the pungent sickening smell of vomit and loose bowels. Damn, somebody shit on the floor.

The prisoners in the holding cells were yelling and shouting, cursing at each other. The cops were screaming obscenities at prisoners, putting them in choke holds, pushing prisoners against walls – doing what they had to do to subdue their charges. The din was frightening, and assaulted my ears with its cacophony of outrage and fear. I now understood how the monkeys at the zoo felt, trapped in their cages. Although I wasn't trapped on an alien planet run by apes, it was all so surreal, and to me it was "a maaaadhouse, a maaaadhouse!!"

The jail and the holding cells weren't pretty, but they had the desired effect on the newly-arrested prisoners. Some of the other prisoners had been there for a while. You could see the despair in their lifeless eyes, and the hopelessness in the way they shuffled, manacled at their feet and wrists. I didn't belong in here with these felonious denizens of the night, sweating out my incarceration on a bench shared with a drug dealer and a pimp.

I thought again, *What the hell am I doing here? A 20-year old Black guy, a newly commissioned second lieutenant in the Army, on my way to law school at the University of Texas, and now I'm in jail?* That just didn't seem fair.

This trip started so well. I had just graduated from the University of Texas, and my brother, Dana, and our two friends Hector and Tony, had just graduated from high school. Dana was going off to West Point to eventually pursue a career in the Army; Hector was going to New Mexico State University on a track scholarship; and Tony was going to Texas Tech University on a ROTC scholarship. So, this was a perfect opportunity to go on a road trip.

My parents had just given me a brand new, special edition, black and gold, Trans-Am, and we were determined to hit the highway going somewhere. We wanted to do something that none of us had ever done before – go on a trip without our parents, and do things that young men had been doing for centuries – you know, sow our wild oats, party, drink, meet new women and have fun. And what better place to do it than Cali. And now here I was, in jail, in Cali, and wondering how it happened...

Into the Desert

The night before we were supposed to leave, I could barely sleep. I spent part of the evening with my girlfriend at her house watching TV, but eventually had to go home to get some sleep before the next day. We were going to get an early start in the morning and I needed to hit the sack, but I was just too excited to sleep well. Every time my head hit the pillow, all I could think about was driving to LA, and who we were going to meet and what we were going to do. This was going to be the adventure of a lifetime, and I couldn't wait to get started.

I woke up to the smell of frying chicken and knew Mom was in the kitchen preparing food for the trip. I got up about 5:30 that morning after just a few hours of sleep. With the adrenaline pumping I was hyped and ready to go.

I went to Dana's bedroom door, knocked, and yelled, "Hey Dana, you awake yet?" Huh, no answer. Then I heard water running in the bathroom. I walked in and saw he was brushing his teeth.

"Good morning, you almost ready?"

"Hm hmph," he mumbled around his toothbrush.

"Okay, I should be ready in a few minutes."

"Okay," he said as he took the toothbrush out of his mouth, "Me too."

As I brushed my teeth and washed up, I contemplated our reflections in the mirror. Dana was tall, brown-skinned, handsome, intelligent and cocky, with a big combed-out Afro. He was extremely personable and liked by most people. He had a way of endearing himself to strangers with his warm, sincere, caring eyes and his personable demeanor. He would always be successful with the ladies.

I looked at my reflection with a critical eye. I've been described physically in a lot of different ways, not all of them flattering. At that time, at 5'10", I was slender [sometimes described as "skinny", mostly by guys jealous of my girlfriend], fairly muscular with my six-pack abs, and I was shorter than Dana. I was light-skinned, with a blondish light brown Afro, and green eyes, that have been described as pretty, piercing and laser-like. I like to think of myself as being reasonably attractive. *Hmm, not a bad package,* I thought to myself – I guess I'm ready for prime time, and ready to take this on the road to Cali.

I finished up in the bathroom, went to my room to get dressed, and yelled back down the hallway, "What are you wearing?"

He yelled back, "My overalls with a t-shirt, and, um, tennis shoes. What are you wearing?"

"Painter pants, Kappa shirt, Kappa running shoes and red driving cap." That was my **de rigeur** driving outfit for this trip. I loved wearing Kappa paraphernalia, which was mostly red, and of course, the red driving cap (like the English, but much more ethnic) perched jauntily atop my 'fro.

"You always wear that Kappa crap."

"Yeah, yeah, you wish you could, so be quiet," I laughed.

At about 6 o'clock, Dana and I walked into the kitchen, the smell of frying chicken wafting into our nostrils. Mom was still rushing around frying chicken and boiling eggs for our trip. "Good morning Mom, the chicken really smells good." I said inhaling the aroma.

"Hope it tastes good," Mom replied. "You know me, I've been up all night frying chicken and getting your food ready for the trip."

"Thanks Mom," Dana chimed in. "We're really going to enjoy eating all of it on the trip."

"You never know where you can eat on the road between here and Los Angeles, so I wanted to make sure you all had enough food to eat." Mom said.

I started laughing, "Well, you know, it's not like it used to be back when we were kids, with plenty of places to eat along the road, like Mickey D's, KFC, and Jack in the Crack."

"Where? What?" Mom asked.

"I mean McDonald's, Kentucky Fried Chicken and Jack in the Box. There're plenty of fast food joints along the way."

"Aren't you all driving through the desert?" she asked. "There aren't many places out in the desert, so you're going to need this food."

"Yeah, true, but it's not like back in the day when we couldn't eat at certain places, but we really love your fried chicken." Dana said joking, "Yeah, we don't have to pee in bottles any more because there're plenty of places for us to go to the bathroom, even in the desert."

"Okay, but you know I worry about you boys, so I just want to make sure you're safe."

Dana and I knew Mom was a worrier. We tried to assuage her fears by agreeing with her concerns. "Mom, we'll be fine, but we'll call you every night, okay?"

"Okay," she said with a little sob in her voice, "I'm sure you'll be fine but you know me, I worry."

"We know, but we'll be alright," Dana assured her.

We helped Mom wrap up the chicken in foil, and put the eggs in sandwich baggies to keep them fresh, and then put all the food in a fairly large blue and white cooler with cold sodas and bags of chips. Mom had outdone herself in preparing food for the trip.

"You boys need to eat something before you leave the house," she insisted.

"Mom, we'll be fine, we figured we'd eat on the road," I said.

Dana agreed.

But the chicken smelled so good, we both kept out a piece to munch on as we left the kitchen. I gobbled mine while standing there. As Dana ate his chicken, I grabbed the cooler, hefted it up and walked to the front door where our bags were packed from the night before. We were seasoned travelers and knew how to pack economically. We packed fairly light because there were four of us. We limited ourselves to one suitcase each, so as not to load us down too much. We were driving a Trans Am, not particularly known for its cavernous trunk space, so we had to pack light. We also needed room in the car for our food; I mean we had to eat, so we couldn't pack too many clothes.

I opened the front door to take the bags and cooler out to the car. It was a typical El Paso morning, with the sun beginning to rise in the east, promising another bright sunny day without a cloud in the sky. This was a great morning to start this momentous trip and it gave the promise of great things to come.

Dad walked into the entry way about that time. "You guys about ready to go?" He asked.

"Yep," I said, "I think we've got it covered."

"Run it down for me," Dad said.

I knew what he meant – he was the master packer and the all-time driver on most of our cross-country trips. He had given us some tips as we went through our planning, and now he was going to grill me on our plan for the trip.

"We're going to drive to Tucson tonight, then to San Diego, where we're going to visit Sea World and spend the night," I replied. "Then we're going on to Los Angeles, spend several days with Hector's aunt and visit some beaches and maybe Universal Studios. We're going up to San Francisco and visit Dr. Witten and his family, Mom got the directions, then back through LA, and back home."

"How are you going to get there?"

"I-10, I-8, going west, then I-5, going north in California. Mom had some Trip Tiks made up for us to help us get around." I had an answer for everything.

"How long will you be gone?"

"Two weeks."

"You have enough money?"

"Yeah, Dana and I used our graduation money and savings, and Tony and Hector came up with their money. Tony had to use some of his savings, and I think Hector either borrowed the money or used his graduation money. Everybody pitched in $500. We figured we'd need about two grand for the trip based on our mileage, food, and hotel calculations. Staying with Hector's aunt and the Wittens will help a lot with the expenses."

"All in cash?"

"No, we took your advice and we're putting half in traveler's checks, just in case."

"Okay good. So, what, is the trip about three or four thousand miles?"

"Yeah, about that."

"What about gas?"

"Umm, probably gas up every 250 miles or so. The Trans Am doesn't get great gas mileage."

"Yeah, you're going to pass everything on the highway except a gas station." Dad laughed.

"Umm hmm, yeah, we gassed up last night."

"Okay, it sounds like you all have a good handle on everything, but just in case, here's a little gift from us to help out on your trip." Dad handed me $200 in twenties.

"Thanks Dad."

"That's from both of us," Mom insisted.

"Thank you Mom," Dana said.

"Need any help loading up the car?" Dad asked. Not that he really wanted to help, but I think he thought he needed to offer to help.

"Nope, we've got it," I said.

Dana picked up our two bags and walked through the open front door taking them out to the car. I grabbed the cooler and followed right behind him. There it was, in the driveway. I smiled at how glossy and sleek it looked – like a night predator ready to leap at its prey.

"Damn," Dana said. "The Trans looks good!"

"Thanks," I said, "I washed and waxed it last night."

Yeah, the car – a shiny midnight-black Trans Am with gold striping and a huge gold firebird on the hood, literally gleamed in the morning light. The car looked like a bird of prey with the rectangular headlights peeking from behind the hooded eagle-eyes and beaked front panel. The TA-6.6 Liter, 200-hp V8 engine made my car one of the fastest stock cars on the road, and just exciting to behold rolling down the highway – it looked fast standing still even without a T-top.

The interior looked just as good. The dashboard shimmered with a kind of gold metallic material with the racing gauges for the tachometer, speedometer, oil, water/temperature, and battery. The speedometer showed the speed in MPH and KPH, which was a first for me, and redlined at 120 MPH/200 KPH. The steering wheel, made of thick leather, was a racing style wheel with three gold lamé spokes designed for agile handling of the car. The seats were a plush, glove-soft velour, and midnight black, as was the entire interior, except for the gold metallic applique accents interspersed in the cockpit of the car. And for our entertainment, the 8-track system boomed out the music through state of the art speakers. I loved this dangerous-looking car.

Dana tossed our bags in the trunk, and put the cooler in the front seat where he would be sitting. We knew the cooler would make it a little tight for him, at least on the initial part of the trip. The plan was to eat up the food the first day, and then store the cooler in the trunk for most of the trip. We also wanted the cooler when we went to the beach. It was an essential commodity. Once we got all the stuff in the car, we went back to the front door where our parents had been watching us load up. I hugged Mom, and said goodbye, then Dana hugged Mom and said goodbye. Mom could barely contain her tears – this was the first time her "babies" had left her to go off on their own on such a trip. Dad didn't have much to say, I think he was happy to see us go. I think he considered this a "rite of passage" to manhood and he was glad to see us getting out and spreading our wings.

He didn't give us much advice, except, "Have a good trip, stay out of jail, and don't get anyone pregnant." Then he laughed as Mom looked at him with that look of "I can't believe you just said that."

Dana and I walked back over to the car, got in, and closed the doors. I felt like we were the pilot and co-pilot of some sort of jet aircraft getting ready to take off. The dashboard certainly resembled a jet aircraft with all the dials and gauges, and with the bucket seats, the front interior gave the appearance of a cockpit. We buckled in and I started the car. That beautiful machine responded with a nice, gratifying growl that settled down to a whisper-quiet idle. Oh yeah!

In preparation for the trip, I had recorded all my favorite jams on several 8-track tapes and put them where I could get to them, and Dana positioned the food for easy access in front of his seat. Before I put in the first tape, Dana and I just looked at each other, and we laughed enjoying the moment.

"Are you ready for this?" I asked.

"Definitely! Let's get this party started!"

"Alright, let's do this!" I pushed the 8-track tape in and the music of Mass Production's *Wine Flow Disco* blared out of the speakers. This was my theme song for the trip – "*Stomp your feet to the rhythm of the drummer, yeah; clap your hands to the guitar and the piano player, Hey, yeah, yeah; let's get down where the wine is flowing freely everywhere you go; let's get down to the music of the Wine Flow Disco…*" We started moving our heads to that driving beat and that great bass line…this was going to be fun!

I backed the car out of the driveway, and waved to our parents who continued to watch from the front door, and then we headed down the street on our way to pick up Hector and Tony. They lived a couple of doors from each other on Wedgewood Avenue, a few miles from our house, so it took just a few minutes to get to their houses.

We'd known Hector and Tony since their early days in elementary school – they and Dana had pretty much grown up as best friends. The three of them spent their high school careers as "brothers from another mother," and at times were inseparable. Tony and Hector were very popular athletes in high school…both on the varsity football team. They both had outgoing personalities, but of the two of them, Tony was the more gregarious. In other words, you always knew when Tony was around. He liked being the center of attention and the life of the party. Tony was tall, in great physical shape, and his complexion was a sort of chocolate brown, with a big wide smile and laugh that could be heard for miles around.

Hector was quieter than Tony, but he was still very visible and liked to have fun. Hector was a little taller than Tony, and also in great physical shape. He was a handsome guy, probably a little darker than Tony with a smile that could light up a room.

We knew with them on this momentous road trip, we'd have a great time. They were the kind of guys you wanted on a road trip to Cali. The decision to include them was an easy one.

We pulled up to Hector's house still jamming to *Wine Flow Disco,* and I honked the horn. Hector came to the door and waved. His mom was right beside him. His mom, Nell, was an attractive dark-skinned woman with an oval-shaped face and well-coiffed hair. He motioned for me to come to the door, so I turned off the engine, got out, and walked up to his front door.

"Good morning," I said to Hector's mom.

She looked a little wistful as she replied, "Good morning. I just wanted to make sure you have all the information for Rose."

"Okay," I said, "I think we've got her address and phone number. We'll call when we get close and get directions to her house."

"That's fine," she said, then turned and looked at Hector, "Make sure you treat her house with respect. You know your Uncle Rudi, he doesn't play, and he runs a tight ship."

"Mom, I'll make sure everybody knows the deal about Uncle Rudi," Hector said, and turned to me, "C'mon Chris, let's go." He hugged his mom, picked up his hard case piece of luggage and started walking towards the car.

We waved good bye to his mom as she watched us from the

front door. Hector followed me to the rear of the car. I opened the trunk, took a look at the available room and stowed his bag into the rear corner, then slammed the trunk shut. We walked to the driver's side of the car.

"You get in behind me since you have the longest legs, and I'll keep my seat forward for you," I said as I slid the seat forward.

Hector squeezed behind the driver's seat into his designated spot in the Trans Am. I closed my door, started the engine, and backed out of the driveway onto Wedgewood Avenue, a sort of busy artery on that side of town. Although Tony's house was only a few houses down, I had to be careful not to hit any fast-moving traffic coming down the street. A few seconds later we pulled into Tony's driveway.

Tony bounded out his front door with his small piece of luggage. No sign of Aunt Loo or Uncle George, at the door. Tony looked eager to get started.

I opened my door and stood up, "Tony, you ready to go?" I yelled.

"Oh hell yeah!" He yelled back.

"Where's Aunt Loo or Uncle George?"

"They're inside, I already said goodbye to them," Tony said as he walked up to the car.

"Okay, hold on, get in on Dana's side."

Dana opened his door, got out and said, "Hey Tony."

"Hey Dana, where do I sit?"

"Behind me. You and Hector will be in the back, me and Chris in front." You could tell Dana was proud of that fact and made sure Tony knew it as he slid the seat forward.

"That's cool, it's y'all's car, I'm just happy to be going."

I walked around to the opposite side of the car and Tony handed me his bag. He slid in behind Dana and folded his long frame into the back seat next to Hector. I went around to the back and opened the trunk to fit his bag into the already crowded trunk. This is where I began to earn my reputation as an apprentice "master packer." I rearranged all four bags to make sure they all fit, and we had room for any additional stuff we might want to put in there later, and then closed the trunk.

I came around to the driver's side, opened my door, and got in. I turned around to Hector and Tony in the back and asked, "Do you all have your money?"

"Yep," they said in unison.

"Okay," I said. "Give it to me now and I'll put it in the glove compartment. At some point during the trip we'll convert half of the money into traveler's checks, okay?"

"Alright," Tony chortled.

"No problem," Hector said as they handed me their money. I didn't bother counting it, but placed it in the glove compartment with Dana's and my money then locked it.

"Buckle up." I pulled my hat down, started up the car, and hit the "play" button on the 8-track – time to get this show on the road. Again I backed out slowly onto Wedgewood Avenue, and we snaked our way through the morning traffic to I-10 West.

"Man I just love this car," Hector said. "I remember the day you got it and brought it around for us to check it out. I thought to myself, 'Damn that is one bad motherfucking ride' and I could just see the four of us taking a trip in it, somewhere." He laughed.

"I guess your wish came true, but this isn't the car I originally ordered." I said.

"What do you mean?" Tony asked.

"Okay, going all the way back to last year. My parents surprised me last year with the idea of giving me a car for graduation. I thought they were going to give me a used car, like a Mustang fastback or something; but they surprised me again and told me I could pick out a new car. Well, at that time, my dream car was the new black and gold Trans Am with the new headlights that made it look like a bird of prey. When I mentioned that to them, they said okay and we went to test drive one last Thanksgiving. The car wasn't black and gold, but a pretty chocolate brown with a TA-6.6 liter engine. Man, I fell in love with that car. I'd never driven a car like that and I knew that's what I wanted."

"Okay, so what happened?" Hector asked.

"When I came home for spring break, Dad, Dana and I went out to the Pontiac dealership to pick out a car. I wanted a special edition, but Dad was only going to pay for a more basic car with black wheels and vinyl interior. I insisted on the 8-track player and the TA-6.6 liter engine. I wanted to be able to jam to my music and outrun anything on the road."

"You said this wasn't the car you originally ordered – so what, the other one didn't come in?" Hector asked as we headed towards I-10.

"Yep. I never waited for anything with so much anticipation as that damn car. I used to dream of driving it on the California coast like the poster I had in my dorm room. I found out, the greater the anticipation, the greater the disappointment."

"Okay, okay, I get it, what happened?" Hector asked.

I looked over at Dana, "After we got back from graduation in Austin, the Pontiac dealership called and told me the car had never been ordered, or never been made or whatever; but the bottom line was – it wasn't coming in. I thought 'Damn!' and told Dad what happened. He called them and they invited us to go down there and pick out another car at a discounted price."

Dana took over the story at that point, "We went down there to look at some other cars. As a matter of fact we just passed the dealership back there on Montana. Anyway, Chris and I looked around the lot until we found this car, and Chris fell in love with it. We went back to the office where Dad was waiting with the sales guy and we told him which car we wanted."

"What happened then?" Tony asked.

Dana continued, "The sales guy looked up the price and told Dad that even with the discount this car would cost an additional $1,500. I looked at Chris and told him I would chip in $500 from my savings and graduation money if he could come up with the rest. Chris said he had $1,000 in savings and graduation money, so we raced out of the dealership leaving Dad there with the sales guy while we ran to the bank before it closed to get the money."

I finished the story as we entered the ramp for I-10 and began accelerating into the left lane, "When we got back, the sales guy had all the papers ready, and within a few minutes we rolled off the lot driving this car. Damn, that was a great feeling. Dana really came through for me, and I appreciate it."

Dana was a little embarrassed, "That's what brothers are for."

"I guess you left before they explained how to open the hood, huh?" Tony laughed.

"Yeah, that was pretty funny when I came by you guys' house to show you the car for the first time, I didn't know how to open the hood. Fuck it, it didn't matter, I had the car and I was driving this bad motherfucker."

"Damn right," Dana agreed as Tony and Hector laughed.

"So, what's this about your Uncle Rudi?" I asked Hector, changing the subject. "What's the big deal?"

"Mom had to assure Uncle Rudi that we would behave ourselves while we stayed with them," Hector said somewhat embarrassed.

"What do you mean?" Dana asked.

"Uncle Rudi is a former Marine gunny, and runs his household like a tight ship. He doesn't like anything that disrupts his household."

"Terrific, a former gunnery sergeant," I said. "You know that's what we do best – disrupt – but I think we can handle him. What do you think Dana?"

"Yeah, I think once we wow him with our military background and future military plans, he'll be alright. We'll just be careful at the house, okay?"

14

"Alright," Hector said, "I just don't want us to fuck up at Aunt Rose's house – Tony."

"What? Why you got to say that to me?" Tony smirked.

"Because you know you're the one always fucking up, so you'll have to tone it down at his house, got it?"

"Alright, let's not get all hot and bothered ten minutes into the trip, I'll be cool." Tony promised.

"Uh huh," Hector said.

"We'll all be cool at Aunt Rose's house, understood?" I commanded. "We're lucky she's letting us stay there so we don't want to fuck it up."

"Okay okay," Tony said. "So, what direction we going in?"

"West you dummy. You don't remember us sitting down at my table, in my kitchen, looking at those maps of the United States and planning this trip? Hell, the maps were even color-coded for you, Tony. Texas was purple, New Mexico yellow, Arizona pink, and California orange. You don't remember us going through that exercise of trying to figure out where we were going on this trip and how we were going to get there? What are you, stupid?"

"Nope. I just wanted to make sure you remembered since you're doing all the driving. I didn't want us getting lost. Who's got the maps?"

Dana chimed in, "I've got the Trip Tiks and the U.S. maps with all the interstates and secondary roads."

"What's a Trip Tik?" Hector asked.

"The Trip Tiks are maps provided by AAA for a specific route," Dana answered. "Mom requested them once we told her we were going to Cali, through Los Angeles and San Francisco. They're "flip" maps of the route that fold out to a larger map if you want more detail on that part of the route. AAA also provides up-to-date information on highway construction, detours, and even maps out ways of going around the construction."

Dana pulled out one of the Trip Tiks for Texas and New Mexico to show Hector and Tony how it looked. He flipped it open between the seats so they could see the map.

"Oh okay," Hector said, "I've got it."

These Trip Tik maps had always been helpful when my family traveled cross-country, and would prove to be helpful on this road trip. But at this particular time, I didn't need the Trip Tiks for the initial portion of the trip. I had studied the maps the night before and knew we had to travel west on I-10 to Tucson, and then I-8 to San Diego. The U.S. Army had shown its infinite wisdom and trust in my abilities as an officer and a gentleman by

15

commissioning me about two weeks beforehand, so I was pretty confident in my ability to navigate on this trip.

As we continued west on I-10, Tony chirped, "When are we going to stop?"

"Are we there yet?" I pantomimed in a mocking voice, "What, you need to stop already?"

"Well, I didn't eat any breakfast because you all wanted to leave so early to get to Tucson. You said we would eat somewhere on the road. So, when are we going to stop?"

"I figured we'd stop near Las Cruces. That okay?"

"Yeah, that's fine," Tony answered.

"Maybe we can visit New Mexico State University while we're in the area?" Hector suggested, "I want to check out the stadium."

"Alright, sounds like a plan, and we're not in any big rush. Okay by me," I said.

Once we left the El Paso city limits I hit the gas and we were rolling. We were listening to the 12" maxi-version of *Dancin'* by Crown Heights Affair, my favorite dancing song of all time. Oh yeah, we were definitely rocking now. I looked in my rear view mirror to see what Tony and Hector were doing because I could hear them laughing in the back. I saw them doing some sort of synchronized sitting dance moves to the music. As silly as it seemed, it also looked pretty cool. Dana watched and began to mimic their moves. Their heads bobbed back and forth to synchronized moves, with their hands to the sides of their heads. Then they switched up and started moving their heads and shoulders from front to back and holding their hands as fists in front of their chests. At every fourth beat they would alternate between the two moves.

"The music is too good to waste," Hector said, "So we're dancing in our seats, like at a club when you can't get a girl to dance with you. You know something about that don't you Dana?" he laughed.

Dana jumped right back at him, "At least I had a girlfriend Hector."

16

"Who, Sonja? I was dating her first, before you were even interested in her."

Uh oh, here we go. I thought. Dana and Hector had both dated Sonja during their senior year and it was a source of contention between them. I needed to nip this in the bud before it became a real issue on the trip.

"Did either of you hit that?"

"Uh, well, no," Dana said with a sheepish grin.

"No," Hector echoed his answer.

"Then neither of you has any bragging rights. It sounds to me like she dated the both of you when it suited her – you Hector during the football season, and Dana during the prom and formal ball season. Am I right?"

"Yeah," they said.

"So, let's move on, okay? Bro's before ho's, right?"

"Damn right!" Hector said, and he and Dana slapped hands through the opening between the seats. Whew – an early disaster averted, maybe now we could get on with the trip.

While all this was going on, I saw a sign for a little roadside picnic area located a little outside the Las Cruces city limits. We'd been traveling about an hour and I figured everybody was hungry.

"There's a picnic area over there." I pointed to the spot.

"Great," Tony said. "I'm starved, let's pull over and eat."

I pulled into the designated picnic area and stopped in front of one of several tables. Each picnic table, covered by a little green-painted corrugated metal shade, was accompanied by a metal trash can with hinged fitted tops held in place by a metal frame bolted to a cement block. The tables were green-painted pine boards that appeared to be pretty well kept. No bathroom facilities, just the picnic tables and trash cans.

As we got out of our black and gold chariot with the cold air-conditioned interior, the dry heat coming off the surrounding dessert hit us like a hot brick wall. The picnic area was like an oasis in the middle of the New Mexico desert. Very little was out there except a multitude of tumbleweeds. There were so many of them it felt like we were starring in *The Attack of the Tumbleweeds*. The desert was also populated by fast-moving jackrabbits, lightning-quick coyotes, and the occasional roadrunner. At that time of the morning the temperature had already begun to climb, and it was going to get even hotter pretty quick. We didn't want to be out in the middle of the desert as the mercury rose to triple digits.

Dana pulled the cooler out of the front seat area, and walked it over to the nearest picnic table. The metal covering gave a modicum of shade and helped protect us from the ascending hot summer sun.

"Okay guys," he said to Hector and Tony. "We've got fried chicken, boiled eggs, chips and sodas in the cooler. We also put some napkins in there."

"You got any plates?" Hector asked.

"Oh crap," I said. "No, we didn't bring any paper plates or utensils. Just use the napkins as plates; you're just going to have to eat with your fingers."

"That's no problem," Tony said cheerfully. "Let's eat!"

"Alright dig in," Dana said.

Everyone reached in and started pulling out foil-wrapped pieces of chicken, boiled eggs, chips and a soda. The early morning quiet was disturbed by the sound of ripping foil as we hungrily attacked the chicken.

"Wow, the chicken's still hot!" Tony exclaimed as he chomped on a large breast. "This is really good!" He laughed, "You know I'm a 'breast man.'"

"Yeah yeah, me too, and I'm a 'leg man' too," I said with a drumstick in my hand.

"Yeah, Mom can really fry chicken," Hector agreed.

"She and Grandmom are the best at frying chicken, we love their chicken," Dana chimed in.

The next few minutes were filled with the sounds of us munching on Mom's wonderful fried chicken, the boiled eggs and chips; and slurping thirstily on the sodas.

"The way you guys are eating, you'd think you all hadn't eaten a meal in years," I laughed.

"Shut up Chris," Hector said as he stuffed chips in his mouth, "We're growing boys, and we're gonna eat. And this is good!"

"Yep." Tony agreed.

"Okay," I said in surrender. "What do you all want to do now?"

"I thought we were going by the New Mexico State campus and look at the stadium," Hector said.

"You mean NMSU?" I asked.

"Yeah, NMSU knucklehead," Hector said.

"I thought that was part of the plan, right?" Dana asked.

"No problem, let's get this stuff cleaned up and we can roll down the road to the State campus," I said.

Once we finished our impromptu meal, we cleaned off the table and tossed our trash in the nearest trash can.

As we climbed back into our black & gold steed, and got settled in our designated seats, Hector said, "You know, there's got to be a better way to get in this car than just kind of climbing in. What do you think?"

"What do you mean?" Dana asked.

"I don't know, some cooler way of getting in here. I mean, look at this car...this car is bad. There's got to be some cooler way for us to get in here."

Tony jumped in, "Next time we get out, let's practice doing it, like in sequence. Right now Chris gets out and slides his chair up so Hector can get out, and Dana does the same thing on my side. Next time, let's try to do it at the same time."

"Okay," I said; it sounded kind of silly to me, but it might work.

"Sounds good," Dana said, "let's try it on campus."

"Alright," I said as I started up the car. The sight of the huge gold firebird on the hood still brought chills to my spine. I just loved to look at it from the driver's seat. I put the car in drive and pulled out of the picnic area. I turned up the AC, stuck in an 8-track tape, and with *Brickhouse* blasting its signature drum roll; we rolled out across the New Mexico desert.

In the rear view mirror I could see the Franklin Mountains surrounding El Paso, and to our front was nothing but desert. As we traveled west on I-10, the terrain was pretty flat with dry-looking sagebrush, brown sand and clear blue skies above. The gray-brown land stretched as far as you could see to the horizon. With a glare from the sun that began to climb in the eastern sky, we continued our trip west. Only the occasional barrel cactus, tumbleweeds and boulders offered any relief to the eye.

Transmanauts

The next stop on the horizon was Las Cruces. The first exit announced we were at the home of the NMSU Aggies, so I turned off on that exit.

"Hector, you been to the campus?" I asked.

"Yeah," he said, "we need to turn right up at the next light, and just follow the signs to NMSU."

"So, where's the stadium?" Dana, the navigator, asked.

"Like duh, it'll be that really big structure once we get to campus." Hector taunted.

"Funny," Dana replied. "Have you been there yet?"

"Sure I have," Hector said. "That was the best part of the tour, since that's where I'll be running track."

"What events will you be running as a part of your track scholarship?" I asked.

"Mostly, the 100, 200, four by 100, and four by 200. I'm really looking forward to this next year."

"You plan on pledging?"

"Oh yeah, you know I have to pledge Kappa as soon as I can. Dad wouldn't let me back in the house if I didn't pledge Kappa!" Hector laughed.

"Let me know when you go on line, 'cause I want to be there when you cross the 'burning sands'" I chuckled.

"Don't pass this turn Chris," Dana interrupted.

Yep, I almost missed it talking about Kappa Alpha Psi, my fraternity at school. The sign read, "New Mexico State University – Home of the Fighting Aggies" we were here, finally.

"Okay, where now Hector?" I asked.

"Over there to the right, do you see the stadium?"

"Oh yeah, okay, I see it." I steered the car in that direction. As we closed in on the stadium, pedestrians stood on the street gawking.

"What's everybody looking at?" Tony asked.

"What do you think, Tony? The car – like duh!" Dana taunted.

"Yeah," Hector said, "no one's seen a car like this before, especially with four black guys driving. This might be the perfect place to practice our getting-in and getting-out routine. What do you think?"

"Maybe in the parking lot of the stadium?" Dana suggested.

"Okay, we can do that," I said as we pulled into the shadows surrounding the west side of the stadium. I parked the car and said, "Let's do this. Hector, Tony, it's y'all's idea, what do you want to do?"

"Hmm, okay, let's sound this out. First, uh, Chris, you and Dana open your doors at the same time, then, simultaneously, you get out of the car, then you both lean over, pull on the seat release to pull the front seats as far forward as possible to let me and Tony get out from the back seat." Hector gestured with his hands.

"Okay, then what?" I said.

"Wait, wait, let me think…then me and Tony kind of duck our heads, and get out of the car at the same time."

"Okay, then what?" I prompted.

"I don't know, I mean, we need to look cool when we get out, right?"

"Agreed."

"So, uh, when Tony and I get out, you and Dana close the car doors at the same time, then all of us kind of stand there at the side of the car in some sort of, I don't know, a 'cool' pose, or something."

"What's a 'cool' pose?" Tony asked, "What's 'cool' in Cali Hector?

"I don't know, maybe if we, like casually lean against the car, with our heads cocked a little to the side, holding our chins with one hand, and give that 'I don't give a damn because I'm cool' look?"

"Okay, let's try it," I said.

We practiced our maneuver several times until our execution was smooth as silk and we looked cool doing it. In the process, we gathered a little bit of an audience, to include one white girl who seemed particularly interested. She was about 5' 5", blonde, quite shapely, wearing a thin white t-shirt, cut-off jeans shorts, sandals, and looked to be about 20 years old. She watched us intently for several minutes. I guess the four of us, with our varied complexions, athletic builds, good looks, and energetic personalities, presented an intriguing package. We were a captivating foursome to any interested young woman, even under these circumstances.

After we got out of the car for about the fifth time, and struck another "cool" pose, curiosity finally got the better of her.

She got up her courage and asked in a melodious Southern accent, "What in the world are y'all doin'?"

We all broke out of our "cool" poses, and Dana answered, "Practicing!"

"Ah can see that, but practicin' what?" She asked again.

Hector laughed and said, "Practicing lookin' cool getting in and out of the car."

"That's a beautiful car," she said. "Are y'all some sort of dance group or somethin'?"

"Yeah," Hector said. "We're the Transmanauts!" He looked at the rest of us for confirmation.

"Oh cool," she said, "after the car?"

"Yep," I added, confirming the name. "Like astronauts, but our spaceship is the car."

She looked pleased with those revelations, "Y'all look really good doin' that routine, you ought to be on TV."

"Yeah, like the Temptations." Tony laughed.

"Thanks," I said also laughing. "We're actually on our way to Hollywood, and just stopped here to practice one of our routines."

She smiled and said, "Well good luck to y'all, ah hope to see y'all on TV one of these days." She walked away with a nicely provocative wiggle.

"Damn." Tony said under his breath as he watched her leave, "She is foine!"

"Yeah," Hector said. "If we can pull her just from getting in and out of the car, what's going to happen when we play ball or do our dance routines?"

"Yeah," I said, "I think we're gonna have a good time in Cali." I added, "We've spent enough time here, its time to get back on the road."

"Transmanauts?" Dana inquired as we got back into the car, "Where did that come from?"

"Cool, huh?" Hector beamed, "I thought we were, like, on this trek to the unknown, and we all like *Star Trek,* so I thought it would be cool to be named after the car."

"I don't know what it is about guys, but whenever we get together, we always got to give ourselves a name. Transmanauts, huh? I like it." Dana proclaimed.

"Yeah," I agreed. "It's cool, I wish I'd thought of it. What do you think Tony?"

"I can't think of anything better, so okay, I guess we're the Transmanauts." Tony agreed.

As I started the car to maneuver the Trans Am out of the stadium parking lot we officially became the ***Transmanauts,*** and from that time everything we did was "Transmanautic."

I retraced our route back to the interstate, and got back on the open road. As I gunned the engine and we hurtled down the highway, we started talking about our favorite subject – girls. And yeah, the discussion can get pretty, um, salacious.

"Hector, if that girl was any indication, you should be swimming in pussy next year," Tony laughed.

"I don't know man, but she did seem kinda eager didn't she?"

"Yeah, college girls can be pretty aggressive if they want you, but they can also be a real dick tease," I said.

"What do you mean?" Hector asked.

"Here's an example – this past year, when me and several frat brothers went down to Lamar University in Beaumont, we were told by the frat down there that their Diamonds were easy pussy, so we went down there thinking we were going to just pick somebody out and hit it."

"So what happened?" Tony asked.

"None of us got any pussy," I said.

"None of you?" Hector was incredulous, "I thought you guys were the 'Pretty Boys' of Kappa Alpha Psi." He laughed.

"Yeah well, none of us got any pussy that night."

"Why not?" Dana asked.

"Fuck, I don't know, but I do know when we got down there the girls seemed really receptive. We went to a party and had a lot of 'Kappa Punch' and were feeling good. The girls invited us to spend the night at one of their apartments, and we thought we were in there."

"What's Kappa Punch?" Hector asked.

"It's a mixture of some clear alcohol with Kool Aid, usually vodka, gin or Thunderbird, in a large container, like a big ol' trash can or something like that. That's what we normally serve at our parties."

"How's it taste?" Hector asked.

"I guess you'll find out next year, but it does taste pretty good. It's one way to get girls feeling good without really getting 'em drunk. They're a lot more likely to give up the drawers when they have a little buzz, you know."

"Okay, I got it, so what happened in Beaumont?" Hector asked as he leaned forward in his seat. I caught his eye in the rear view mirror.

"We all got up in the apartment and were invited to sleep in the same room as several of the girls. It looked like a pajama party. All the girls seemed to have these baby-doll pajamas, you know with the matching panties, and we just knew we were about to get into some serious pussy."

"And?" Dana prompted.

"And nothing. The girls got up on the beds, probably about four of them on each of the beds in the two bedrooms, and went to sleep, while we lay on the floor next to the beds."

"What? You all didn't hit *any* of that?" Tony asked.

"Nope, and all night we would make comments like, 'Damn, I thought we going to get some pussy tonight,' or 'Why aren't we fucking right now?' or as Mayfield said, 'These bitches were just fucking with us and we need to fuck with them.' But nothing happened, and we eventually fell asleep."

"The next morning, what happened?" Hector asked.

"We got up to the smell of frying bacon and eggs, and found that most of the girls had left. We ate breakfast and left. The irony was, almost all the Lamar frat thought we had been fuckin' all night and we just let them think that as we took off back to Austin. But we were suffering from a major case of blue balls."

26

"Damn, you all got screwed," Tony laughed.

"I wish," I laughed.

"Have you gotten any pussy at UT?" Hector asked.

"Not yet," I said, "I was being faithful to Melanie, sort of. But I think that's going to change when I show up this year in law school and with this pussy mobile."

"You think you'll get some pussy just because you drive this car?" Tony asked.

"Hell yeah," I said, "Why else would you have a car like this?"

"You got a point," Hector admitted.

"What about you and Melanie?" Dana asked, changing the subject.

"What about us?"

"Well?"

"Well what?"

"You know, have you done it with her yet?"

"Nun ya, and that's all I'm going to say." I laughed. *Although her house will never be the same*, I thought.

"C'mon," Dana said.

"Nope," I replied.

"Well you know me and Greta are just about there," Tony said.

"So what's stopping you?" I asked.

"Nothin' we're just waiting for the right opportunity," Tony said.

"Try the drive-in," I said.

"Yeah, but you need a car," Tony said.

"Yeah, I guess that would help," I laughed.

Dana and Hector were kind of quiet during this part of the conversation. I turned to them and said, "You guys think you might score in Cali?"

"Isn't that why we're going out there?" Dana said.

"Definitely," Hector said, "It's time to sow some wild oats, and there's no better place than Cali."

"Yeah I hear you. I'm looking forward to hitting some of that California pussy myself," Tony said, "I hear the Cali girls are pretty easy."

"Alright, that sounds like a plan – our main objective is to get laid in Cali." I laughed.

"Yep," Tony said.

"Hey, we're getting close to the Arizona state line. Just a few more hours to Tucson." I announced.

It's good we had plenty of music, because the deserts of New Mexico were vast and seemingly unending, unbroken by any type of interesting or unusual terrain. The desert was brown, dotted by tumbleweeds and sometimes framed by a backdrop of drab-looking mountains. New Mexico was almost depressing in its drabness.

"What's that in the distance?" Tony asked.

"What?" I asked.

"There," he pointed to the north, "that whirling, tornado-looking thing."

"Oh that," I said, "That's called a 'desert devil,' or 'whirling dervish.'"

"I've never heard of that, what is it?" Tony asked.

"It's a whirling wind that picks up a lot of desert sand and looks like a small tornado in the distance, sometimes they reach several stories in the air. It's different from a tornado because it doesn't come from the clouds, it's created by various factors on the ground," I said.

"It looks like the Tasmanian Devil," Tony laughed.

"Yeah, you better hope it doesn't come any closer." I gripped the wheel a little tighter.

"Why, what can happen?" Hector asked, now interested in the conversation.

"I've seen Volkswagens knocked over by one of those things," I said.

"Where?" Hector asked.

"El Paso, on the freeway."

"Yeah, I remember that," Dana said, joining in.

"Damn, that thing looks like it's moving towards us," Tony said with some trepidation. "Can't you go any faster?"

"Look, I'm doing the speed limit, I don't need to outrun the thing. If it looks like it's going to get close I'll either pull off the road or try to outrun it, okay."

"Alright," Tony conceded, "Just don't run up in it, okay?"

"Stop being a pussy," I said. "Nothing's going to happen to widdle Tony."

"Fuck you Chris," Tony said as we all laughed.

"Damn, there's just nothin' out here is there?" Hector said, saving Tony some embarrassment.

"Nope, it's a lot like the desert area near NMMI," I said.

"That's right, you went to military school in New Mexico, didn't you?" Tony added.

"Yeah, Chris was at New Mexico Military Institute for two years, went through Fort Knox Basic Camp, and Fort Riley Advanced Camp. He was the youngest guy to go through those two ROTC camps." Dana said with quiet pride.

"Really?" Hector said. "That was kind of before we got to know you."

"Yeah," I confirmed, "I went through a special two-year ROTC program at the age of 16, and they'd never had anybody go through the program that young."

"How was that?" Tony asked.

"Oh man, it was hard at the beginning because I was so young and small, but as I got older and bigger and faster, it got easier."

"Where is NMMI?" Hector asked.

"Roswell."

"You mean where the aliens crashed?" Tony laughed.

"Yep, it was a big secret when I went to school, and we went out to the site where the aliens supposedly crashed."

"I didn't know that," Dana said. "What was that like?'

29

"Nothin' big, we just looked around and went out to the air force base where they supposedly took them and walked around on the bunkers."

"Wow," Hector said. "Did you see anything?"

"Nope, but it was still kinda scary."

"Yeah, I'll bet. Did you spend any time out in the desert?" Dana asked.

"Yeah, part of our training was to bivouac out in the desert. We did field training out there, including tactical training, land nav, orienteering and live fire exercises."

"Was that pretty tough?" Dana asked.

"Not really, but it could get tough after a while. We would spend like a whole week out there in the desert. The temperatures could range from freezing in the morning to really hot in the afternoon."

"What do you mean?" Hector asked.

"Well, like one day out in the field, I saw one of the cadets taken away in the morning with a case of hypothermia, a cold-weather injury; and that same day, in the afternoon, a cadet collapsed from heat exhaustion. The temperatures out in the desert can be pretty extreme." I paused for a moment to let them digest that information. "And it looks a lot like this desert, except more rifts and canyons," I continued. "But it was a lot of fun."

"How long 'til we get to Arizona?" Tony asked.

"Hmm, less than an hour," Dana answered.

"Once we get to Arizona, can we stop for lunch?" Tony continued.

"Sounds good," I said, as we drew nearer the Arizona state line.

After several minutes we crossed the Arizona state line. Right away I could see that Arizona was different from New Mexico. At times, it presented spectacular desert landscapes that, in the early morning or late afternoon sunlight, are the stuff that you see in postcards. The oranges, reds and the browns combined for a beautiful palette of colors.

As we burned through the afternoon air, we passed areas that were studded with boulders and rock formations that fired the imagination of other-worldly landscapes. I imagined being on the moon or on Mars, or some other alien planet.

"Wow," Hector said. "It's just like we crossed into a different world when we crossed the state line."

"Let's stop and take a look at some of these boulders," Dana suggested.

"Anyone bring a camera?" I asked.

"Nope," Tony answered.

"No, I didn't think about it," Hector said.

"Damn, that was dumb," I said.

"Maybe we can pick up an Instamatic while we're in Cali," Dana suggested.

"Okay." I pulled over to one of those viewing sites along the highway. This was our first stop after Las Cruces, and we needed to stretch our legs.

"Hey, do we do our Transmanautic unassing of the car?" Hector asked.

"Yeah, even if no one is watching, I think we need to keep working on it to get it right." I said.

"Okay, then you call it," Dana said.

"Alright," I turned off the car. "Here we go – now." Dana and I simultaneously opened our car doors, got out, bent over and slid our seats forward, then held the seats forward to let Tony and Hector out of the back seat. When they got out at the same time, Dana and I exchanged a nod and closed both doors with a resounding "thump" and all four of us struck our Transmanautic pose. This was done to the delight of the various denizens of the Arizona desert. I'm sure we entertained many a rattlesnake, iguana and prairie dog with our routine.

As we wandered over to the viewing area, the phantasmagorical rock formations dominated the scenery. But almost as prominent were the large Saguaro cacti which are featured in movies and on television. They're the ones that look like large people from a distance, well, a very long distance. These cacti loom high in the air and seem to grow in groves out in the desert.

"They look like they could come to life like the apple trees in *The Wizard of Oz,*" Dana said.

"What are they called?" Hector asked.

"Big-assed cactus," Tony said.

"Cacti, you idiot," I said, "Big-assed cacti."

"Is that what you learned in college?" Tony asked.

"No, that's what you learn when you crack open a book, you ought to try it Tony." I laughed.

"Shut up Chris," Tony scowled.

"You all seen enough?" Dana asked.

"I'm good," Hector said.

"Alright, let's get back on the road, we still have a couple of hours to go to Tucson," I said.

As we approached the car, we got into position to perform our Transmanautic entrance into the Trans. Me and Dana on both sides of the car with our hands positioned on the car handles. At a nod from me, we opened the car doors at the same time, and pulled our seats forward. Tony and Hector ducked their heads below the top of the door opening, and slid into their seats. With another nod, Dana and I slid into our seats, and then closed the doors together. Yeah, that looked pretty cool. I cranked up the car, started up the music, and we got to rolling with *Love Roller Coaster* by the Ohio Players.

After spending most of the day traveling through the desert, we finally saw Tucson in the distance. The city rose like a shimmering oasis in the distance and was the first large city we had seen since leaving El Paso. As we drove into the city we sought out the downtown area to find a hotel and to get a feel for the city.

"Where we going to stay?" Tony asked.

"Dana and I have stayed at either Howard Johnson's or Holiday Inn when we travel with our parents, so I thought we could stay at one of those two." I said.

"Okay," Tony said. "Do you know where they are?"

"Yeah, well sort of," Dana said. "The Trip Tik gives addresses of the major hotels and they're marked on the blown up part of the Trip Tik.

"Cool," Hector said. "Where's the closest one?"

"Hmm," Dana studied the map. "It looks like it may be the Howard Johnson's on Southwest Freeway. Take a left up here Chris and then a right at Southwest Freeway."

"Okee dokee," I said as I followed his directions. We spotted the hotel after a few blocks and pulled up to the lobby area. I unlocked the glove compartment and pulled out the envelope that contained Dana's and my money. As I got out to see if they had available rooms, I called back into the car, "Hey, do we want one room with two queen size beds or two rooms?"

"One room, two beds," Tony said.

"Yeah, I agree," Dana said.

"What about you Hector?"

"Yeah, that makes sense, and it's probably cheaper…okay."

I went inside the lobby and spoke to the pretty, black-haired receptionist about getting a room.

"How many guests?"

"Four," I answered.

"How about a double queen-sized room? We have one on the back side of the hotel on the second floor. Will that be alright?"

"That's fine. How much is the room?"

"That will be forty-four dollars," she replied.

"Okay." I paid for the room in cash.

She handed me two keys and gave me directions on how to get to the back side of the hotel.

I went back out to the car and started up the engine.

"Where's the room?" Dana asked.

"Other side of the hotel," I said. "Second floor, room 245."

"This isn't a bad looking hotel," Tony said. "I've never stayed at a Howard Johnson's."

"Yeah, they're normally pretty nice," Dana said as I pulled up to a parking space in front of our room.

"Okay, out." I turned off the engine. We then executed our signature dis-embarkment of the Trans Am, and began to unload our bags out of the trunk.

"What do we do with the cooler?" Dana asked.

"Bring it up, we can snack on the food tonight," I said.

"Okay."

Tony and Hector got their bags and bounded up the steel-framed stairs and stood waiting at the door to the room until I could catch up with them, since I had the keys to the room.

"Hurry up," Tony said, "I've got to take a leak."

"Okay, okay, don't wet yourself," I said, and then unlocked the door, and watched with amusement as Tony rushed through the door to the bathroom. We immediately heard the loud sound of streaming and splashing water.

"I guess you did have to take a piss pretty badly," I laughed.

"Shut up Chris," Tony yelled from the open bathroom door.

"Hurry up," Hector said, "I've got to pee too." The sounds of Tony relieving himself had its effect on the rest of us and we all lined up to go.

Dana brought up the rear with his bag and the cooler, "Whew, here's the food, where do you want it?"

"Over there by the closet is fine," I said.

"What time is it?" Hector asked after we had all visited the bathroom.

"Four o'clock." I said.

"Yeah, but that's Mountain Daylight Savings Time, what time zone are we in?" Hector asked.

"You're right, I think we're in the Pacific Time Zone, so we should turn our watches back an hour," I said.

"Good idea," Hector said, and all of us turned our watches back an hour.

"What do you all want to do now?" Tony asked.

"I want to get out and explore downtown Tucson," Dana said. "Chris and I haven't been here in a long time, so I'd like to get out and see the city."

"When did you all come through Tucson?" Hector asked.

"Back in 1969 when we came through here on our way to El Paso from Oregon. We stayed with some of our friends from Fort Totten, New York." I said.

"Are you going to call them?" Dana asked.

"No, we didn't plan on it, so I don't think we ought to."

"Okay, well, let's go," Hector said.

As we left the room, I gave Dana the other key for safe keeping and closed the door behind us. We went down the stairs a little slower than going up since we didn't have the same urgency to get to the bathroom.

Down at the car, we again executed our patented maneuver for getting into the Trans Am and buckled up for our tour of downtown Tucson.

"That looks like the center of downtown," Dana said, pointing towards the tall buildings not too far from the hotel.

"Okay," I said, and steered the car in that direction.

As we approached the center of downtown Tucson we saw an X-rated theater.

"Hey, you guys want to check out that theater tonight?" Tony asked.

"What's showing?" Hector asked.

"Wait a minute, that title looks familiar," I said.

35

I pulled over to the curb in front of the theater so we could get a better look at the name of the movie and the theater itself.

"I recognize that movie title from one that I read about in *Hustler* magazine," I said.

"*Hustler?* You read *Hustler*?" Tony asked.

"Well yeah, I've read *Hustler, Playboy, Penthouse* and whatever magazines show titties and pussy, just like any other red-blooded American male my age," I said. "It's funny you should ask that since we brought those X-rated cards back from New York last year showing all those people fucking and sucking. Why the hell wouldn't I read Hustler?" I said.

"True," Tony said.

"And it's not like the first time we've gone to a porno movie," Hector said, "We went to a few in El Paso, right?"

"Yep," Dana agreed. "So are we going to this one?"

"Yeah, I want to go," Tony said.

"What did the Hustler review say about this movie?" Dana asked.

"Hmm, if I remember right, it was a Japanese movie with subtitles, kind of soft-core porn, and uh, well, it's about this guy who cheats on his wife and she finds out about it."

"Okay, so what's the big deal about this movie other than it's in Japanese?" Hector asked.

"Well," I explained, "once she finds out he's been cheating on her, she waits 'til he's asleep, then she, uh, cuts off his dick, and the last scene is her walking down the street with his dick in her hand."

"Yuck!" Tony exclaimed. "Let's go see it, I want to see that."

"What time does it start?" Dana asked.

I peered at the sign with the movie times and said, "It looks like it starts at 7 o'clock."

"Okay, we'll come back at seven," Dana said.

It was decided, we were going to check out this strange-sounding movie. On the way back to the hotel we stopped to fill up the tank, since we were driving on fumes. I think we'd gotten about 20 miles to the gallon, maybe. We didn't need to run out of gas on this next leg of the trip through the desert, so we needed to keep an eye on the gas gauge the rest of the trip.

We had wasted about an hour, so we went back to the hotel to eat more of the fried chicken and eggs and take a nap. We watched TV in the room for about two hours, and decided it was time to get up and go to the theater.

I retraced our route back to the theater, and parked in the private parking lot reserved for customers of the theater. When we walked up to the box office window I noticed there weren't many patrons.

"I need four tickets for the seven o'clock show," I said to the ticket-taker.

The ticket-taker was a very cute white girl. "You know the show is not for another hour, right?" She said.

"What do you mean, what time is it?" I said.

"Six."

"Wait a minute, what time zone is this?" I asked.

"Pacific, but not Pacific Daylight Savings time."

"What do you mean?"

"Arizona doesn't do Daylight Savings, so we're an hour behind California," she said.

"An hour behind California? Is that the same time as, like, Alaskan Daylight Savings time?" I joked.

"I don't know about that. All I know is we're an hour earlier than Pacific Daylight because we didn't 'spring forward' like the rest of country, so we're an hour behind California."

"Damn, that's confusing." I turned to the other guys, "We've been running around here an hour ahead, they're on a different time than anyone in the country."

"Okay," Hector said. "What does that mean?"

"While we're in Arizona, we're an hour behind California,

which means," I did the calculation in my head, "we need to put our watches back another hour. Arizona, during the summer, is two hours behind El Paso, not just one hour like during the winter."

"Man that's weird," Hector said as he adjusted his watch. "That's just crazy."

"Well, we've got another hour to kill, what do you want to do?" Dana said as he adjusted his watch.

"There was that huge dip a few blocks back, you remember?" Tony said.

"Yeah, what about it?" I queried.

"I want to run through that thing a few times. It looked like fun."

"Okay, we've got nothing better to do." I agreed.

We got back in the car and drove around until we found the really huge dip in the road – it was really more like a depression than a dip, it was just that big. I drove through it slowly at first and made a U-turn down the block to drive over it again.

"C'mon Chris, drive faster," Tony shouted.

"Yeah let's hit this thing faster," Hector agreed.

"Okay, here we go," I said, and kept driving over it faster and faster until we got a roller coaster feeling of weightlessness.

"Oh shit, this is great," Tony said. "It feels like a ride at the carnival."

"Alright, watch this," I said, and I kept driving through the dip until I increased the speed from 30 to 50 mph. At that point, we actually left the ground, and I heard Tony and Hector in the back of the car, yelling, "Ohhhhhh shit!" And then we landed with a jolt.

"Oh shit," Dana said. "That's enough."

Yeah, it probably was enough; it felt like one of those scenes in *Smokey and the Bandit* where Burt Reynolds's Trans Am went airborne over the sheriff's car – yeah, what a rush! We decided that was enough excitement with the car. It was time to go to the movie.

We got to the theater and parked in the theater parking lot. This time when we went to the box office there were more patrons buying tickets. The ticket-taker asked for our ID's and we provided drivers licenses for proof of age. Once we bought our tickets we sauntered into the shabby-looking lobby to buy some snacks and drinks at the concession stand.

"Hey, this floor is sticky," Hector commented.

"Yeah, what is that stuff on the floor?" Tony asked.

"Damn, I don't know, I hope it's just spilled soda. Yuck." I said.

"What else could it be?" Dana asked.

"Well, based on where we are, some sort of ejaculative body fluid?" I said.

"You mean cum?" Hector asked in disbelief.

"That's just nasty," Dana said.

"Let's get in the theater before we step in something really disgusting," I said as we gingerly stepped through the goo on the floor.

The movie began soon after we took our seats in the seedy, dark theater.

The movie, as advertised, was in Japanese, and there were subtitles. It was X-rated, although not very graphic; but we were paying rapt attention to the action on the screen. There's something about watching sex on a movie screen, bigger than life, with the louder-than-life moaning and groaning, the sounds of sucking, and the wet, obscene noises of the in-and-out movement of penises in vaginas, and the slapping of pelvises during the act of intercourse that is just surreal. But it had our attention and the natural reaction of red-blooded guys watching porn.

As the movie progressed and it got closer to the moment of truth, you know, when she was going to cut off his penis, we started getting a little nervous.

Dana who was sitting next to me whispered, "I don't think I can watch this next sequence, it looks like she's going to cut off his dick."

Yeah, she had just found out about her husband's infidelity. You could see that I'm-going-to-cut-his-dick-off look in her eyes. In the next scene, she went into the kitchen and found a huge butcher knife while her husband slept.

"Yeah, me too," Tony said speaking across Dana, "It makes my dick hurt just thinking about it. Let's get the hell out of here."

Now, on the big screen, she was sharpening the knife using a leather strap – back and forth, making the knife razor sharp. The bitch sliced the knife across her thumb to test its sharpness and drew her own blood. Then she sucked on her blood with an obscene slurping sound. Then she headed back towards her bedroom, where her husband slept with blessed unawareness that he was about to get his dick cut off. Damn.

"I'm with you guys, let's go now," Hector said.

Obviously, we couldn't take the idea of watching some guy, no matter what he did, get his dick cut off. That hit way too close to home. We got up near the end of the movie, before we watched her do the deed, and ran out holding our crotches like we'd just been castrated. Whew! Catastrophe averted. When we got outside the theater, you would have thought we'd just run a marathon we were breathing and laughing so hard. That was enough for one night; it was time to go back to the hotel.

We decided to get an early start the next day for our final leg to Cali.

Finally – Cali

The best way to get to know your friends is when you have to spend a night in a hotel room sharing two beds. I had that experience in college with my fraternity brothers, and now with Tony, Hector and Dana.

Unfortunately, guys don't have the same kind of restraints on emitting bodily sounds and gases as do women, so during that first night the room was filled with snoring, and silent but deadly farting. I'm glad I wasn't in the same bed with Tony and Hector.

We got up at seven o'clock that morning to get ready for our next leg of the trip. I was the first to get up and got into the bathroom before the other guys. When I came out they were starting to stir.

"Hey guys, time to get up," I said.

"What? What's the rush? It's only seven in the morning," Tony grumbled.

"Yeah, well, we're going to get an early start to get to San Diego by four or five."

"Alright, alright, we're getting up," Hector mumbled.

"You up?" I looked at Dana. I could see his head still on his pillow and his face turned away from me.

"Yeah, yeah, I'm up," he growled.

"Good. I'm done in the bathroom, so you guys need to figure it out."

Tony, who was the most awake, said, "I'm going to the bathroom now, Hector can use the sink while I'm taking a crap."

"Yeah, thanks for that," Hector said as he started for the sink to brush his teeth and wash up.

Once everyone had finished their morning ritual we got dressed in the same clothes we had on the first day. No need to change yet, except our underwear.

"Dana, check the room, make sure we didn't leave anything behind, okay? We'll take the bags and cooler and load 'em up," I said.

"Okay."

"C'mon let's go," I said as the three of us picked up our bags and the cooler, and headed out the door. "Dana, lock it up when you're finished."

"Okay."

The three of us went down the metal stairs to the car and dropped the bags and the cooler by the trunk.

"You know, it may be a good idea for us to park with the front of the car facing out. It might make it easier to load up," Hector suggested.

"Yeah that sounds like a good idea," Tony said. "You never know when you got to make a fast getaway," he laughed.

"Sounds like a good idea, that's called combat parking, and the military uses that technique for that very reason, to get the hell out of Dodge in a hurry, like when you're under fire or have to get away," I said as I unlocked the trunk. I looked into the trunk and decided to rearrange the bags from the day before to accommodate the cooler. We'd finished off the chicken and the rest of the food the night before, so we didn't need it up front any more. By that time, Dana had made it down to the car and I threw him the keys.

42

"Start it up, and get the AC going, it's already getting hot," I said. The only other person I let drive my car was Dana, because I trusted his driving and he helped me pay for it. He was a great brother. I had no problem giving him the keys and letting him start the car.

Once he got it started, he stood outside the car waiting for me to finish packing the trunk.

"You didn't lock the car did you?" I asked suspiciously.

"No," he said as he looked back in the window to make sure the locks were up, "We're okay."

"Alright, let's do this," I said, and we again executed our Transmanautic entry to the car.

"I'm going to drive around to the lobby and check us out of the room," I said as we all buckled up.

"Where we going to eat breakfast?" Tony asked.

"I don't care, I'm not really that hungry, but we can stop if you all want to," I said.

"Let's eat once we get outside Tucson," Dana suggested.

"Sounds like a plan," I said.

"Do you think they still have the Sambo's restaurants? I think we went to a Sambo's the last time we were in Tucson," Dana said.

"Sambo's? You're kidding right? Sambo's? You all ate at some place called Sambo's?" Hector laughed.

"Yeah, for some reason I thought it was here in Arizona," Dana said.

"What? Is it named after Little Black Sambo?" Hector continued laughing.

"Yep," I said, a little embarrassed, "They even had coloring books and placemats that showed the whole Sambo story."

"What story is that?" Tony asked. "I've never heard of Little Black Sambo."

"Terrific," I said, as I pulled up to the overhang in front of the lobby. "I'll break it down to you when I get back." I slid out the car, and marched into the lobby to return the keys and get the final bill. As I came back out of the front entrance I heard them laughing.

"What's so funny?" I asked as I got back in the car.

Tony was laughing so hard he was almost crying, "Dana," he gasped, "Dana, was just telling us the story of Sambo."

"Too funny," Hector laughed. "I'd forgotten some of the

details."

"Yeah, especially that part about the tigers running around the tree after the little Black kid until they turned into butter and were served on pancakes," Tony added.

"Yeah, it's pretty funny," I said. "And you know white people call us Sambos, right?"

All the air went out of the car.

"What are you talking about?" Tony asked.

"Sambo is another racially derogatory term white people use for us, like nigger, spear-chucker, jungle bunny – and Little Black Sambo," I said.

"You're kidding," Hector said with some disbelief.

"Look it up, ask your parents," I said, as we snaked our way through downtown back to I-10, "They'll tell you all about it. Unfortunately, I heard that shit while I was at NMMI."

"Oh man, well we can't eat at some place called Sambo's," Hector said.

"Oh, hell no," Tony added.

"Yeah, probably not a good idea," Dana concurred.

"I agree," I said. "I don't think my parents were aware of the significance when we ate there almost a decade ago, but I don't think they'd eat there now."

"Okay, so Sambo's is out, where do we eat?" Dana asked.

"Eh, we'll figure it out as we go along," I said,

"Well, don't wait too damn long," Tony scowled, "I'm already getting pretty hungry."

"Okay, okay. Damn, are you always this hungry in the morning?"

"Yes."

"We'll start looking as soon as we clear downtown, okay?"

"Sounds good." Tony said, a little calmer.

In the next few minutes I guided the car smoothly onto I-10

heading west and accelerated towards San Diego. Within several minutes, once we left downtown Tucson, we saw a pancake house right off the highway not named Sambo's, and decided to stop for breakfast.

I parked near the front and we sauntered in after having disembarked from our bad-assed vehicle. The interior was typical IHOP with booths and tables, and smelled of frying bacon, eggs and pancakes. Our mouths watered at the prospect of fluffy pancakes covered in syrup, sausage, eggs and bacon.

The hostess seated us at a window booth where we could keep an eye on the car and had a bird's-eye view of the surrounding desert. She then handed us menus. A few minutes later the waitress approached our table.

"You all ready to order?" She asked looking at me.

"I'll have the three-stack pancakes, ham and orange juice," I said.

She turned to Dana, "And you sir?"

"I'll have the three-stack pancakes, eggs and bacon, and orange juice."

Tony was next, "Uh, let me have your sampler breakfast."

"With everything sir?"

"Yep."

"Very good sir," and she looked at Hector, "And you sir?"

"I'll have the same."

"I'm sorry sir, the same as what?

"The same as him." Hector pointed at Tony.

"Very good sir – with everything?"

"Yes, please."

"Very good, your orders will be out shortly," she said. "And would you two like something to drink?" she asked Tony and Hector.

"Orange juice please," Hector said.

"I'll try some apple juice," Tony said.

"Very good, I'll be right back with your drinks."

"We used to go to these pancake houses in Austin after our parties," I said. "Usually we'd walk in about 2:30 in the morning and within a few minutes the Austin police would arrive."

"Really? Why?" Tony asked.

"I guess when you had about twenty black people walk in at 2:30 in the morning, no matter how nicely they're dressed or how well-behaved, management's going to make sure the police were around. Never failed," I laughed.

"You thought it was funny?" Hector asked.

"Yeah, we got mad the first time, but after a while we got to the point we would time it from the moment we walked in to see how quickly the police arrived. I think the fastest time was about five minutes," I laughed again.

"Damn, I didn't know it was like that," Hector said.

"Uh huh, you'd better get used to it. Wherever you go, especially if there's a bunch of you, you can expect the police to show up at some point," I said.

"Yeah, but damn," Hector continued.

"Yeah."

"So what's our next destination?" Tony asked, changing the subject.

"San Diego," I answered.

"I thought we were going through Phoenix," Tony questioned.

"Nope, Phoenix is the next big city if we went I-10 to LA, but we're going to take I-8 about halfway between here and Phoenix, and then head further west to San Diego," Dana answered.

"How long to San Diego?" Tony asked.

"About seven hours, it's about 400 miles from here; we should be there before five."

"You good to drive Chris?" Hector asked.

"This is a piece of cake. I've driven a lot farther with Mom before, remember Dana?"

"Yeah, you know back in summer 1971, Mom drove all the way from El Paso to Philadelphia by herself, with just us and the dog. It took about a week because we stopped in a few places, but she did all the driving," Dana explained to Tony and Hector.

"She used to do over a hundred miles per hour out there on the Texas highways," I laughed. "She's the one who taught us how to drive really fast."

"But that's Mom, where've you driven?" Hector asked. Tony and Hector called my mother "Mom" because she was like a second mother to them.

"What makes you think you can drive the whole way?" Tony scoffed.

"Fuck you Tony."

"Fuck me? Fuck you. What experience do you have to drive the whole trip?"

"For one, it's my fucking car, and two, I've had a lot of experience driving on the road and in big cities."

"Like what?"

"Okay dummy, right after I got my license, we drove with Mom to Colorado Springs at Easter in 1973. Mom wanted to take a nap and she turned the wheel over to me. That was my first time on the open road like that, it was a little scary. I remember going about 100 down this long hill and thinking, *wow, this is really fast,* and just loving it."

"We survived your driving," Dana laughed. "And Mom let you drive a lot of the way from El Paso to Philadelphia at Christmas in 1974."

"That's right. It was on the way back I got pulled over by DPS for speeding, me and another car doing about 75, outside of Sweetwater, on I-20."

"Oh yeah, I remember that," Dana said. "You looked pretty scared because it woke Mom up and she was not happy."

"We had a CB radio and those knuckleheads on the other side of the highway said it was clear, but this guy came up behind us and that's how we got caught."

"Did Mom let you drive again?" Tony asked.

"Yep, me getting a ticket wasn't a big deal. I helped her drive to Philly and New York last year when we went to the AKA Boulé, and then Dana and I drove around in both cities."

"I tell you what," I continued. "The New York drivers were pretty creative, but the Philly drivers were dangerous and just plain stupid."

"What do you mean?" Hector asked.

"Oh man," Dana chimed in. "Those Philly drivers, especially black folk, would just run stop signs, go the wrong way on one-way streets, wouldn't yield on the left turns at green lights, double park on narrow streets, and just sit there and look at you like you were crazy. So we had to be just as aggressive and sometimes drive just as stupid. I don't know how many times we said, 'These niggas are crazy,' when some of them would just do stupid stuff."

"What about New York?" Tony asked as our food was being served. The smells were wonderful, and we started salivating.

As the waitress placed the dishes on the table, Dana answered, "Ha! There was one time we were on 5th Avenue, and there were four lanes, two double-left hand turn and two lanes that went straight. When the light turned green, through some unseen communication, all four lanes made a left turn at the same time."

I laughed, "We'd never seen anything like that. I saw the drivers making gestures before the light turned green, but I had no idea they were coordinating this complicated turn which could have been a real fuck up if someone didn't get the message. But it turned out okay, and every one made the turn and we got a show."

We thought about that for a moment, and then got to the business of eating breakfast. Over the next several minutes the air around the table was filled with the sounds of silverware clinking against plates, and teeth and jaws chomping on a great-tasting breakfast. Not much conversation; and no complaints from us.

Once we finished breakfast, it was time to get back on the

road towards San Diego.

We got into the car in our stylistic Transmanautic manner, much to the delight of restaurant patrons watching from their tables at the front windows. Once inside, I asked, "What do you want to hear?"

"Ohio Players." Tony immediately said.

"Okay." I put in *Fire,* a favorite of ours from 1974.

"Yeah baby," he said as the lyrics sung by Sugerfoot blared out. And again to the delight of the window-seat patrons, we did a little in-seat dancing – *"When you shake what you got, and girl you gotta lot, you really somthin' child,"* we sang along with the song. After a few minutes of our little routine, I put the car in gear, backed out of the parking lot, and aimed the beak of the golden firebird towards the west, and Cali.

As the song came to an end, it was followed by another favorite of ours from 1975, *Get Down Tonight* by K.C. and the Sunshine Band.

"Man, that reminds me of the summer of '75 when we used to dance on the *Crosno Show*," Dana said, as I rolled up the entrance ramp to I-10 West.

I accelerated to about 65 mph to match the flow of traffic and settled into the fast lane with other cars going about the same speed. The first sign I saw was for Phoenix, 116 miles, but I knew we'd be cutting further west to San Diego at I-8, in about 60 miles, and on to San Diego, and another 350 miles after hitting I-8.

"I remember seeing you guys on TV back then, and being a little jealous," Hector said.

"Yeah, I used to go over to Hector's house to watch you guys, and wondered why I wasn't on the show with you. I'm just as good a dancer," Tony added.

"He used to cuss you guys out because you were on TV and he wasn't," Hector said laughing.

"How did that happen?" Tony asked, "I never asked you guys about that."

"What, getting on the show?"

"Yeah," Tony said.

"It's kind of a long story," Dana said.

"We got time, and we're not going anywhere. C'mon tell us," Tony prodded.

"Okay, here goes," Dana began to explain.

I let Dana take the lead telling this story because it was going to take some time and I had to concentrate on driving down the highway.

"You guys remember when me and Jaime, Steve, Sonja, and some other guys performed at the talent show our sophomore year?"

"Yeah, I remember," Hector said, "You all didn't win."

"Yeah, okay, but the experience showed me how to develop a dance routine, to do different types of moves, and how to put together a dance group. So, when Chris came home from college that summer, he and I were talking about something to do during the summer, and I showed him part of the routine we had performed to *Machine Gun* by the Commodores."

"When Dana showed me those dance moves and told me about the dance group I thought that looked pretty cool. I told him I thought we could put together something like that, and we decided to put together a dance group of our own." I interjected, "Dana's group had performed one routine during that talent show, but what I had in mind was more long term and would involve different types of dancing. Dana told me about another group in the talent show that performed to *Funky Stuff,* by Kool and the Gang – Tommy and the Batsons. But the way Dana described their performance it was more along the lines of freestyle using "Lockers-like" dance moves. I envisioned our group doing choreographed group hustles, and individual freestyle dancing."

"The Lockers, what's that?" Hector asked.

"Yeah, you know, the dance group featuring "Rerun" from *What's Happening*!! You know, the fat guy always breaking out in those dance moves during the show," I said.

"Okay, I didn't know their name. Yeah, those guys had that

really unique style of dancing with them jumping in the air, doing jazz splits, and making all those leg and hand moves," Hector said.

"I remember those crazy multi-colored dance shoes, caps, and clothes," Tony added.

"That summer everybody was doing the Robot, the Bump, and the Hustle, and every week we watched Soul Train to see what those guys were doing," Dana said.

"Did you guys have a name? I don't think I ever heard one," Hector asked.

"I tried to keep it simple, we called our dance group, THE GROOP, in all caps and spelled G-R-O-O-P," I said.

"That's kind of stupid," Tony laughed, with Hector joining in.

"Yeah okay, but when Crosno asked me what our name was, I had to come up with something on the spot, and that was it," I also laughed.

"Who was in the group?" Hector leaned forward in the back seat.

"You probably know most of them – Jaime, Steve, Jaime's sister Ruth, Sonja, Melanie, Clara, me and Chris, Steve's sister, and a few others," Dana said, "Hey that reminds me, we're supposed to visit Clara in LA, right?"

"Didn't you call her before we left?" I asked.

"Yeah I did. She's staying with her brother and she said she's looking forward to seeing us when we get to LA." Dana replied.

"Okay, sounds good, we'll call her when we get there and get directions." I said.

"That's right Clara was in your group. I guess you had a pretty mixed group, huh?" Hector relaxed back in his seat.

"Yeah, it was made up of blacks, whites, and Hispanics, so, yeah, pretty diverse, I guess," I added. "Didn't really think about it, but that may have been part of the attraction with Crosno."

"How did you all get on *Crosno*?" Hector asked.

"You guys know Steve's dad is the weatherman on Channel Five, right?" Dana turned around facing Tony and Hector.

"Yeah," Tony answered, "So what?"

"Unbeknownst to a lot of people, he's also El Paso's own Bozo the Clown," Dana said.

"What!?" Tony screeched, "Steve's dad is Bozo? That's crazy." He laughed.

"Yeah, I didn't know that either," Hector said, "I guess that's not something Steve wants everybody to know, huh?"

"Hey don't laugh, it sounds like a pretty good gig if you can get it," I said, "And, it meant Steve's dad had some 'juice' downtown with the TV community, including Steve Crosno. Our dad also knew some folks at the various TV stations and between them we were able to get free tickets to the *Steve Crosno Show*. You know, we performed for six weeks straight and actually had people tell us they watched *Crosno* just to watch us. We'd developed somewhat of a following during those six weeks. I thought that was kind of funny."

"I guess that includes me, 'cause I watched just to see you guys dance. When I watched the show it looked like you guys had rehearsed or practiced your routines, how did that work out?" Hector asked.

"Actually it was a lot like what the four of us did this summer before coming on this trip. You know how the four of us practiced our dance routines at the house to *Wine Flow Disco* and *Slide*? In fact, the idea of the four of us doing dance routines to specific songs kind of originated from our experience with the Groop," I explained.

52

"How's that?" Tony asked.

"We didn't have much else to do during the summer, so we would get together and practice different hustles and routines to most of the hit songs of the day like *Get Down Tonight* and *Love Rollercoaster*. We also wanted to feature individual dancers, and we would feature Steve, the only white guy, but probably the best individual male dancer, and Sonja, who was by far, the best individual girl dancer in the group." I said.

"He and Sonja were really good on the dance floor, and when we wanted to showcase the best of our dancers, we put them out there," Dana said. "Y'all know they were voted 'Best Dancers' for our senior class. Gee, I wonder how that happened?" he laughed.

"Okay, we get that Sonja and Steve were the best in the group. What was it like being on the show?" Tony now asked.

"Yeah, what was that like?" Hector followed.

I continued to talk about dancing on the show to help fill up the time as we continued to drive through the seemingly endless desert on the way to the California border.

"The first time we went down to the studio, Steve and I went to find Crosno to identify ourselves. Once we identified ourselves at the entrance, we were let in and Steve Crosno treated us like celebrities; I guess because he knew Steve's dad," I said.

"When we got in the studio, it was really cool. We'd never been on TV before and all the lights and cameras were exciting. Some of us were a little nervous, but most of us had performed on one stage or another, so we were looking forward to showing our stuff," Dana said.

"When we first got in there and the show started, Crosno played some "warm-up" songs and we danced as couples, but then he played *Get Down Tonight,* and that's when we turned it out. We formed our square and started doing our hustle to that particular song and the other dancers gave us the floor. As we went through the routine I would sing out directions to make sure we got in formation and on beat." I continued, "Then he played another song that was the "Soul Train" line song of the day. That's when we really showed out!"

"That was really cool coming down the Soul Train line," Dana said. "It gave us a chance to show off our 'signature' dance moves. We would just take over and line up on two sides facing each other, forming an aisle for the dancers to move through. Everyone was clapping, moving to music, and shouting encouragement to the dancers coming down the aisle." Dana continued, "It was really a lot of fun because we practiced doing the Soul Train line at the house and already were paired up. Steve and Sonja had even made up a routine to go through the Line. As each pair of

53

dancers entered the dancing lane, the next two dancers moved up to the head of the line, so it becomes a continuous flow of dancers coming down the aisle. We usually went through the Line at least twice – the first time with our dance partners, and then the second time was to show off individual talent. Yeah, we had a great time on the show doing the Line."

"Uh huh, I remember that – a cameraman was stationed at the end of the Soul Train line to get a good view of each dancer as they came down the aisle in front of the camera. I remember thinking it was just like on *Soul Train*. That was pretty cool," Hector said.

"Yeah, that was nice. The other dancers on the show gave us room to really 'get off' and we danced up a storm. Steve did his 'Robotics' and Chris and I did our 'Locker' steps with jazz splits," Dana laughed. "Something you couldn't see on TV was the ovations we got from the other dancers. And that was really cool."

"After the Soul Train line, Crosno interviewed me about The Groop, and I explained that we were friends that had gotten together with a common interest in dancing, and we'd developed several of our own dances. That's also when I made up the name for the group on the spot. I think I made some of us kind of nervous with my bragging about our dancing, but hey, we had already proven ourselves on TV."

"Yep," Dana said, "in fact, since we danced really well that first week, Crosno invited us back for as many times as we wanted to come and we were able to get in free each time."

"I think he wanted us to show up every week." I added.

"Why's that?" Tony asked.

"We gave Crosno a ready-made group of dancers that he knew would dance on just about every song, and we didn't disappoint him. We showed up for several weeks, and had a lot of fun dancing on the show that summer," I said.

"What happened at the end of the summer?" Hector asked.

"I had to go back to school, and I didn't dance with The Groop again, but I think you did, right?" I looked over at Dana.

"Yeah, we continued to perform on the *Crosno Show*, at Basset Center mall, and at freshman orientation at Eastwood. We were known as *The Crosno Kids*. I hated that name, but it's how people knew us. In November, 1975, like right before Thanksgiving, The Groop broke up. It was a lot of fun while it lasted."

"It'd been nice to have been invited to be a part of The Groop." Hector frowned.

I glanced back at Hector, "Yeah, but now you're a Transmanaut, and you're on a road trip in a special edition, black and gold Trans Am, so I think that's better than dancing on TV."

"You're probably right, but I still would like to have been invited."

"Me too," Tony chimed in.

"Okay, sorry," I said, "Next time we get a chance to dance on TV, we'll make sure you're invited," I laughed.

We finally made the turn onto I-8, and headed directly for San Diego. The further west we drove, the more we felt a little like the guy in the old B-movies who's crossing the Sahara Desert and sees an oasis in the distance and hopes it's not a mirage. Between Tucson and San Diego there's not much to see. No trees, no animals, just desert.

I took the exit ramp to Yuma, Arizona. We needed gas, a bathroom and snack break. Again, we exited the car in our normal manner, auditioning for the California crowd we hoped would be out there when we arrived. The desert tortoises, lizards and cacti didn't seem impressed – everybody's a critic. Once we got back in the car, we headed west again, only a few miles from the California state line.

55

There wasn't much difference in the terrain even after we crossed into California. We were still in mountainous desert with signs telling us to keep our air-conditioning on and to drive a certain speed; I guess so you don't run out of gas or break down because of overheating in the desert. We were in the southernmost reaches of the Mojave Desert, and that's not a place you want to break down or be stranded.

As we crossed into California, we all cheered, and Tony

asked, "How much farther to San Diego?"

"Probably another couple of hours," Dana answered, yawning.

"Sleepy?" I asked.

"A little," he said. "Not much out here."

"Yeah, I hear you," I agreed.

"Need a break?" he turned and looked at me. "I can take over."

"Nah, I'm fine, just a little bored." Then a moment later, I said, "What's that coming up behind us?"

"What? Where?" Tony said, looking through the back window.

"There," I said, as I pointed in my rearview mirror. "I don't know where he came from, maybe from behind one of the large Coppertone ads, I don't know – but one minute he wasn't there, and one minute he was – shit, a California Highway Patrol car."

He smoothly came up behind us, no more than a car length between us. When I saw him getting closer in my rearview, I nervously told everyone in the car, "Be cool, we've got a state trooper on our tail!"

Tony turned around to look again, and I said, "Don't look at him, you might provoke him!" Tony hurriedly turned around.

"What do you think he wants?" Dana asked.

I said, "I don't know and I don't want to find out, just be cool."

Hector added, "Just stay at the speed limit, and we should be okay."

Like, duh! In the first mile the CHiP was on our tail, and then in the second mile he smoothly rolled up next to us on the left like a great white shark looking over its next meal. Of course I had been in the right lane the entire time, doing the 55 mile speed limit, and staying well within the boundaries of my lane, just to make sure I didn't provoke this guy into stopping us. Maybe he was just curious about the new car, the Texas tags, or the fact there were four young Black guys in the car. As he drove by on the left, the car assumed a deadlier profile, it was painted black and white and festooned with a myriad of antennae. Unlike the Texas state troopers, this guy was not wearing a Stetson cowboy hat, he wasn't wearing a hat at all, but he was wearing the requisite aviator sunglasses. I looked over at him, just a peek, to check him out, and he looked back at me without expression.

"I feel like throwing him the 'finger,'" I said.

"Are you crazy?" Dana said. "Don't do anything stupid."

After looking us over, he sped up to a position to our front, and looked back at us through his rearview mirror. This little tableau of police harassment went on for about 15 minutes until he saw something on the other side of highway, crossed over into the left lane, and made a U-turn through the median to take off after some other poor sap. We thought we were in the clear until a few minutes later, some "county mounty" got behind us driving a white and blue police car. He hung back behind us for about ten to fifteen minutes, and then when he peeled off, a few minutes later another CHiP car joined in behind us.

"I've never seen this bull shit from highway patrolmen and sheriff's deputies," I scowled. "I don't know what the fuck is going on, but it seems like we're the flavor of the month."

"Why don't you put the car on cruise, that way you don't have to be as nervous about the speed limit." Dana suggested.

Yeah, that sounded like a good idea, so I put the car in cruise control at 55 MPH just to make sure I didn't exceed the speed limit and give them an excuse to pull me over.

As we continued to be slowly pursued by these various cop cars, Tony got nervous and asked, "What the hell's going on Chris?"

"I don't know," I said. "But this is some weird shit."

"You know they're probably in radio communication with each other, and they're just fucking with us because we're four Black guys driving this great car," Hector said. "Police are always fucking with black guys driving nice cars 'cause they think they're either stolen or drug dealers or something. This is pure racism."

"Yeah," Dana said. "They're probably jealous and racist."

Whatever the reason, we didn't play our music, didn't talk much and really held our collective breaths until we saw San Diego in the distance. Although the police harassment only lasted about an hour, it felt like it had been a week. I had never gripped the steering wheel as hard as I gripped it during that hour we were being tailed. When the last CHiP car peeled off without so much as a friendly wave, we all let go of our collective breaths. Whew, it seemed like it was over.

"It's about time," I breathed in relief. "I'm glad that's over."

"We still don't know what that was all about, but I'm glad it's over too," Hector said.

"How many cop cars followed us?" Tony asked.

"I think we were stalked by at least five CHiPs and county mounties," I said.

"Damn, what a welcome to Cali," Dana said. "I hope the rest of the trip is less eventful. We don't need anymore run-ins with the law."

"Yeah, I'm looking forward to getting to San Diego and just relaxing in our room," I said.

As we approached San Diego, you could see the landscape begin to change. There were trees and irrigated farmlands and greenery in the distance. And of course, the closer we got to San Diego on I-8, the more CHiPs we saw. We were just amazed at the number of CHiPs there were on the road. Even though we had just seen a few in the last hour up close and personal, this was wall-to-wall state troopers.

58

"What the hell is going on?" Hector exclaimed, "There are swarms of these guys all over the place."

"They're pulling over cars left and right," Tony said. "Maybe they got a quota to meet."

"I don't know, but I'm keeping us at 55, to make sure we don't become a target again," I said.

Unfortunately, we didn't have a CB radio with us, so we had to depend on the speed of traffic to hide us if we intended on speeding on the highway. President Nixon had imposed the nation-wide 55 MPH speed limit on all the interstate highways, and it had yet to be rescinded by either Ford or Carter, so we were stuck with either creeping at 55 mph or moving with the traffic. If the traffic was moving fast, we were moving fast; if the traffic slowed down, so did we. And if we were traveling by ourselves with little traffic around, I stayed pretty close to the speed limit. Our earlier introduction to CHiPs was an instructive one.

As we headed to downtown San Diego, I followed behind some cars that were going at a pretty good clip when out of nowhere this black & white CHiPs car swooped down like a diving sea hawk about to grab an unsuspecting mouse in its talons, and pulled over the lead car in our speeding procession.

"Oh shit, where did that guy come from?" Dana said nervously.

Tony and Hector were looking out the windows looking for where he came from.

"Look up there, above us, there're these little perches where the CHiPs are hiding in the hills above the highway. They have a bird's-eye view of the cars speeding beneath them," Hector pointed behind us.

"That might explain where that very first CHiPs car we encountered at the state line came from," Dana said.

"Yeah, that's true," I said. "There weren't many hills back there, but there were a lot of hiding places."

In this case, these guys wasted no time in bringing down the heat on any car breaking the speed limit and that gave us another object lesson not to screw around on the California highways. Huh, our first lesson had been personal, and now we saw these guys meant business with every driver that thought about breaking the speed limit.

After negotiating the I-8 gauntlet, we finally made it inside the city limits of San Diego and headed towards downtown.

Dago

We arrived in downtown San Diego around mid-afternoon, just in time to try and figure out where we were going to stay. Since we had just stayed in a Howard Johnson's the previous night we looked for a similar hotel in San Diego. When we saw a Holiday Inn we decided to stay there, instead of Howard Johnson's. Little did we know we were right near the "red light district" where all the sailors from the San Diego Naval Base seemed to hang out.

After we checked in and got our two room keys, we took the elevator to the fourth floor and collapsed in our room. We took a short nap, and headed out to the street at about 7 o'clock. We were dressed the same way as earlier in the day – we didn't feel like getting dressed up just to get something to eat and explore downtown San Diego. As the four of us got to the lobby, the bell captain at the main bell stand – a bespectacled older white guy, balding, and wearing a hotel uniform – gestured for us to come over to his stand.

"I saw you guys check in. You going out tonight?" He inquired, smiling.

"Yep," I said. "We want to explore the night life offered by your beautiful city."

"You know where you are, right?"

"No, where?"

"This is right off the 'red light district' here in Dago."

"Dago?"

"That's what all the sailors call it when they come in for shore leave."

"A lot of sailors out tonight?" I asked.

"Every night," he said, "but particularly on Fridays and Saturdays, and this is a Friday night in June, so, yeah, they're going to be out like fireflies, just like the street walkers."

"Street walkers?" Tony asked. "Where?"

"Over about a block, west," the bell captain said.

Hector had been quiet up to that point. "Let's go check it out," he said.

"Okay," I said, and thanked the bell captain for his information.

"No problem," he said with a knowing smile, and went back to his regular duties.

We walked west out of the entrance of the hotel. Once we got over to the epicenter of the red light district, we were pretty much surrounded by sailors in their whites and blues, and prostitutes making propositions and counter offers for services. The hustle and bustle reminded me of 42nd and Broadway, the "ho" capital of Manhattan. Guys were hanging out of doorways drinking whiskey and beer, having a good time.

There were bars and lounges with garish neon signs blaring out music from disco to country, something for everybody's tastes – just like the streetwalkers, a myriad of women for everybody's tastes as well. We walked around with that wide-eyed look taking in the sights and sounds.

"Guys we can't be over here," Dana said. "This could jeopardize me going to West Point. You know I report in a few weeks."

"Yeah, you and your mommy are going to West Point," Tony laughed.

"Shut up Tony, I'm not going to be a 'momma's boy' while I'm at West Point."

"Uh huh, who else's mom is going to college with him?" Tony taunted.

That was a sore subject with Dana. If you wanted to piss him off call him "a momma's boy."

He said, "That wasn't my idea, she wanted to be closer to our grandparents, and that was the closest assignment."

"Sure…sure it was," Tony laughed.

"Leave him alone Tony," I said, then turned and gazed at Dana. "Look, I'm a commissioned second lieutenant in the Army, and going to law school, so who's got more to lose? Just chill out, we're not going to do anything except talk to some of the ho's and watch the action."

"Okay," Dana said, still a little apprehensive.

"So okay, how you go about talking to the ho's?" Hector asked.

"You basically just walk up and talk to them, like regular people." I said.

"What, they just talk to you about being ho's?" Tony was incredulous.

"Yep, that's been my experience." I replied.

"What experience?" Hector challenged.

"Look, you know I was at Fort Riley, near Junction City. Well, Junction City was known for its red light district. Me and another cadet went downtown to experience Junction City's limited night life, and while I was downtown I talked to several prostitutes. They were pretty cool and had no problem talking about being a prostitute. I learned a lot talking to them."

"Okay, so how do you know who's who?" Tony asked.

"Dana and I walked around New York last year, and I think we can tell the prostitutes from the other girls. Plus, the prostitutes dress a hell of a lot more provocatively. They're trying to put their best 'ass-sets' on display." I chuckled.

"Got it. You lead the way." Hector said.

"Okay, just walk like you know what's going on. We're all old enough to be sailors on shore leave, even though we're not in uniform, we can pass as sailors," I said. "Just be cool."

"I can do cool," Tony said, and he started walking in that sort of slow "pimp walk" with an exaggerated swagger. We all walked doing our notion of a "pimp walk" just so we wouldn't stand out from the crowd.

We walked the walk, and talked the talk, but didn't participate in the thriving night business of those working girls. We found a place to sit along the main thoroughfare and watch the prostitutes at work. They were white and black, dressed in mini-skirts, hot pants, halters and tube tops. They were walking in high heels, and platform boots, all in outlandish colors and with plenty of make-up, to show off their assets and attract potential customers.

"Damn," Tony said, "I didn't know ho's could be so fine."

"I thought you had all that experience being from the bad side of Knoxville," Hector said. "What, you never saw ho's before?"

"Nah, I was too young for that, but I saw enough crime in the hood to know about drugs, shootings, and robberies. That's how I ended up in El Paso with Aunt Loo and Uncle George," Tony replied.

"Yeah I know. I've heard your stories about hearing gunfire at night and huddling in your bed under the covers," Hector said. "What does that have to do with this?"

"Nothing," Tony shot back. "You brought it up. Like I said, these ho's are fine."

I joined in, "You know some of these ho's may not be women, some of them could be men in drag."

"Oh hell no, what makes you say that?" Hector said.

"Different strokes for different folks," I said.

"What do you know about that?" Tony laughed.

"You guys really don't know about Austin and UT, do you?" I asked.

"What do you mean?" Hector said.

"We're on our way to San Francisco, the gay capital of the country, right? I mean everybody knows that, right?"

"Yeah, okay, so what? You plan on fucking somebody in the

ass in Frisco?" Tony laughed.

"Not hardly," I said, "I've had enough of that scene in Austin and at UT."

"Like what?" Tony asked.

"When I first got to Austin, I found out it was the gay and lesbian capitol of Texas, like San Francisco East, and UT was just as bad. I was on the 'Freshman Experience' floor of Jester Dorm, maybe the largest dorm in the country at the time, with 3,000 residents. What I didn't know was there was a section on my floor where many gay guys, many of them transvestites, lived together."

"What? You were living on the same floor with a bunch of faggots?" Tony laughed. "You?"

"Yeah, that was a new experience for me, considering I had just graduated from NMMI, an all-male, redneck, military junior college, and had been through all that ROTC bull shit. I didn't know much about the gay and lesbian lifestyle, especially where men were transvestites."

"You mean guys dressing up as women?" Hector asked.

"Yeah, in drag – drag queens. That was something different – watching guys dressed as women walk past my dorm room to get to the elevators."

"Damn, how did you handle that?" Tony asked.

"Sometimes I was just dumbfounded because some of these guys made for decent-looking women and I was kind of shocked by it all at first. Initially, I didn't have any feelings about it until I started getting approached by gay guys who thought I was gay."

"You? I guess I never thought of you as a gay magnet," Hector laughed.

"Fuck you Hector," I said as I continued my story. "Yeah that was sort of surprising since I had always thought of myself as kind of a macho guy. But, apparently, maybe because of the really short shorts I used to wear – you know those cutoffs, or maybe my really youthful good looks, or whatever, I was getting propositioned every so often by gay guys. Not only on campus, but just walking around Austin, near some of the gay clubs. I wasn't always aware of where the gay clubs were until I started getting propositioned, so I found out real quick where they were and avoided them."

"That is too funny," Hector laughed.

"There was this one time when some nigga thought I was gay and wanted me to suck his dick, and that wasn't too funny," I said.

"How'd that happen?" Hector asked.

"This past spring, I was leaving the Jester Dorm cafeteria when I was approached by a kind of rough-looking nigga that had 'Eastside' written all over him."

"The Eastside?" Hector inquired.

"Yeah, the Eastside is where most of the black folk in Austin lived because of segregation, and where much of the black population still lives. You almost always knew when you were talking with someone from the Eastside. They normally had this look that identified them as being from the Eastside, whether it was their clothes, mannerisms, attitude, their walk, speech or a combination of all those. In this case, this guy was definitely from the Eastside.

"His first words left no doubt he was from the Eastside. He asked me, 'Do you live in the dorm?' And stupidly, I said, 'Yeah, why?' And he said, 'Well you look like a faggot, so I thought you would take me up to your room and suck my dick.'"

"What'd you say to that?" Tony asked.

"Now, okay, this is one of those moments when a whole lot of thoughts run through your mind. I was dressed in my usual short shorts with the knee-high white socks and the red stripe at the top, red running shoes, nice Afro and my normal clean-shaven good looks. So I guess to this guy, who was dark skinned, uh no offense guys, butt ugly, and dressed in some worn out looking jeans, raggedy-ass T-shirt, tired looking Converses and scraggly-assed beard, I must have looked gay. In order to get past the shock of hearing this out-of-the-blue, ridiculous proposition, I asked him, 'What did you say?' He repeated himself, 'You heard me nigga, take me to your room and suck my dick!'"

"At that point, I got pissed. I told this guy, 'Okay, let's go up to my room, and if you pull your dick out I'm going to cut that motherfucker off, so get the fuck out my face!'"

"How'd he react to that?" Hector asked.

"You guys know I keep that machete under the seat in the car, right? Well, unbeknownst to this guy, but pretty well known to anybody who's spent any time in my dorm room, that's where I normally keep it, under my bed. I keep it really sharp and used it as a prop in some of our fraternity rituals. I was trained to use it at Fort Riley, and I just liked to have the thing around. I was serious about using it on this nasty motherfucker. After I told him what I would do to his dick, that fuck wad just shrugged, laughed it off, and walked away."

"That's pretty good Chris, are you looking forward to getting with any gay guys on this trip?" Hector laughed.

"So with all that experience with faggots, I guess you'd be able to recognize them if we ran into some of them down here, right?" Tony laughed.

"Will you both shut the fuck up," I said. "I have this fine-assed girlfriend back home, so I don't think there's any doubt about my persuasion. But it was kind of fucked up getting propositioned by gay guys like that all the damned time."

We got up and resumed walking amid the raucous sights and sounds of the sailors and prostitutes, when we found ourselves on a side street off the main drag. There wasn't a lot of action on this street, and it seemed unnaturally quiet compared to the main artery of activity. In front of us there was a neon sign for a massage parlor, proclaiming in flashing red, yellow and green, "Best Massages in San Diego!" and "Sailors Welcome!" and "Beautiful Girls, Girls, Girls!"

Tony looked up, "Ever been in a massage parlor?"

"Nope," I said. "You all want to go in?"

"Yeah, let's do this," Hector said enthusiastically.

Dana wasn't as enthusiastic, but he was curious, "Okay, let's go in and see what's going on."

I opened the door, which was decorated with pictures of pretty Asian women in various stages of undress. I wasn't sure we were walking into a massage parlor or a strip bar. We walked in and were greeted by a very nice looking Asian-looking woman, probably in her 30s.

"You gentlemen here for massage?" she asked in her slightly accented voice.

I looked around the lobby and saw we were surrounded by red and gold brocaded furniture, love seats, wingback chairs, straight back chairs, and a carpet that felt three inches deep, in a beautiful burgundy color. The walls were decorated in gold and burgundy striped textured wall paper, with crystal chandeliers falling like ice crystals in their intricate designs, showering us with twinkling patterns of light and color. The air was intoxicating with the fragrance of some lightly exotic incense that was burning from candles strategically placed around the room. The Asian lady had come from behind an ornate desk that sat near the entrance to two or three different hallways branching from this main area.

"Uh, yeah," I said. "How much?"

"Well, for you sir, it would be fifty dollars for one hour."

"And if we all want a massage, how much?"

"For all four, I give you discount, maybe one-hundred and fifty dollars for all four."

"You guys want a massage?" I asked the other guys.

Tony and Hector's eyes got big, and Dana said, "Probably not right now, I think we'll wait on the massage."

"You in town for a while, or just overnight?" she asked.

"Overnight," I said.

"Then tell you what, I discount you twenty-five dollars if you want massage right now."

"Do you all offer more services than just a massage?" I asked slyly.

"What you mean, more services?" she replied just as slyly.

"Well, my friends were more interested in getting with some

women in a nice environment, and we thought this might be such a place."

"Ah so, you want to have sex," she said, just putting it right out in the open.

"Well, yeah, I guess when you put it like that, yeah, sex," I answered. You could see Tony and Hector just panting with the possibility of having sex with some of the girls whose pictures were on the door. I'll give Dana credit – he was as cool as a cucumber, listening to this exchange.

"Oh no, we don't have sex out here," she said. "But if you get massage, you make private arrangements with girl, okay?"

"So, we have to pay for the massage first, then make private arrangements with whoever gives us the massage to have sex at some other location?"

"Or in one of our rooms," she said, "on massage table, very erotic."

Damn, I was getting hard standing there trying to be cool, but the vision of having sex with some beautiful Asian girl on a massage table, especially after the movie last night, was just getting to me. I could see a similar look and reaction was affecting the other three as well. *This might be a good time for a well-executed retreat before we get into a difficult situation*, I thought.

"You know, it's getting pretty late, I think we'll call it a night," I said.

"No, you come in, have nice time. I charge you just one-hundred dollars for all four."

Wow, one-hundred dollars for all four of us? But that told me something – the real business was sex, the massage was just the cover to get you in the massage rooms. No telling how much that might cost.

"Uh, no thanks, I think we'll be going," I said.

"Last chance," she said. "Only fifty dollars for all four."

Tony and Hector looked at me with that, 'I-really-really-want-to-go-in-and-fuck-somebody' look, but I declined again, and thanked the madam, as I'm sure she was, for the generous offer, and we got the hell out of there before it got real expensive.

"Why'd we have to leave?" Tony asked once we got back on the street. We started walking back to the main artery.

"Look guys, we came a long way in two days, and have even farther to go. If you want to pay for some pussy, that's fine, but let's see where this trip takes us. You may end up getting some free pussy. Isn't that what you want?"

"Yeah, okay," Hector said. "I hate it when you're right."

"I agree." Dana said, as we walked down the main drag towards the hotel, "Let's go to Sea World tomorrow, and then get to LA."

"Sounds like a plan," I added.

When we dragged back into the hotel, the ubiquitous bell captain was still on duty. "Gentlemen," he said, "enjoy yourselves? You're back a little earlier than I expected."

"Yep," I said. "Thanks for the tip, that's a real happening scene out there."

"Anything to oblige our hotel guests," he laughed. And we laughed too as we made our way to the elevators. This was definitely a night to remember.

When we got back to the room I turned on the TV and we flopped on our beds.

"Hey, you guys hungry? We haven't eaten since Yuma and I'm really hungry." Tony said.

"How about room service?" Dana suggested.

"Is there a menu on the desk?" I asked.

70

Dana got off the bed and walked over to the desk next to the TV. "There's a lot of stuff on the menu, take a look." He threw the guest services book on the bed.

I looked at it, "The cheapest stuff on here is burgers and fries on the all-night menu – about six bucks."

"Damn, that's expensive, but if we don't it means going back out there and I didn't see any fast food places nearby," Tony said.

"So I vote for burgers and fries from room service."

"Sounds good." Hector said.

"I'm in," Dana agreed, "I'll call down and order it."

"It's going to take about forty-five minutes," Dana warned us after he hung up with the restaurant.

"Damn, I don't know if I can wait that long," Tony whined. "I'm starving."

"What choice do you have? Just chill, it'll be up here soon enough." I said.

"What's to drink?" Hector asked.

"I think there's a soda machine down the hall with the ice machine," Dana answered.

I looked over at Tony and Hector, "Why don't the three of us go down and get the sodas and Dana can stay here in case the waiter shows up."

"Okay, let's go," Tony said, as he and Hector got off their bed and went to the door. Tony unlatched the chain and turned towards the sound of the whirring ice machine and soda machine to his right.

"Keep the door locked," I said to Dana. "We'll be right back."

"Negro, I'm not some little kid. Just go and get the sodas. I want something orange or grape if they've got it, if not then a Coke."

"Okay, will do," I laughed.

The three of us walked down to the vending room and got our sodas. Hector looked around and asked, "Did you bring the ice bucket?"

"No," I said, "I guess I assumed one of you would get it."

"Shit, alright, I'll get it when we take the sodas back to the room." Tony said.

We walked back to the room with our hands full of sodas and I knocked on the door.

"Who is it?" Dana said in a falsetto voice, like some little girl.

"It's the Big Bad Wolf. Open up or I'll huff and I'll puff and I'll blooow your house down." I laughed.

"Dana open the fucking door," Tony said impatiently, "Quit playing games."

"You gotta get a sense of humor Tony," Dana said as he unlatched the chain and let us in the door.

"Fuck that, I'm going back down the hall to get the ice." Tony snapped.

"No wonder you're pissed, you forgot the ice," Dana laughed.

"Yeah, yeah, I'll be right back." Tony picked up the ice bucket and stormed off back to the vending room. Dana closed the door behind him as we continued to wait for our room service.

A few minutes later Tony was back in the room with the ice and we filled our glasses with ice and poured the sodas.

"That tastes good," Tony smacked his lips. "Where's the fucking food."

"I'm sure it'll be here soon," I said. Obviously everyone was getting pretty hungry waiting on the damned food.

By the time we heard the knock on the door announcing the arrival of the food, we were starved. Dana rushed over and unlatched the door to let the waiter in the room. The waiter, a younger white guy in black pants and shoes, white shirt and white jacket, pushed in a cart filled with silver-topped plates, silverware wrapped in linen napkins, with ketchup, mustard, salt and pepper. The waiter spread out the dishes on the desk and table on the other side of the TV and uncovered each dish with a flourish to reveal the mounds of burgers and fries with lettuce, tomatoes and pickles on each plate.

He stood back and said, "Dinner is served gentlemen." The smells were delicious. "That'll be thirty dollars which includes tax and the automatic gratuity of fifteen percent."

"Okay," I paid for the meal in cash, tipped the guy, and he pushed the cart towards the door as he showed himself out the room.

Tony and Hector grabbed the plates on the tray closest to their bed and Dana and I did the same. As soon as we had the plates arrayed in front of us on the bed, we ravenously attacked the food. The next several minutes were filled with the sounds of us wolfing down the nicely-charbroiled burgers and crisp fries. Once satiated, we set the empty plates outside the door, called it a night and went to bed.

The next morning I woke up around 8 o'clock wondering if the previous night really happened. As before, I woke up first to get into the bathroom first, and then woke up the other three guys. This time Dana got in the bathroom second, and Tony and Hector flipped for the next turn in the bathroom.

Once we finished getting dressed, we made our way down to the lobby to check out. The desk clerk was a pretty, chocolate-skinned, black woman, with beautiful expressive brown eyes, who had a mischievous glint in her eye.

"Did you all have a good night in our fair city last night?" she asked.

"Yes, thank you." I handed her the room keys. "We had a great time."

"Good," she smiled. "I would hate for our guests to be disappointed during their stay here at the Holiday Inn."

"We weren't disappointed," I said, "thanks to the bell captain."

"Yes, he does a great job in directing patrons to various activities." She winked as she rang up our final bill.

"No extra charges gentlemen, you're all set."

"Thank you," I said.

"Did you get the feeling she knew we had been directed to the red light district?" Tony said on our way out to the car.

"Yeah, I'm sure she knew," I said. "But she looked pretty good, I think if we'd had more time I could have hit that."

"Yeah okay, 'Pretty Boy,' who couldn't score at UT. What

makes you think you could have scored with her?" Hector challenged.

"Different persona. She already has an image of us as being out on the edge, so I would have played that card and I bet I could have gotten her out," I said.

"Yeah, yeah, but we'll never know will we?" Tony scoffed.

"Not this time, but I bet we'll have plenty of other opportunities on this trip," I said.

"I hope you're right," Hector said as we approached the car.

We loaded our bags back into the car and checked the Trip Tik for the route to Sea World San Diego. Luckily it was off I-5 North on our way to LA, so we wouldn't have to waste any time getting back on the road. Hector had called his Aunt Rose the night before to give her an approximate time for our arrival. San Diego is about 90 miles from LA, and then another 40 minutes or so to get to Redlands where Aunt Rose lived. Hector told her we would be there about six in the evening, just in time for dinner. That only left us about six hours to spend at Sea World, but that was probably enough time. There's only so much time you can spend seeing Shamu and his friends.

As we motored out of the hotel parking lot, we drove by the same area we had spent so much time last night. It looked so drab and deserted – there was no magic at this time of day, and certainly no prostitutes out this early in the morning. We didn't see the street with the massage parlor…probably a good thing.

We followed the signs out of downtown San Diego to I-5N towards Sea World and Los Angeles. Once we got on I-5N, we began to see signs for Sea World – it was located in the Mission Beach/Ocean Beach Park area west of I-5N. Once we got to the correct exit we veered to the west to get to the park.

After a few minutes we arrived at the stylized entrance to Sea World with the world-famous logo of a leaping Shamu, the killer whale. Once we entered the park we were greeted with an army of pink flamingoes, and a beautifully landscaped park that featured water mammal shows with dolphins, killer whales, seals, otters, sea lions, and walruses. There were plenty of rides, and a water park area for swimming and enjoying the artificial beach. There were also glass-encased exhibits showing various fishes from around the world, as well as, non-performing aquatic mammals. In one of the glass-encased exhibits we saw a large sea mammal, probably a humpback whale trying to mate.

Just like a guy, Hector had to comment. "Look at the size of his dick, my goodness, he's built like a horse."

"He is a whale. What, you jealous?" I laughed.

"Maybe," Hector admitted. "But I don't know if I want to have a dick the length of my arm."

"You know my nickname in the fraternity is 'Mr. J,' I said, "And some of the girls say 'J is for Jumbo because that's what I do best,'" I laughed.

"Get out of here, you already admitted you didn't get laid at UT," Tony chuckled.

"That was on that one occasion, I've been there for two years. You don't think I've gotten any pussy the entire time I've been at UT, you got to be crazy," I said, just lying my ass off.

Other people around us were getting interested in our conversation, mostly young white teenaged girls.

"This isn't the time or the place," I said to Hector. "Why don't you keep on dreaming of having a dick the size of your arm."

"Cut it out you guys, who cares about the size of any of your pencil-thin dicks?" Dana laughed, "Especially when you haven't done anything with them."

"Oh, and you have?" I challenged, "Please, Super Cadet, you haven't gotten any pussy yet, 'cause you're hoping to score on this trip."

"Hey, quit calling me 'Super Cadet,'" Dana said with some irritation.

As his brother, I knew exactly how to get under his skin, and I knew he hated to be called "Super Cadet."

"Alright, you guys ready to go see Shamu?" I said, "I think we've gotten all the humor we're going to get out of ol' 'whale dick' here."

"Okay, let's see how high Shamu and his buddies can jump, then let's get on the road to LA," Hector suggested. "I'm kind of excited to see the family."

"Sounds good," I said, and we ambled over to Shamu Stadium, the centerpiece attraction at Sea World. We enjoyed the show, and enjoyed watching people getting splashed in the "Splash Zone" near the pool. The killer whales were obviously well-trained and responded obediently to their trainers. I admired the trainers for being brave enough to not only get in the water with killer whales, but to work with them daily to get them to this level of perfection in their performances.

Once the performance was over, we decided to hit the road. Los Angeles beckoned to us and we answered the call. LA here we come.

On to LA, the First Time

Finally, that afternoon, we arrived in Los Angeles, the home to movie stars, swimming pools, pretty women, and beaches. We were going to take L.A. by storm, a Texas-sized storm, and the denizens of the City of Angels would never be the same.

Instead of driving directly to the city, we drove north on I-15 and then east on I-10 to Redlands; a town located 65 miles east of Los Angeles. This is where Hector's Aunt Rose, his mother's sister, who was like a second mother to him, lived with her husband, Uncle Rudi, and his California cousins.

Hector had gotten directions from his uncle the night before and guided me to a specific exit off I-10.

"Pull up over here," Hector said, "at the Amoco station, we'll call from there."

"What's the plan?" I pulled into the gas station close to the telephone booth located on the other side of the pumps.

"I'll call them from here, and Uncle Rudi will rendezvous with us here and lead us to the house."

"While we're waiting, I'm going to fill up."

"Alright," Hector said.

I scooted my seat forward to let him out of the car.

He laboriously climbed out of the backseat, and walked over to the telephone booth.

The door was still open, "You got change?" I called out.

"Yeah, I'm fine."

"Okay, we'll be over there," I pointed at the pumps.

"Okay," he said as he fed coins in the phone. I closed my door and drove over to the closest pump.

"Dana, go inside and tell them we want to fill 'er up," I said.

"Okay, anything else?"

"No, we'll eat at Aunt Rose's, I guess."

"I need to take a piss," Tony added. "I'll go in with Dana."

"Alright," I said, opening my door. The passenger door slammed shut as Dana and Tony got out and walked to the office. I got out and stood by the car, striking a cool pose as I waited to fill the gas tank. A few seconds later the pump was turned on with a distinctive ping.

I began to pump the gas, each gallon going in with a ring of the bell, until the gas seeped out around the metal nozzle of the gas pump handle.

Hector walked up and said, "Uncle Rudi's on his way, he'll be here in a few."

"Cool, once Dana and Tony get back, we'll be set."

"I need to piss too. I'll be right back," Hector said, and took off toward the building.

I turned back to the car, got in, and started it up. I moved the car around to face the street and waited on the other guys. They came out in a few minutes with some bags of chips and bottles of soda.

78

"Y'all couldn't wait 'til we get to Aunt Rose's?"

"Nah man, we're hungry now, no telling when we might eat next," Tony said. "We haven't eaten in like four hours."

"Whatever." I turned to Hector, "What kind of car they driving?"

"I forgot to ask. Why?"

"Did you tell them what we were driving?"

"No, they didn't ask."

I looked towards the street, "Maybe that's them pulling up now."

An older brown Cadillac pulled into the gas station parking lot and idled as the driver looked us over.

"Yeah, I think that's them, roll down your window, so I can see."

I rolled my window down to give Hector a better look, and once the window went down, the driver of the other car apparently recognized Hector and the car slowly drove over to us.

The driver's side window lowered and an older, dark-skinned man's face appeared. "Hector?" he said.

"Hey, Uncle Rudi, it's us."

"Good to see you son. Okay guys follow me to the house. Make sure you keep up," Uncle Rudi said.

"No problem." I rolled up my window. "Make sure you keep up," I said in a gruff voice mimicking Uncle Rudi's overly officious tone. "He sounds like kind of an asshole."

"Well, I warned you," Hector said. "Uncle Rudi is a retired Marine Corps gunnery sergeant, you know the type – he gets up before the crack of dawn and everything's about total discipline in his house. I told you he runs a tight ship, and it's not going to be any different because we're here."

I looked over at Dana as we followed Uncle Rudi's car through the streets of Redlands. "I guess you'll get a taste of Beast Barracks a few weeks early," I chuckled.

"We'll see." Dana said.

"What's Beast Barracks?" Tony asked.

"It's like basic training at West Point," Dana explained. "All plebes go through it. It's like six weeks long during the summer and starts the day we arrive on 'R' Day."

"What's 'R' Day?" Hector piped in.

"It stands for Reception Day, it's just the first day we get there. Our families get a chance to see us march at the end of that first day after they go through orientation."

"The families go through orientation?" Tony asked.

"Yeah, so they get an understanding of the whole West Point experience, and particularly what we're going through that first day – the day the transformation begins from civilian to plebe."

"But you were a cadet colonel in ROTC," Hector protested. "Weren't you like the highest-ranking cadet in the district?"

"Yeah," Dana said, "But that's not going to mean shit when I get to West Point. I'll be just like all the other plebes."

"No, you'll be different because you'll have four years of junior ROTC under your belt, and that'll put you ahead of other guys who don't have that experience," I said. "It really helped me out when I got to Fort Knox, and NMMI after that."

"I remember Dana mentioned Fort Knox once before. What was at Fort Knox?" Hector asked.

"Basic ROTC Camp -- it's like basic training for ROTC cadets going through the two-year senior ROTC program. It's designed to teach them the basics of the Army before going through the last two years of ROTC before commissioning," I said.

"Kind of like Dana's Beast Barracks?" Tony observed.

"Yeah, except Beast Barracks is run by cadets and Chris' basic was run by drill sergeants, but they're both six weeks long." Dana added.

"Oh, so you've had experience dealing with guys like Uncle Rudi." Hector laughed tapping me on the shoulder.

"Yeah, and that wasn't a lot of fun, so this should be interesting," I stated.

"I think we're here." I turned onto a nicely mature-looking residential street. The Cadillac pulled into the driveway of a ranch-style home with a perfectly manicured front lawn, dotted with shrubs, trees, and flowers in bloom – a very nice looking house.

I parked next to the Cadillac and got a better look at it. The Cadillac was spotless, with chrome shined to a mirror-like finish, and the white walled tires gleaming in the early evening sunlight. Apparently, Uncle Rudi meticulously maintained his car, and took pride in its appearance.

Uncle Rudi got out of his car accompanied by a young black woman. He was a barrel-chested, dark skinned man, who wore his hair in that same Marine Corps buzz cut, and stood about six feet tall. You could imagine him still in uniform, because he seemed to march to the beat of military drums wherever he walked. The young woman was also dark-skinned, with a short black afro, attractive face, about 5"6" with a slender build. She was wearing shorts, white blouse and sandals.

We executed our Transmanautic exit with our normal panache and showed we were a precision drill team, at least when getting out of the car. We were still dressed in the clothes we'd been wearing since the first day. We'd changed t-shirts and underwear, and maybe our socks, but I'm sure we were still a motley crew to the critical eye of Uncle Rudi.

"Hey Uncle Rudi, hi Audrey," Hector said as he walked over to his uncle and cousin and gave them both hugs.

Uncle Rudi looked at us with some amusement, "Cute maneuver. You all figure that out on your own?"

Uh oh, here we go. I thought.

"Yes sir," Hector said. "It's kind of our special way of getting out of the Trans Am. We even call ourselves the Transmanauts."

Uncle Rudi laughed, "Okay, Transmanauts, welcome to our casa."

"Thank you," I said. "We really appreciate you allowing us to stay at your home."

"You're quite welcome. Hector is his Aunt Rose's favorite nephew, so we looked forward to entertaining him and his friends. Get your bags and come on in." Uncle Rudi started towards the front door, and ordered Audrey, "Stay out here and show them into the house when they get their bags."

"Okay. C'mon guys," I said. We walked to the back of the car and popped the trunk. We grabbed our bags and followed Hector's cousin, Audrey, into the house.

As we approached the front door, with its decoratively painted storm door, Aunt Rose stood there, the spitting image of Hector's mom. She gave Hector a big hug. She hadn't seen him in a while and it showed.

Aunt Rose greeted us and said, "Please call me 'Aunt Rose' while you're here, Nell tells me you're just like Hector's brothers, and that makes you family. Make yourselves at home."

Aunt Rose turned to Audrey, "Show them where they'll be sleeping, and then we can eat dinner."

"C'mon Hector, I'll show you your room." We followed Audrey through the nicely appointed house back to one of the four bedrooms.

"There's only one bed," Audrey said. "But it's a queen and three of you should be able to fit on that, and we put a sleeping bag on the floor for one of you." There were three pillows on the bed, and a sleeping bag rolled up on the foot of the bed.

"Okay," I said, "We'll figure out who sleeps where." We dropped our bags in the room and followed her to the dining room.

Uncle Rudi, Aunt Rose, and another of Hector's girl cousins, Veronica – Ronnie, as they called her, a younger version of Audrey, and wearing a similar pair of shorts and blouse – all stood waiting until we entered the room, and then, on some sort of unknown signal, all sat down together. The whole tableau reminded me of NMMI and our "family-style" dining in the mess hall.

The dining room was well appointed with an 8-person, ornate, dining table that reminded me of the orient. There were other artifacts that hailed from the four corners of the world and showed the extent of Uncle Rudi's service in the Marines.

82

We quickly found our seats. Dana, Tony and me on one side, Hector and his two cousins on the other. Aunt Rose sat at the foot of the table, and of course, Uncle Rudi at the head of the table.

"Please bow your heads," Uncle Rudi said, and the family all held hands as he delivered the blessing. Once the food had been blessed, Aunt Rose and the two girls got up to bring out the dishes to be served.

Yeah, I thought, *this was a lot like NMMI in its flavor and tone. Uncle Rudi was the squad leader and the family his obedient squad.*

We could hear the clattering of serving dishes and platters from the kitchen and when the kitchen door swung open our nostrils were inundated with the delicious aroma of homemade spaghetti sauce, seasoned noodles, garlic bread, corn on the cob, and tossed salad.

"Wow, Aunt Rose, that smells delicious," Hector exhorted.

Yeah, we were salivating; it really looked and smelled great.

"Thank you Hector, I hope it tastes good as well." Aunt Rose said as she passed the bowls and platters of food around the table. We began to heap the food on our plates, and started eating as soon as we had enough on our plates to fill our hungry stomachs.

Uncle Rudi took this opportunity to get some information from us about ourselves. "Nell tells us you boys are heading to college, what are your plans?"

Hector looked down at his full plate, sighed, and said, "I don't know if you know Uncle Rudi, I'm going to New Mexico State University on a track scholarship."

"That's great Hector, what are you going to major in?" Uncle Rudi asked.

"History."

"What do you plan on doing with a history degree?"

"Not sure, maybe teach or work with kids in some capacity."

"That sounds admirable, what about the rest of you?" Uncle Rudi panned the rest of us for our responses. That got Hector off the hook, so he started eating.

Tony was next, "I'm going to Texas Tech University on a ROTC scholarship," he said as he swallowed a forkful of spaghetti.

"Really?" that got Uncle Rudi's attention. "What service? Army?"

"Yes, sir, and I'm majoring in political science," Tony answered anticipating his next question.

"Very good, and what are you doing with your degree?" Uncle Rudi continued.

"I'm not sure. I'm going to be an Army officer, so I thought I would get a better understanding of how our government works and the civilian command structure over the military. Maybe run for office."

I was shocked, that was a pretty astute answer from Tony.

Uncle Rudi must have thought so, "Very good answer young man, what about you two? You're brothers right?"

"Yes sir," I said. I'd already put down my fork, anticipating the questioning would come to me, "Unlike these guys, I just graduated from the University of Texas. I'm a commissioned second lieutenant in the Army, air defense artillery, and I'm starting law school at Texas this fall."

"Impressive," he said. "Quite impressive…that shows a lot of promise. And you?" he said staring over at Dana.

Thank goodness – I could get back to eating.

"I start at West Point next month," Dana said and picked up his fork, ready to spin some more spaghetti into his mouth.

"I didn't know that. The United States Military Academy at West Point, very impressive," Uncle Rudi said almost to himself. "What branch?"

"Probably Armor, I really like tanks, and see myself as a tank commander," Dana replied, starting to sound a little annoyed with the questioning.

I tapped him under the table to remind him to be cool.

84   "Do you have any prior military experience or training?" Uncle Rudi asked Dana.

Before Dana could answer, Hector jumped in and said, "Yes sir, Dana was a cadet colonel in high school, was the student council president, and president of each class in high school."

I think Hector also sensed Dana was not enjoying the interrogation from Uncle Rudi.

"That's interesting, did your father serve?" He asked Dana.

"Yes sir, our dad is a retired lieutenant colonel in the Army." I answered, "He was an air defense officer, that's how we ended up at Fort Bliss and El Paso."

Aunt Rose stepped in at this point and said, "That's enough interrogation Rudi, let the boys eat, I'm sure they're hungry."

"Okay, okay," Uncle Rudi said. "I don't want to get between hungry young men and your great cooking…dig in boys."

We dug in. I think we tried to hurt ourselves the food was so good, and we ate so much…it was really excellent.

With my face full of spaghetti, I finally said, "This is great Aunt Rose, thank you so much."

The other Transmanauts agreed with their mouths full as well, "Really good Aunt Rose," "Delicious," "Thank you," they chorused.

We finished up dinner, and retired to the family room looking for something to do for the rest of the evening.

"There's still some daylight, would you all like to see some of the neighborhood?" Audrey asked.

We looked at each other, "Yeah, that sounds like a plan, but I need to hit the bathroom first. Where is it?" I said.

"Down the hall, on the right, before you get to your bedroom."

"Okay," I said, "be right back."

My going to the bathroom had a sympathetic reaction with the other three guys because Audrey was quickly directing them to another bathroom in the house.

Once we attended to our personal needs, we went out to the car. This was when we saw more of Audrey's personality. She actually had the audacity to ask me if she could drive my car since she was going to take us around the neighborhood. Her request elicited what would become our famous response to any request to either get in the car, or certainly if anyone actually asked to drive the Trans Am.

I said emphatically and with no hesitation, "Not only NO, but HELL NO! Not only HELL NO, but FUCK NO!" and then I laughed.

Looking like we were going to bust, all the Transmanauts started laughing uproariously. And once Audrey closed her mouth from the shock, she started laughing with the rest of us.

Once her laughing died down, she asked, "I saw the way you all got out of the car when you pulled up, do you get in the car the same way?"

"Yeah," I said as the four of us got into position around the car, "Watch." I nodded to Dana and we went through our patented Transmanautic ingress into the Trans Am. Once Dana and I closed our doors, we then reversed the process to get out the car to let her ride in Dana's seat so she could act as our guide. Dana, being the shortest of the three, and having lost his designated seat, squeezed between Tony and Hector, looking really uncomfortable.

"You okay back there?" I asked Dana.

"Yeah, I'll be fine, just don't take too long, I want to have children some day," he laughed. His legs were wrapped tightly around the console that nestled between the front bucket seats, and it was up against his groin.

"I'll try to avoid any potholes or big bumps," I said.

"'Preciate that," he said. "Let's go."

I started up the car and the engine settled into its whisper-like quiet when it idled.

"When you pull out the driveway, turn to the right. We'll go in a different direction than the way we came in from the interstate." Audrey said.

I followed her directions out the driveway, and she guided us around the neighborhood so we could get our bearings. We had driven in from the highway, so we knew that route, but we wanted to get more familiar with the hangouts.

"Where do the guys play ball?" I asked.

"At the rec center, it's not too far from here. Make this next right and I'll direct you," she said. "I work there during the week, and some day I would like to become a rec center director or manager."

"Do you go to school to learn something like that? Is it a profession?" I asked.

"I'm studying business classes and taking classes in management at Cal State San Bernardino, not too far from here. Maybe you all can make it out to the campus this week, if you're not too busy."

"That sounds good. I always like going to new campuses and meeting women. Where do you live on campus or at home?" I asked.

"On campus, I just come home on the weekends," she said.

"Chris is a Kappa," Hector said, "And me and Tony want to pledge when we get to campus."

"Oh, a 'pretty boy', okay, well, no wonder you're so cocky," she said.

I laughed at her response. I normally get that reaction when college girls find out I'm a Kappa...we do have a reputation to uphold with the ladies.

We rolled past the rec center, and spotted guys playing basketball on the asphalt courts. I parked the car as we watched these guys play.

"You know California has the best basketball players, right?" Audrey commented.

I let Hector handle that comment, "Yeah, yeah, that's all we've heard is how good the ball players are out here, well we know how to play ball in Texas, and the four of us are pretty good."

"Pretty good isn't going to be enough. I tell you what, my boyfriend Bobby normally plays on Sundays, around 11 o'clock, right out here. So if you boys want to run, I'm sure they'll give you a game. And I hope you got game 'Mr. FUCK NO.'" She laughed at me.

"Don't worry about me," I said, "I was introduced to basketball in the fifth grade and played a lot of schoolyard ball through high school, and then intramural ball in college. The one thing I can do is 'jump out of the gym,' and I'm cat-quick, so I can play one-on-one ball pretty well. I was the only person on my college intramural team at UT that could dunk the ball, and that made me the guy who jumped the tip-off at games."

"Okay, you can jump. You got any other skills?" she taunted.

"Yeah, I do," I said. "Like I said, I'm very good at one-on-one, and have a great outside shot." I continued, "I spent hours and hours shooting jump shots and driving on the hoop, practicing my crossover dribble, and shooting and dribbling with both hands. I'm a pretty good schoolyard player, and, yeah, I think I've got game. I can shoot 'the rock.'"

She laughed, "Uh huh, all I hear is you woofin', I need to see some game. I tell you what, I'll make sure some of my girlfriends are out there tomorrow so you guys can meet them, and we'll see if you've got any game."

I was pretty confident in our ability to play ball, but we'd not been challenged like this, and this was coming from a girl.

I turned and looked at her, "That's fine, bring 'em on, I love performing in front of a crowd, especially women."

"What gives you that kind of confidence?" she inquired.

"I succeed at everything I do, so I feel confident we'll perform well tomorrow. We've got a good team, Tony and Hector were both varsity football players at Eastwood High School, the largest high school in El Paso. Tony played defensive back, Hector was a receiver, and they both ran varsity track." I pointed at them in the back seat, "I mean look at them, they're over six feet, and they're in great shape."

"Okay, what about him?" Audrey pointed at Dana.

"Dana's also pretty tall, and he ran B-team track."

88

"But what about their game?" she insisted.

"We've all got game, and we play well together," I continued, "Tony and Hector can both dunk the ball and have a great inside game. Tony has a really good outside shot. When we play together, my game is one-on-one defense, and a good outside shooting game. I normally guard whoever is playing point. Dana is great at defending the lane, and is money close to the basket. All of us defend well, and we're not afraid to take on anyone, including those guys." I pointed to the guys on the court.

Tony added, "We have a lot of fun playing ball and the four of us can beat anybody, so, yeah we look forward to beating your boyfriend and his friends – especially in front of their girlfriends. I look forward to embarrassing them on their home court."

"You sound pretty sure of yourselves, but we'll see," Audrey smiled.

I put the car in drive and we pulled out of the rec center parking lot. It was starting to get dark and I suggested we start heading back to the house. Audrey gave me directions on how to get back.

Once we got back to the house, Audrey made sure we heard her call and tell her boyfriend all about us, so we knew it was on for the next day. We were definitely going to pick up the gauntlet Audrey had thrown down in the car by beating her boyfriend and his posse.

Across the country, particularly in urban neighborhoods, most brothers play ball. Getting good at basketball was almost a rite of passage itself, and was definitely a sign of manhood. If you couldn't hang on the court, you would get punked, and we weren't going to let that happen, by anybody. So yeah, bring 'em on.

Playin' Ball

Our sleeping arrangements made it easy to get up early Sunday morning. Three of us slept on the bed, and poor Hector, the loser of the coin flip, stayed on the floor in the sleeping bag. On second thought, he may have had it better than the rest of us because he had the sleeping bag, a pillow, an inflatable mattress, and more importantly, he was by himself on the floor. Above him, on the bed, we slept head to toe, with Tony in the middle, with his head at the foot of the bed, and Dana and I with our heads at the head on opposite sides of the bed. It really made it tight sleeping under those conditions, and we didn't spend more time in that room than we had to.

I woke up at seven that morning while they still slept. I rolled off the bed towards the closet and wandered to the bathroom to take care of business. The smell of frying bacon and eggs greeted me as I left the bathroom and drew me to the kitchen.

Aunt Rose stood at the stove over a hot frying pan spitting grease and fat from the frying bacon. She wore a flowered apron and pink, fuzzy, slippers and stared intently at the frying bacon with a fork in her hand. In another small pot something else was bubbling, maybe gravy. Uncle Rudi sat at the kitchen table reading the Sunday paper with a bowl of grapefruit sections to his side.

"Good morning," I said, savoring the smell of the frying bacon.

"Good morning young man, up early I see." Uncle Rudi replied.

"Hi Chris," Aunt Rose said as she turned the bacon with the fork.

"Have a seat," Uncle Rudi gestured to one of the open chairs at the table.

"Thanks, the bacon smells really good," I said.

"It'll be ready in a minute," Aunt Rose said, "and I'll have eggs ready to go in a few minutes, and after that some biscuits and gravy."

"I thought I smelled something baking." I said, "Biscuits and bacon are fine for me, I don't eat eggs."

"No eggs?" Uncle Rudi said skeptically, "If you're going to be in the Army, you'll learn to eat eggs."

"I went through Basic at Fort Knox and Advanced Camp at Fort Riley and didn't eat eggs," I said. "I just don't like the taste, but I eat just about everything else."

"Uh huh. I've eaten stuff that would make a billy goat puke, and let me tell you, when you're really hungry, you'll eat whatever's put in front of you, I guarantee that."

"Yes sir," I said, not wanting to argue with the old guy. "This is a pretty kitchen. I like what you've done with the ducks and wallpaper." I looked over at Aunt Rose. The kitchen was decorated in pretty blues and yellows, with ceramic ducks and wall paper that matched the paint and tiled floors and counter tops.

"Thank you," Aunt Rose said as she finished up with the bacon. She placed the freshly fried bacon on a platter covered with paper towels to absorb the grease, and started whisking the eggs and pouring them into the pan. About that time the rest of the Transmanauts straggled in rubbing their eyes and yawning.

"Good morning everybody," Hector said with a yawn. He had on a t-shirt and shorts, dressed like the rest of us for the morning.

"Good morning gentlemen," Uncle Rudi said. "Have some breakfast. Your Aunt Rose should be finishing up in a few minutes."

"Thank you," Dana said. "This is nice."

"Yeah," Tony said. "We really appreciate you all letting us stay here."

"You're certainly welcome boys. How did you sleep last night?" Aunt Rose asked.

"I think Hector had the best of it on the floor," I laughed.

"Yeah, it's a challenge on the bed," Dana agreed, "but we're fine."

"Easy for you to say," Tony grumbled. "You don't have to smell y'all's stinky feet."

"Sorry about the sleeping arrangement boys," Uncle Rudi laughed. "One of you could sleep on the couch, but you'd have to get up by six every morning."

"That's okay," Tony said, "I'll smell the feet. You guys just make sure you wash your feet every night."

We all laughed at that as Aunt Rose finished scrambling the eggs. She put the eggs on the platter with the bacon and brought the platter to the table.

"Eat up, there's more where that came from. I'll get the biscuits and gravy. If you want some orange juice or milk it's in the fridge. The cups are over here in the cupboard by the stove," she pointed toward it.

We all got up to get cups and something to drink from the refrigerator as Aunt Rose pulled the baked biscuits from the oven. There's nothing like the smell of frying bacon and baking biscuits, nothing.

"Every thing smells and looks great," Hector said. "Thanks Aunt Rose."

"Thank you Hector, eat up." She smiled as we devoured breakfast.

During breakfast we discussed our strategy for playing basketball that day.

"Okay," I said between mouthfuls of bacon and biscuits, "we stick together on this, right?"

"Yeah, just us," Tony agreed. "No five on five, just four

on four. We don't want anybody to mess with our vibe and our groove when we play ball."

"You think they'll agree to that?" Hector asked.

"Who cares," I said. "Those are our conditions, if they want to run with us, they do it on our terms."

"You going to challenge these guys on their court?" Uncle Rudi interjected.

"Yeah, we haven't heard nothin' but woofin' from everybody out here about the superiority of ball players on the West Coast, and how baaaad they are, particularly, here in LA. So now we're going to show them how we do it in Texas." I said.

"Well, these boys are pretty good out here, I hope you guys got some game," Uncle Rudi retorted.

"We got game," I said, having heard this same song from Audrey. "We're in pretty good shape, so we thought we'd play these guys full court and run 'em off the courts."

"Nice plan, won't work," Uncle Rudi said. "These guys are in pretty good shape, and all they do is play ball."

"That's cool, but just so you know, almost every day for the past two years, when we weren't playing Ping-Pong, playing cards, swimming at our house, or hanging out at the mall, we were playing basketball, either at Tony's house, at the school, indoors or outside," I explained. "We played each other with no holds barred, playing either one-on-one, or two-on-two developing our game. We got to know each other's game extremely well, each of our weaknesses and strengths." I continued, "When the four of us get together to play basketball it's serious. We each have different types of games, but our games mesh well, and we play well as a team – and we take on all comers."

"Sounds good, you let me know how it goes today," Uncle Rudi chuckled.

"Yeah, we'll let you know how bad we beat your local boys before we move on to bigger game in LA," Tony bragged.

Dana and Hector looked over at Tony's braggadocio and exchanged glances. Hopefully, we weren't biting off more than

94

we could chew. We were about to find out as we finished up breakfast and got ready to hit the courts.

Oh yeah, it's time to play ball!   We felt we were ready to play these guys out here. We jelled as a team and made every game we played hard fought and close.

The first game we played was at the rec center near Aunt Rose's house, the one Audrey had pointed out to us last evening. When we drove up, it was late morning, and there were several young brothers already out on the court. They were playing that brand of basketball that made you go "Whoa!" – dunking on each other, making "no look" passes behind their backs and crossover dribbles.

As we rolled up in the Trans Am and I looked at the courts, I thought, *This is going to be interesting.* Last evening in the waning sunlight I didn't get a clear view of the rec center. This morning it was in clear relief. I saw a weathered, low-level building that may have, at one time, been painted blue. There were two courts, each with its own set of wooden grandstands facing the courts; and water fountains by each court. The courts were standard asphalt with the chain mail nets and wooden backboards that were pretty typical of outdoor basketball courts across the country.

When we drove up, there were guys on one of the courts, so we drove up next to the grandstands in front of that court. The guys all seemed to be in good shape, playing "shirts and skins;" with half of them going shirtless and the other half with shirts on, thus the name "shirts and skins." You know when you weren't always playing with guys you knew well and you didn't have uniforms, the best way to tell who was on your team was going shirtless or with shirts. If you went shirtless you better look good or you were going to hear about it, not from the guys, but from the girls. The women who liked to watch their men play ball were not shy in making comments about how some of the guys looked without their shirts. Boy, they could be brutal.

We had stopped by a do-it-yourself car wash on the way to the courts; and when we drove up in our shiny, new, just washed,

Special Edition, black and gold, Trans Am, the action on the court stopped. We rolled up like a black bird of prey, silent and deadly, with nary a whisper from the engine. I parked next to the grandstands in full view of the courts, and I held us in place, milking the moment, until we got out of the car. Nobody moved – the moment frozen in time. I guess we sort of helped create that phenomenon by doing our "Transmanautic extra-vehicular activity" – in other words, we got out of the car in our own inimitable fashion. Audrey was there, as were several other girls in the stands.

Once we struck our "cool" pose, we sauntered over to the stands, in our athletic shorts and muscle shirts. When we got to the first row, Tony jumped up into the stands closer to the girls.

"Hey, how're you all doing?" Tony said grinning. "I'm Tony, and this is Hector, Chris and Dana." Tony continued in his braying voice, "Yeah, we came out to find out how good you all play ball. We've heard so much about LA ball, we want you all to see how we do it in Texas." He laughed.

We just looked at each other – okay, I guess it's on now. The girls were apparently amused by Tony and they all laughed too.

Audrey introduced us to several of the girls in the stands and they seemed impressed by us. One of the nicer looking girls was Brenda Blanchard, who eyed us with some interest. We were in good shape, looked pretty good, and at least three of us were six feet or taller, so I think we presented an interesting package to these California girls. And, of course, we showed up in the Trans Am, so that made us different.

The guys on the court paid rapt attention to all of this, considering we were talking to either their girlfriends or friends of theirs who were girls. Regardless, we were certainly not welcome at their court and they didn't seem to appreciate us talking to their women.

After our surprising advent, the game in progress continued, and we sat down in the stands with the girls to watch. This gave us a chance to see how these guys played and the level of competition. Most of them looked pretty good, but we believed we were just as good, and could beat them. They were playing "five on five" ball, but we knew we weren't going to play "five on five" because there were only four of us.

When the game in progress ended, we unfolded ourselves from the stands and approached the guys on the court.

"We've got next," I said.

One of the guys on the winning team said, "Cool, let's run."

"That's fine but we're only going to play "four on four." I said. If they wanted to run with us they had to play using four guys.

After a few minutes discussion, the leader of the winning team, a brown-skinned brother, about six feet, two inches, with a pretty big Afro and muscular physique, came back over to us and said, "Okay, we'll play 'four on four.' Audrey told me about you guys, I'm Bobby. You're from Texas, right?"

Okay, so this was Audrey's boyfriend. He looked like he had game.

"Yeah, you got your four?" I asked.

"Almost, we're going to pick some guys to play you all." Bobby said. He and another young brother picked out two more guys to play us, sort of an all-star team of their best players – not just from the winning team, but from everybody present; and then we discussed the rules of the game.

As the spokesman for our team, I asked Bobby, "What're the rules?"

"Make it, take it. You know what that means?" he challenged.

"Yeah, it means whoever scores a basket keeps the ball," I said.

"Make it take it" also meant that the side with the ball got to inbound the ball at half court on their end of the court; and the ball is "checked" by the other side before bringing it in bounds.

"How do you all check the ball?" I asked.

"Your guy throws the ball to my guy and he holds it until we're ready to play the next point." Bobby said.

"Make it, take it" also meant that the only way the ball changes possession is by getting the rebound off a missed shot, or the ball being turned over through a steal, going out of bounds or some other turnover.

"What about fouls? How do you call fouls?" I asked.

"What do you guys do in Texas?"

"Hard fouls only," I said. That meant only hard fouls could be called, and they had to be pretty blatant to be called. And no, there were no refs out there; this was self-policing by the players.

"It looked like you guys were playing half-court; we want to play full court. Can y'all keep up?" I asked, challenging their manhood.

"Oh yeah, we'll run your asses off the court," Bobby said, getting a little pissed at the challenge. "I heard you all think you got game, we'll see. Let's do this, c'mon."

"Wait, win by two, each basket is one?" I asked, further clarifying how we were to win the game.

"Yeah, first to ten, need to win by two; any more questions?" He looked eager to get started.

"Naw, I think we got it," I said, "Let's play. We'll be skins, who gets out first?"

"You the visitors, you take it out first," he said, and pointed to the far goal. "And that's your goal, so bring it in down here. Now, let's run."

If all this rule discussion sounds tedious, it really wasn't, because it was required. Since we were in Cali, we wanted to make sure we knew what the rules were before we started. In Texas everyone knows the local rules, and in Cali everyone knows the local rules, but there are always different versions of the rules depending on where you're playing. It's always necessary to sort that out before you start so there won't be any "misunderstandings" leading to fights. Dana and I had problems with that issue playing street football in Philly, so we knew the deal beforehand.

Once all the rules were decided, we walked back over to the stands and took off our shirts to become the "skins" team. We really didn't need to do that because we all knew who we were, and who they were, but we wanted to show off our physiques to all those girls. What can I say, we did look good. So, alright, it's time to get it done. Play ball!

We took the ball out first to begin the game, and found out even guys in Cali can run. They weren't in better shape than us, and weren't better conditioned, but they kept up with us. As mentioned earlier, Tony and Hector were varsity football players and ran varsity track, and Dana ran track. And although I didn't run track in college, I had been running three to five miles at least three times a week for four years as a part of my Army training. I could run with the best of them. We tried to run these guys off the court, but couldn't – they were in pretty good shape themselves.

We took the ball out at the near end of the court and drove down to the other end to run our offense. They were waiting for us in what appeared to be a man-to-man defense. I was the point for the Transmanauts, and the guy guarding me was about my height, dark-skinned with his dark hair cut short against his gleaming scalp. He was a muscular guy and seemed able to keep up with my speed.

I ran our offense driving down the middle of the lane towards the basket, and as I passed the top of the key I looked for Tony or Hector cutting to the basket. Both of them moved well without the ball, making their cuts trying to get open. Hector got by his man first, and I saw him streaking towards the basket. I faked my guy left and passed the ball back to the right where Hector caught it in midstride and made an easy lay up. When we made the first basket I felt good about our chances of winning the game. Based on the rules, we took the ball back in at half-court and tried to keep it, to score as much as possible before they got it back.

I brought it in at half court and passed the ball to Dana to the left of the basket where he had a clear shot, but he missed, and Bobby, who was playing forward, snatched the ball off the board. Bobby looked down the court and saw one of his teammates who had gotten behind us on a fast break to their basket, and threw a long pass to the guy who scored an easy lay up.

One thing to our credit – we made them a jump-shooting team in the half-court. They scored that one fast break, but no others. None of them dunked on us in this first game, and we didn't dunk on them. Our defense was tight. We didn't play a zone or any of that other crap, we weren't that sophisticated. We played one-on-one "D" and everybody was responsible for their man. On occasion we would double team, but that was rare. When we were guarding our man, we were hand slapping as they dribbled the ball, body checking and using hard fouls to keep them from making easy baskets.

Dana, in particular, was death in the middle of the lane. On one play, their point guard had gotten past me and was dribbling down the lane like he was going for a layup. Dana came off his man, and literally flew into the air to block this guy's shot. Dana went up with his right hand to block the shot, and knocked the ball out of bounds. In the process Dana just knocked the snot out of the guy, and put him on the ground. That guy got up off the asphalt fighting mad, he was pissed!

"Hey motherfucker that was a fuckin' foul!" He shouted. This guy was pretty muscular, and was ready to hit someone.

"Bullshit, it was a clean hit, let's play ball!" I scowled.

Bobby jumped in the middle before it went to blows. "Hey forget it, let's play ball."

So everybody cooled down a little and they took the ball out from the sideline. They didn't come down the middle very much after that. Of course, they didn't need to come down the lane because they definitely had radar in that basketball – they didn't miss much from the outside. We, on the other hand, were able to drive to the hole, but our outside game was not as good and we lost 11 to 9. We kept it close in all our games, but in the end we still lost all of them.

After the game they were pretty good sports and showed respect for our game. They won the game, but we beat the crap out of them physically. That was our "Texas" brand of defense and our claim to fame. You weren't coming down the lane without some blood being shed – your blood, not ours. So even though we didn't win, there was no doubt they knew we had come to play. There wasn't a lot of trash talking. As a matter of fact, there was no trash talking at all – surprisingly. As a sign of good sportsmanship, Bobby invited us back for a rematch the next day and we accepted.

Once the game was over, since we had acquitted ourselves so well on the court, we reaped our reward for a good showing. Brenda Blanchard motioned us over as we walked to the grandstands. I think she liked the idea of us surrounding her with our glistening, sweaty bodies.

"You guys played well, I'm sorry you lost. But I like your style, and I want you to meet my sisters. We're giving my younger sister, Debbie, a graduation party Thursday night, would you all like to come?" she asked.

Well, like duh! She was nice looking and where there's one nice looking girl, there's more. They sort of hang out together in herds.

"Sure." I said keeping my cool, "It sounds like fun. What time and where?"

"You're staying at Audrey's parent's house right?"

"Yeah." Hector said, "My aunt and uncle."

"Oh you're her cousin? Oh, okay, yeah, I'll call you guys over there with the details."

That sounded like a plan, and we definitely looked forward to partying out here in Cali. However, before Thursday night rolled around, we had plenty of business to take care of, like winning the rematch with these guys.

When we got back to the house, Uncle Rudi was watching TV. "How'd it go?" he asked with a twinkle in his eye.

"Well, we didn't win today, but we have a rematch for tomorrow with the same guys." Hector answered.

"Did you meet Bobby?" Uncle Rudi asked.

"Yeah, he played us," I said, "and will probably be out there tomorrow."

"He's good. Played varsity in high school and some college ball," Uncle Rudi chuckled. "Should have warned you, but I thought you needed a little lesson in humility."

"Okay, thanks," Dana said. "We'll beat them tomorrow."

"We'll see," Uncle Rudi said, and then turned to me and asked, "Can you all take Audrey out to campus? I usually take her, but I thought you might want to get out and see more of the area, sort of a recon."

"Okay," I said. "How'd she get here from the rec center?"

"Bobby brought her home," Uncle Rudi replied.

"Oh, that's how you knew we'd lost. Is she ready to go?" I asked.

"I think so. She's in her room," Uncle Rudi said.

"Before we get all cooped up in the car, let's get cleaned up," Dana said.

"Yeah, I think Audrey would appreciate that." Hector said.

"Alright," I said to Uncle Rudi. "We'll get cleaned up and get some lunch and then we'll take her out to campus."

"I'll let her know, thanks guys," Uncle Rudi said.

While we got cleaned up, Aunt Rose fixed us a nice lunch of cheeseburgers and French fries, which we wolfed down in a few minutes. We were famished from playing ball all day.

Once we finished, Audrey had her overnight bag packed and ready to go by the front door. After loading her bag in the trunk we got in the car and she squeezed between Tony and Hector. We then headed out of the driveway on our way to Cal State San Bernardino.

As we pulled out of the driveway, I asked, "How do we get there?'

"I'll give you directions. Just get back on I-10 heading west, and we'll go from there." We retraced our route back to the freeway and headed west until we intersected with I-215 which we took north to the city of San Bernardino. Audrey directed me to an exit that read "California State University at San Bernardino" and within a few more minutes we were driving onto the pretty little campus.

"Nice campus," I said looking around. "A lot of students?"

"Several thousand, but it's mostly a commuter school. There're a few dorms on campus, and I live in one of the all-women's dorms."

"Yeah, that pretty much figures." I smiled. "I am sure Uncle Rudi wouldn't let you live in a coed dorm."

"You got that right," she said. "Pull up over there, that's my dorm." She indicated a building over to the right. I steered over towards the curb to park.

"Okay." I pulled up in front of a nicely appointed building that looked like a dorm from the outside. We saw several women going in and out of the front doors dressed in shorts, sandals and halter tops – a typical summer Sunday on campus.

"Summer school?" I asked.

"Yep," she said as she got out of the car on Dana's side.

"I'm surprised. I would've guessed most folks don't stay on campus during the summer." I said as I got out of the car and walked back to the trunk.

"They keep some of the dorms open during the summer, but it's not as busy as the school year." She said as I got her bag out the trunk, "Thanks for the ride. I might need you all to come back out to pick me up tomorrow, is that okay?"

"Sure, okay, why not?" I said looking around, "I think we could hang out tomorrow. What time?"

"Probably about four o'clock, but I'll call you guys. Good luck playing Bobby and those guys tomorrow."

"Yeah, thanks. We'll see what happens," I said as she walked into the dorm.

103

As I got back into the car, we watched all the girls walking by, going in and out of the dorm.

"Audrey asked us to come pick her up tomorrow and I said yes."

"Why?" Hector asked, "You don't think she's taking advantage of us?"

"Maybe," I said, "but have you been checking out the

women? I definitely want to come back out here, and picking her up gives us a great excuse."

"I never thought of it that way," Hector said wonderingly. "I guess I've got a lot to learn about being in college."

"All of you do, and maybe your education starts tomorrow." I laughed.

"I can't wait to come out here tomorrow," Tony said. "I saw some fine babes. I bet we can score out here."

"Yeah, well, don't get your hopes up high-school boy, but you never know." I said.

"Yo, I'm a college man now," Tony laughed.

"Yeah, I guess you're right," I said. "We'll introduce you all as freshmen in college, at Texas Tech, New Mexico State and West Point, okay?"

"I'm in," Hector said.

"Cool," Tony echoed.

Dana had been studying the Trip Tik, "You remember how to get back?"

"Yeah, I think so; we make a few turns to get back to I-215 going south then I-10 east to Redlands." I said.

"Yep, that's what I see here on the Trip Tik," Dana agreed.

"Okay then, let's go. We'll be back out here tomorrow." I put in an 8-track, rolled down the windows, and turned up the volume to let the passing students hear us jam to *Slide,* by Slave, and watch us do our in-seat dancing. After a few moments, I put the car in drive, rolled up the windows, and we pulled out of the curbside area in front of the dorm to head back to Redlands.

104

The drive back was uneventful, and we spent the rest of the evening watching TV and talking about playing ball the next day. We came up with a few different strategies to try to get Tony or Hector the ball down low below the basket, and ways of defending those guys on the outside to keep them from raining those outside shots on us.

Unfortunately, the rematch turned out a lot like the first one, with us on the losing end. Again, we faced the same team or a team with some of the same guys with the same results. Unlike the first game, we didn't have as big an audience, which was okay since we didn't win. Also, like the first game, we played pretty physical defense and made sure that the other team respected our physicality. Although we lost the second game we were not beaten. We gave them a beat down and walked away with our heads held high. As in the poem "Invictus," "our heads were bloody but unbowed," well figuratively "bloody" because of our consecutive losses to the same group of players. We decided for the next game to play some other guys in a different location, with hopefully better results. Unfortunately, that wasn't the case – different location, same result. Damn.

Goin' on the Yard

On Monday, after we lost the second basketball game, we were hanging out at the house. We had just eaten lunch and were lounging in Aunt Rose's family room watching some mindless TV and bored out of our skulls when Audrey called from the Cal State San Bernardino campus and asked to speak to Hector.

Hector called over to me, "Audrey's on the line and wants to know if we can go back out there and pick her up."

"Sure, we're not doing anything this afternoon. What time?" I said.

"About four?"

"Okay, we'll be out there. It'll give us something to do."

"Let's hit the shower and dump these sweaty clothes," I told the guys. "I got first; you all figure it out so we can get dressed and get out to the campus."

There was a mad scramble to the bathroom when I got out.

"What're you wearing Chris?" Tony shouted as I headed down the hallway towards the bedroom.

"Same shit I always wear, painter pants and t-shirt," I said.

"Shouldn't we be better dressed going out to campus?" Dana asked.

"Hey, it's summer, and we're just going out there to pick up Audrey. We don't need to be well-dressed for that," I responded.

"I guess I'll wear my overalls," Dana said.

"You'll be fine, and even if we do see some women, based on the way they were dressed yesterday, we'll be fine." I said.

"Okay, jeans and t-shirts," Tony said as he made his way into the bathroom.

"Yeah, okay, you know more about being on campus than we do," Hector conceded as he came out of the shower.

I got dressed and turned to Dana, "You need to hurry up and shower so we can get out of here."

"Waiting on Tony, then I'll be ready."

"Why aren't you wearing a Kappa t-shirt?" Tony asked as he came out a few minutes later.

"Don't feel like it, plus I think they're all dirty. I only brought a couple." I said.

"That reminds me, we need to do laundry before too long; I'm running out of clothes," Hector said. "We should be able to use Aunt Rose's washer and dryer."

"Good idea." I agreed. "We'll do it before Thursday's party."

"What time is it?" Hector asked, "Shouldn't we be going?"

"Dana, you about ready?" I shouted.

"Yeah, I'm finishing up in here," he called from the bathroom.

"Alright, let's get up out of here," I said a few minutes later. "Everybody good?"

Dana had finished dressing, so we were ready to go. We said goodbye to Aunt Rose and rushed out of the house.

"You remember how to get out there?" Dana asked as we got settled in the car.

108

"Yeah, I-10 west, then I-215 north, and look for the sign for Cal State San Bernardino." I said.

"That sounds about right," Dana added. "Let's go."

I popped Parliament-Funkadelics into the 8-track player. *Give Up The Funk (Tear the Roof off the Sucker)* from The *Mothership Connection* album blasted throughout the car as we took off down the road – "*Tear the roof off, we're gonna tear the roof off the mother sucker...tear the roof off the sucker..."* Oh yeah, funk doesn't get any better than that.

After a few minutes of funk, I turned the music down so we could talk. I wanted to school the newly graduated high school guys about who we might meet on campus. Obviously, I was the only one who had any experience dealing with college women, but the other three thought they could dazzle college-age women in California the same way they had high school girls in Texas. I had to disabuse them of that erroneous notion.

"You guys know we're talking about significantly different groups of women. Like I've told you guys before, high school girls are nothing like college girls. Once you move up to college, you're in a whole different league. You guys need to come across like you know what you're doing and not like you just graduated high school." I lectured, "Just be cool and we'll see how things go. No way to know how these college girls will react to us, but if we walk in confident we'll be fine."

"Yeah, we know, you're the guru on college women," Tony laughed, "That's why you got so much pussy at UT." They all laughed.

"Alright, you got me, but I'm telling you the truth – just be cool and we'll be fine." I said, "It's a lot different 'on the yard' than it is in high school."

"The 'yard'? What's that? Sounds like a barnyard." Tony laughed.

"It's what black folk call the college campus, I don't know the origin." I laughed.

"Where did you hear that?" Dana asked.

"The first time I heard it was at HT," I said. "Huston-Tillotson, on the east side of Austin."

"What were you doing over there?" Hector asked.

"Oh boy, that's a long story." I said.

"Well, we've got time, so let's hear it." Tony leaned forward in his seat.

You know I pledged Kappa last spring, right?" I explained,

"Well, there were these two Big Brothers at HT, Yank and Ozby, that eventually found us over at UT."

"What do you mean 'found you'?" Hector asked.

"We were being pledged by the Austin Alumni Chapter, under the HT charter of Gamma Lambda to help rejuvenate that chapter and eventually charter a chapter at UT. We were told there were two Kappas at HT named Yank and Ozby, and we were to avoid them at all costs. I guess the grad chapter told them to leave us alone; they were like renegades. They weren't financial and they really didn't have a chapter. So, we stayed at UT to avoid them and didn't go anywhere near the HT campus." I continued.

"What happened?" Tony prodded.

"One day someone knocked on my door and there stood Charles Yancy aka Yank. I thought to myself, *Oh shit what're we going to do now?* He invited himself in and ordered me to call my line brothers. I was the president of our Scroller line and I called all the guys to come to my room. That's how we met Yank; and then later that week we met Charles Ozby over at HT."

"What's a 'Scroller'?" Tony asked.

"That's what Kappa pledgees are called."

"Okay, so what happened next?" Hector chimed in.

"There was a step show that same week at HT and those two wanted us to attend. So, with a lot of trepidation, we went over there for the first time."

"How many of you were there?" Dana finally said something.

"Five from UT and one guy from HT; but we never saw him while we were pledging and he never went over – an eternal Scroller."

"What then?" Tony asked.

"I'd never been to a HBCU before, so it was kind of an eye-opener for me." I said.

"What's a HBCU?" Tony asked

"Historically Black College or University," I explained, "Basically, a black college."

"Alright, so you guys went over to HT, then what?" Dana asked.

"Apparently, Yank had been smoking dope, which seemed to be almost an extracurricular activity amongst a lot of the students at HT, and he was high when we got there. Initially, we were just watching in line from the audience, but at some point, Yank told us to go to one of the restrooms."

"Why?" Dana asked.

"He said he was being laughed at because we were standing there but we weren't scheduled to step. He said he was getting a lot of shit, and he didn't feel like fucking with that shit any more, so we were going to step. He had a rep on the yard and we were fuckin with his rep."

"Had you all stepped before?" Hector asked.

"No, and no one had taught us any steps."

"What did you all do?" Hector asked.

"Yank showed us this one step where we were supposed to do a step and yell 'Nupes-Nupes goddammit' and then once we got in front of the audience, we were supposed to introduce ourselves and do some sort of individual dance move."

"How did that work out?" Dana asked as we approached our exit on I-215.

"Not well. I've never seen so many black folk laughing and literally rolling on the floor with hilarity at our expense."

"Why, what happened?" Hector asked.

"Apparently, and unbeknownst to us, Kappas were also known as 'Nupes' and because Yank was high and he slurred his words, we thought he said 'Noose' not 'Nupes.' So when we stepped out on the floor of their cafeteria/auditorium, we were yelling the wrong name. We were yelling 'Noose-Noose goddammit' at the top of our lungs. In addition, some of us had never stepped or danced or anything before and didn't have much rhythm. We were so out of step and out of rhythm that we looked ridiculous. It would have been better for Yank's rep had we not stepped, because now we embarrassed him and ourselves."

111

"You all did something individually?" Dana asked.

"Yeah, that was my only saving grace. Me, Cornell and Mayfield were able to somewhat redeem ourselves because we could play to the crowd; but Reecy and Joe just didn't have any experience doing that and just didn't look good."

"What did you do?" Tony asked as we pulled off the exit ramp.

"Hold on Tony." As we came off the exit, I asked our navigator, "Where do we go from here?"

"I thought you knew where you were going." Dana said.

"If I knew where I was going, I wouldn't have asked you. These little streets look all the same," I said as I made a left at the light.

"Hey, back there, you missed the sign for campus," Hector pointed behind the car.

"Okay, hold on." I made one of my "famous U-turns" to get going in the right direction. Once I got back on track I followed the signs until we got to campus. I searched the campus until I found Audrey's dorm. This time I parked in the parking lot rather than on the curb, because I thought we might be in there for a little while.

"Finish the story before we go inside." Tony said.

"Okay. When it came time for me to introduce myself, I did some Locker steps and ended with a jazz split sliding up to the crowd as part of my introduction. But we were so embarrassed by our performance we promised ourselves we would never allow any UT Kappa or Scroller to ever perform unless they were prepared. This past spring, we won the Delta's inaugural step show with our signature red and white canes and with steps we learned from Craig, a Brother that transferred in from Morehouse. We looked good and we'd come a long way from that embarrassing introduction to both stepping and my first black college campus."

"Wow, okay, that explains your stepping at UTEP with the Kappas up there." Dana said.

"Yeah, I'm comfortable stepping in any environment now.

My experience in high school on the drill team and on the *Crosno Show* helped me become a Kappa 'Cane Master.'"

"Okay 'Cane Master' let's go inside and see if we can't take over this yard." Tony laughed.

"Alright, let's go." I said.

We exited the car with our Transmanautic bravura, and boldly strode in to the dorm. As we entered the lobby there were several young women lounging around along with a few guys. The lobby was pretty well appointed, with several sofas and love seats scattered around the spacious room with end tables and individual lamps. The room was tastefully decorated with artwork on the walls, drapes, tables and chairs. There were several girls sitting in the lobby with the television playing over in the corner. Almost all the girls were black, as were all the guys. Audrey was there, as well as all these other women. This was definitely the right place, and it was time to take over this joint.

We spotted a group of women talking to each other with some animation. They looked like they might know what's happening. We strutted over, and I initiated the conversation.

"Hi, we're Chris and Dana, Tony and Hector; we came to pick up Hector's cousin Audrey, and we wondered if there's anything going on tonight or this week on campus," I said.

One woman spoke up as the others just stared. She was caramel colored, with fine features, about 5'6", her hair in curlers, and a little overweight.

She turned to Audrey, "You know these guys?"

"Yeah, they're staying at my parent's house, and Hector's my cousin." Audrey said.

The woman exuded confidence, and smoothly moved into a conversation with us. "Okay, I'm Cee Cee, and this is my sister, Aurianna, and her best friend, Latisha," indicating the two girls sitting next to her, "They're graduating high school in a couple of days, and they're hanging out with me today 'cause it's 'Senior Ditch Day.'"

That was quite a mouthful. Cee Cee was garrulous and had no problem talking with us. Once she introduced Aurianna and

Latisha we focused our attention on them.

My first impression of Aurianna was light brown skin, without blemish, about 5'10", cut off shorts, long legs, a frilly white blouse and long, black hair that she tended to twirl at times. My *goodness*, she was fine! She was the prototype girl that we came to meet in Cali. Her friend Latisha was cute, brown-skinned, with a short curly Afro, wearing blue jean shorts and a horizontally-striped top. Latisha was shorter with a nice figure, and the two of them looked good sitting there together. Oh yeah, I was looking forward to spending some time hanging out at the dorm.

We hung out at the dorm lobby for quite a while talking, laughing, watching TV and otherwise engaging all the young women. Several of the girls gravitated towards me, and I had no problem talking to all of them together.

I stood next to the couch where Aurianna and Latisha sat. Dana was immediately attracted to Aurianna and somehow squeezed onto the couch between her and Latisha. I detected an immediate electricity between them that caused the air to literally crackle. Uh oh, it looked like Super Cadet was smitten. Those two were just talking and talking, while Tony and Hector roamed around the room spreading their charm amongst the rest of the girls.

"You guys just graduated high school?" Aurianna asked.

"Yep, just a couple of weeks ago." Dana replied.

"What part of Texas are you guys from?"

"El Paso."

"Where's that? I've never heard of El Paso."

"It's like at the most western edge of Texas on the border with Juarez, Mexico and near Las Cruces, New Mexico."

"Oh, okay, I think I know where that is. I'm more familiar with Dallas and Houston," Aurianna said.

"Yeah, no one ever thinks of El Paso as a part of Texas," Dana laughed.

Aurianna smiled, "So what brings you all out here to California? Just taking a trip after graduation?"

"Yeah, my brother got a Trans Am for graduation, and we just decided to take a road trip to see California," Dana answered, "and to meet people like you."

"What have you all done so far?"

"We spent one night in San Diego, and walked around the red light district down there and visited a massage parlor. And we've played some basketball since we've been here. Not much so far, but we're looking for other things to do."

"The red light district? A massage parlor? You mean prostitutes?" Aurianna gasped.

"Yeah, but we didn't do anything," Dana said a little embarrassed.

"Okay, I didn't mean to embarrass you," she laughed.

"I know, I know, it's pretty funny." Dana laughed along with her.

"Where did you play basketball?" Aurianna asked.

"Redlands, at some rec center."

"Did you all win?"

"No, and we played them twice, but couldn't quite beat them." Dana said, kind of embarrassed again.

"I played basketball and ran track for Fontana High School," Aurianna said.

"Wow, I bet you really looked good playing basketball. I would've loved to see you play." Dana adjusted his body and crossed his legs. "You know with a name like Aurianna and your looks you could be a model or something," Dana added shyly.

Aurianna blushed, "Thank you. My mom thought it was a pretty name for a little girl, so here I am." She gave a shy grin, "Actually I've won six beauty pageants in the last few years. Maybe one of these days I can be a model. Who knows?" She pointed at the local guys standing around the room. "You know, you guys are so different from these other guys around here."

"Thank you, we like to think so." Now it was Dana's turn to blush.

Oddly, Dana seemed uncomfortable talking about himself to Aurianna. Now that was unusual. But, she seemed full of questions and kept up the conversation. About this time Latisha got up and walked over to where Hector and Tony were holding court.

"How long will you all be out here?" Aurianna asked.

"About two weeks, then we'll go back to Texas and go our separate ways."

"What do you mean? You won't be staying in El Paso?"

"No, we've got other plans that don't involve staying in El Paso. El Paso was a great place to grow up, but we can't stay there and accomplish our goals in life. We've got to get out into the world."

"What plans? What are you talking about?"

"We don't talk about it much, but Chris and I have a plan we call 'the Work,' and that guides us towards the future," Dana explained.

"Okay, I've got to ask, what's 'the Work'?"

"It's a concept we developed. We conceived this plan for changing society through both the military and the civilian side. I'm going to West Point and my goal is to become a general officer. But not just any general officer; my plan is to eventually command large numbers of troops in combat, and eventually end up in the White House."

"What House?"

"The White House, you know, where the President of the United States lives?" Dana smiled.

116

"Are you crazy?! The White House? What makes you think you'll ever get anywhere close to the White House?" Aurianna exclaimed.

Everyone in close proximity looked to see what they were talking about that caused her to raise her voice.

"Why not?" I interjected as I pulled up a chair facing the two of them. I was tired of standing and was interested in their conversation. The girls I had been talking with leaned over a little to catch what we were saying.

"This whole thing about Dana being in the White House someday is unbelievable," Aurianna interjected. The other girls tittered with laughter.

"What's so unbelievable about that?" I inquired.

"There's never going to be a black man in the White House except as a butler or something," Aurianna remarked.

"You need to expand your horizons," I said. "You know Andrew Young is the U.S. ambassador to the U.N., right? The next step is to get someone elected as Vice-President and then eventually President. Has he told you anything about his high school career?" I nodded at Dana.

"No, we haven't gotten that far yet." Aurianna said.

"Did he tell you he was the class president of every class in high school except his senior year, and that's because he was the first Black Student Council president in the history of our high school? By the way, our high school is the largest in El Paso; one of the largest in Texas, and is mostly white. So Dana was the first Black student council president of one of the largest high schools in the state of Texas. Dana was also the Cadet Colonel in our school district, the highest ranking cadet in the entire district, and top ten percent in his graduating class. He received a Congressional appointment to the United States Military Academy at West Point, and will be going there right after we get back to Texas." I continued, "Dana has all the makings of a great general and politician in the mold of such generals as Dwight Eisenhower, Douglas McArthur, and George S. Patton. He has all the potential of being the first Black Chairman of the Joint Chiefs of Staff or even the President."

"My head is swimming." Aurianna shook her head, "You guys aren't talking about getting a 'good job' and settling down, you're talking about influencing the world we live in and being players on the national and international stage. I've never heard guys talk like that about their own futures and actually believe they will accomplish their goals," she gushed.

"Dana truly has the potential to go all the way." I said.

"What about you?" Aurianna asked, "Do you have a role in 'the Work'?"

"Yeah, I have the civilian side." I said.

"What's that mean, 'the civilian side'?"

"In order to effect real change we have to do it from the inside," I began, "The plan is for me to run for office, hopefully Congress as a U.S. Representative or Senator."

"No, really? A congressman? You're really kidding, right?" Aurianna said in disbelief.

"Yeah, from Texas. You ever heard of Barbara Jordan or even Shirley Chisholm? They're both Black congresswomen and I think I have as much talent or ability as them." I had no problem talking about myself. I continued, "I was in speech and drama in high school and college, and just about graduated with honors from the University of Texas at the age of 20. I'm a commissioned second lieutenant in the Army and I'll be starting law school this fall at the University of Texas School of Law, one of the best law schools in the country. That's why I have the civilian side of 'the Work.'" I paused to let all this sink in with Aurianna and the other girls.

"Those are the two sides of 'the Work.' We believe we can change society and possibly influence events on the world stage, and we're not going to let the fact that we're Black stop us. In fact, being Black may be an advantage in light of the wave of civil rights laws and opportunities being offered Black people." Dana further explained.

"What about those two, are they a part of 'the Work'?" Aurianna nodded her head towards Hector and Tony who were across the room talking with Latisha and some other girls.

"No," Dana said. "They have their own plans. They're going to college on scholarship. Hector is going to New Mexico State University in Las Cruces, New Mexico on a track scholarship; and Tony is going to Texas Tech University on an ROTC scholarship to be eventually commissioned a second lieutenant like me and Chris."

"Gosh, everyone has goals and plans to meet those goals,"

Aurianna said. "What gives you all the motivation to do these things? Your parents?"

"I'm not sure where we get the motivation," Dana explained. "It may come from our parents. We're, like, third generation college graduates or attendees. My grandmother attended college in South Carolina and was a teacher. She also ran the day care for one of the largest Black churches on the east coast, Zion Baptist in Philadelphia, and was part of the civil rights movement in Philadelphia. My mom graduated from Howard University in D.C. as a mathematician, and our dad is a retired lieutenant colonel in the Army, and he attended Virginia State in Petersburg, Virginia. Dad inspired us to become Army officers like him. After retirement, Dad became an entrepreneur and owned his own mobile security force, a Texaco gas station that he sold to Hector's dad, and a professional cleaning company." Dana continued, "We've been exposed to a lot of Black people that are doing important things, like Leon Sullivan, founder of OIC, and the pastor of Zion Baptist Church; Major General Ed Greer – Uncle Ed – recently retired from the Pentagon; and Donald Hollowell, my godfather's brother, who is a civil rights attorney in Atlanta. He even helped get Martin Luther King out of jail at one point."

I picked up where Dana left off, "Yeah, they're all members of my fraternity, Kappa Alpha Psi, and Uncle Leon and Uncle Don were awarded our highest honor, the Laurel Wreath Award. Uncle Ed was one of the first ten Blacks to be promoted to general officer. Our Fraternity motto is 'Achievement in every field of human endeavor' and I try to live up to that credo."

"Are you in the fraternity?" Aurianna looked at Dana.

"No," Dana said, "But if I were to pledge something it would be Kappa. They don't have Black fraternities at West Point; but Tony and Hector will probably pledge Kappa; they're like brothers, and Hector's dad is a Kappa as well."

"I guess that explains a lot about you guys. You really seem motivated to accomplish your goals. I'll bet your parents are really proud of you." Aurianna said.

"Probably so; I think they feel we're going in the right direction." I laughed and that made Aurianna laugh too.

I turned to the other girls and continued my conversation with them. Aurianna continued her conversation with Dana.

"Do you have a girlfriend back home?" She changed the subject as she stared at Dana.

Uh oh, I thought, *this might get real serious real fast.*

"No, not really, just some girls I dated, but nothing serious right now." Dana said.

"I can't believe someone hasn't captured your heart," Aurianna said playfully, obviously hoping for the right answer.

"Nope," he said looking right into her eyes, "not until now."

Hmm, I might need to break this up, I thought.

I spoke up. "I think it's about time we took Audrey home."

"I'd like my mother to meet you guys. Can you come to my house tomorrow afternoon?" Aurianna asked. Apparently she didn't want to let go of us, especially Dana.

Cee Cee, who had come over to where we were sitting, looked at her sharply, and Aurianna looked right back at her. I don't know what all that meant, but it looked significant.

"No problem, just give us directions and tell us what time." I said.

"You all will be coming from Redlands right?" Aurianna asked.

"Yeah," I said.

"Okay, take I-10 West, to I-15 North, then you'll see an exit for Highway 66 in Fontana. Take that exit and get on 66 going east. Look for the turnoff for Beech, then take a left and then a right on Base Line Road. We're on the left on Oleander about a mile down the road. If you get to Riverside you've gone too far."

"You got that navigator?" I asked Dana.

"Yeah, I got it," he said.

"Is two o'clock okay?" Aurianna asked.

"That should be fine." I said.

After giving us directions to her house, she and the rest of the girls who followed us out had their first opportunity to see the Trans Am.

I must admit, the Trans Am looked good. I heard Aurianna gasp when she saw this brand new, sparkling, black and gold Trans Am sitting out in the parking lot with Texas dealer tags still on it. The lights around the dorm were just coming on and there was still a little daylight, so you could get a good look at the car.

Yeah, it was beautiful – midnight black, with gold trim, and the honey-combed gold wheels, and the flashy gold firebird on the hood. It looked like something out of the movies, and we walked up to it like we owned it. Oh yeah, that's right, I *did* own it.

I don't know for sure, but I think the girls were impressed based on the comments we heard as we walked up to the car.

"Wow, that's some ride."

"I didn't know black guys owned cars like that."

"I guess it's theirs, they walked up to it like they owned it."

"That's a beautiful car."

As they continued to watch, we gave them another show as we got in our namesake car. This time we tried to do it with a little more flair.

The car was actually facing the dorm from the front, so the girls standing on the sidewalk could see both Dana and I going to either side of the car to get into position. Hector and Tony stood right past the door, and when I nodded my head Dana and I simultaneously opened our car doors and leaned in to pull the seats forward to hold them, while Hector and Tony slid into the back seats at the same time. We pushed the seats back and slid the front seats up at the same time. This time, it's almost like we had rehearsed this next move, Dana and I just stood there for a moment, milking the drama, then we slid in to the front seats together and closed our doors at the same time.

The girls started clapping, especially Aurianna. I think we wowed them. I smoothly rolled down the car windows and cranked up the magnificent Trans Am sound system in full effect blasting out *Brickhouse*.

121

"Hey, you forgot about me." Audrey was still standing on the sidewalk, so we had to let her get in the car. Hector got out and Audrey squeezed in between him and Tony.

As we drove off, we waved and Dana yelled, "See you tomorrow!"

Aurianna

I could still hear Dana yelling back, "See you tomorrow!" as they drove off, and it sent shivers down my spine. I couldn't wait to see those four unbelievable guys from Texas again.

As we walked back to the dorm, I turned to Cee Cee, "What'd you think of those guys?"

"They were pretty cocky," she started, "but if even half of what they said is true, they're impressive."

"Well, they do have that car, and they seem to know exactly what they want in life."

"Yeah, especially Dana, huh?" She winked at me.

"Yeah, he's cute isn't he?"

"You certainly think so."

"Uh huh, I can't wait to see those guys tomorrow."

"You think Momma's gonna let them come to the house?"

"I hope so. I'll talk to her when we get home."

"Okay, good luck with that. You and Latisha ready to go?'

I looked around for Latisha as we walked back in the dorm and motioned for her to come over.

"You ready to go?" I asked.

"Yep," she said, "I don't think there's any reason to hang around anymore."

I turned to Cee Cee, "We're ready to go."

"Meet you at the car," Cee Cee said.

Cee Cee was a little older than me, but we were still tight. She could tell by how I kept talking about those guys from Texas that I was kind of smitten.

"You really like those guys, huh?" Cee Cee said as we left campus.

"Yeah, especially Dana." I said. "He's tall and he has the most delicious chocolate skin, sparkling brown eyes, an expressive face, and such a nice 'fro. Oh, and what a beautiful smile."

"He was cute," Latisha chimed in from the back seat, "but I thought Chris was almost too pretty."

"Light skin, green eyes, flawless complexion, yeah he looked good. I just hope he's not gay." Cee Cee said.

"I don't think so," I said, "He seemed way too interested in all the girls in the room."

"Yeah, you're right," Cee Cee laughed. "He did seem interested in getting with every girl in there."

"So did what's their names – Tony and Hector?" Latisha added.

"Yeah, they all seemed interested in getting with whoever was in the room." Cee Cee laughed again.

"All except Dana, he seemed to only have eyes for Aurianna," Latisha teased.

"Be quiet Latisha. You really think so?" I asked.

"No doubt. He couldn't keep his eyes off you the whole time he was in the room." Latisha replied. "He was like a little bright-eyed puppy dog."

"Most definitely," Cee Cee added.

"Okay. I'll convince Momma somehow to let them visit tomorrow."

"If you need me to say something let me know." Cee Cee offered as we pulled up to our house.

"No, I think I can handle it." I said getting out of the car. But

I knew convincing Momma to let these guys visit was going to be a daunting task.

Growing up in Fontana, a steel mill town where everybody settled down and got a "good job" was what was expected of people raised in that town. But that was never good enough for me. Momma tried her best to keep me in line, but I was kind of the rebel of my eleven brothers and sisters.

Momma's job was cleaning houses, and her goal for me was to be her helper. Every year from the third grade until the spring semester of my senior year I didn't complete a full week of school because Momma had me cleaning houses to bring in extra money. I knew there was something better out there for me. I always envisioned a different future, but never really had the wherewithal to figure out how to get out of Fontana. That is, until these four confident, cocky guys from Texas, driving this beautiful Trans-Am, and calling themselves the Transmanauts changed my life.

When I walked in the door, Momma was sitting in the living room watching TV.

"Hey baby, how was your visit?"

Okay, here goes. "We met these four guys from Texas, driving this brand new Trans Am, who were visiting their cousin at the dorm."

"Really! And?" she asked.

Momma, who is bigger than me and darker skinned, never liked me to bring guys to the house, and she never approved of any guys I dated, so, this would be a first for her.

"Well two of them are brothers, Chris and Dana, and their two friends Hector and Tony."

"What's so special about these four guys?"

"You had to listen to them talk Momma. Chris is going to law school, and he's already a commissioned officer! Dana's going to West Point military academy, and the other two are going to college on scholarships!"

"That's nice, but so what?"

"Momma, you had to hear them talk about their plans for

their futures. These guys were talking about being lawyers and generals and all kinds of stuff!"

"They certainly got your attention didn't they?"

I dropped the bomb. "I invited them over tomorrow at two so you could meet them."

"You did what? Without asking me first? You know I don't play that!"

"Momma, I couldn't wait to ask you, I didn't know how to get a hold of them and they were getting ready to leave and I really wanted you to meet them," I said in one breath.

"Okay baby. I see this is something you really want; and I'm curious about these four guys from Texas that've gotten you so riled up. Alright, I'll go get some snacks and stuff in the morning, and we'll be ready for your four Texas guys." She smiled.

I was surprised Momma okayed the visit. I guess she was curious about these four guys who had so impressed me. I couldn't wait for the next day.

In the morning, just as she promised, Momma went to the store and picked up chips, dip, soda and iced tea, in preparation for their visit. I spent some time getting the house ready and making myself look good before their arrival. I decided on a yellow V-necked sleeveless blouse that buttoned down and tied off at the bottom. And for an added feminine touch, a flower in my hair. As I twirled in front of the mirror examining my appearance, I had to smile – *they were actually coming to my house.*

126   As two o'clock grew closer, I just couldn't stand waiting inside the house, so I went outside to the porch to look for the Transmanauts. I didn't tell them that I lived in a very small, two-bedroom house, out on a farm with chickens, pigs, cows and other livestock. When I first invited them over, I did it with a little trepidation because I felt these guys were "privileged" and came from an upscale background; but I really wanted Momma to meet these four guys who had made such an impression on me so quickly. I could hardly breathe when I finally saw them pull up

into the yard. They were actually here. Wow!

They rolled up in that beautiful black and gold Trans Am and came to a stop in front of the house with music blasting again, this time I could hear *Slide* by Slave. Getting out of the car, they gave me the same show they had given the night before. Chris and Dana got out first, with the car doors opening at the same time. Then those two pulled the seats forward for Tony and Hector to get out. Then Tony and Hector got out at the same time, and then the four of them just stood there for a few seconds striking a pose. I loved their showmanship. I squealed in delight and clapped my hands like a little girl.

I jumped off the porch to meet them. "Can I ride in the car?" I asked.

"Not only **No,** but **Hell No!** Not only Hell No, but **Fuck No!**" they responded in unison.

That was pretty funny! And no, I didn't ride in their car.

I was a little nervous as I invited them in the house for the first time. The living room was really small, but clean and presentable. Momma stood right inside the kitchen, located right off the living room. As I led the guys in the house she strolled into the living room and stood in the middle of the floor.

Chris stuck out his hand, "Hi ma'am, I'm Chris, this is my brother Dana, and our friends Hector and Tony."

Momma shook his hand and replied cordially, "Make yourselves at home. I'm Adena, would you all like something to drink?"

"Yes, thank you." The Transmanauts said in unison.

Momma walked back into the kitchen to fix glasses of iced tea for everybody. As Momma disappeared back into the kitchen, the Transmanauts arranged themselves around the room with Chris and Dana sitting on a love seat. Tony and Hector sat in two easy chairs near the TV, leaving the sofa for me and Momma. Dana sat in such a way I could see him without being too obvious.

Momma came back in with the iced tea and served everyone. I wasn't sure how she would react to these guys. As I watched her serving the tea, I thought, *hmm, she's handling this pretty good.*

No one was more surprised than I was when Momma finally settled down on the sofa after serving the iced tea, and just jumped right in the conversation.

"I understand you all are from Texas?" Momma inquired.

"Yes ma'am." Dana said.

"I've got some people in Texas, what part of Texas are you all from?"

"El Paso," Chris said, "far west Texas; where are your people?"

"East Texas, around Texarkana."

"One of my best friends, Mike, lives in Texarkana," Chris replied. "I've visited up there several times. He lives in Wamba outside Texarkana."

"Never heard of Wamba. Sounds like it's out in the country."

"Yeah, it's out there," Chris nodded his head, "sort of like out here."

"What, you don't like being on a farm?" Momma said in a teasing voice.

"No ma'am, I've actually spent some time on farms in Kansas and Missouri. I like farms, although I've never worked a farm." Chris replied quickly, obviously to mollify Momma.

She wasn't easily mollified, but Chris's easy manner and sincere voice kept her from getting angry. She smiled and seemed like she was having a great time talking with the four of them. Unbelievable!

My fears about how small the house was or what the Transmanauts might think vanished after a few minutes. Just like last night, at the dorm, they seemed to be as comfortable in my home as they might have been in their own houses. And again, they just sort of took over.

"Aurianna tells me you all are going off to college," Momma changed the subject.

"Yes ma'am, three of us are, and Chris is actually starting law school this year in Austin," Dana answered.

"Where are you going to school young man?" She looked directly at Dana.

"West Point," Dana said with a little pride.

"Where exactly is West Point? I know it's not in Texas, but somewhere on the east coast, right?" Momma asked.

"Yes ma'am, it's actually called the United States Military Academy at West Point, and it's located on the Hudson River about 60 miles north of New York City." Dana explained.

"New York! That's a long way from California." Momma now looked at me. "Does that mean you'll go off to the Army as an officer?"

"Yes ma'am." Dana said.

I'm sure he didn't miss the look Momma gave me. "What about you two, are you going to college in Texas?" Momma turned her head towards Tony and Hector.

"Yes ma'am," Tony said, "I'm going to Texas Tech University in Lubbock on an ROTC scholarship. When I graduate, I'll be commissioned as a second lieutenant in the Army like Dana."

"I'm going to New Mexico State University in Las Cruces, on a track scholarship," Hector added.

"That's very nice," Momma said, "So, let me get this straight, one of you is going to law school, two of you are going to become Army officers, and one of you is going to run track in college, right?" She ticked off one of her fingers for each of them going to college.

"Almost ma'am," Chris said, "I'm a second lieutenant in the Army and eventually plan on being a JAG officer in the Army."

"What's JAG?" Momma asked.

"Judge Advocate General Corps, basically the Army's lawyers." Chris answered.

"Chris also wants to run for office sometime in the future, maybe for Congress," I jumped into the conversation.

"Congress! What makes you think you can run for Congress?" Momma said with disbelief on her face.

Uh oh, I thought, *here goes Adena again. She looks like she's getting ready to pounce on poor Chris.* I held my breath waiting on his answer.

"Well, I'm a good public speaker, I'm going to be a lawyer, and I've had some moderate success running for office in school, but nothing like Dana." Chris said.

I exhaled, that was a good answer. Momma seemed okay now.

"What do you mean?" Momma inquired.

"Dana was the class president for his freshman, sophomore, and junior classes, and was his school's student council president, and ran for Texas State Student Council President. He's really got a future in politics if he wants." Chris said with undisguised pride.

"Dana's high school is one of the largest in the state of Texas," I said with a hint of pride in my voice.

"Really? Very impressive," Momma said, again looking at me and Dana.

I could tell Momma was impressed by these guys, but something else was bothering her. Within a few minutes after she sat down, she began watching Dana like a bird of prey watches an unsuspecting mouse who she's about to swoop down and pounce upon. After several minutes, I could see Momma getting into pouncing mode. She hadn't pounced on Chris, but she turned her attention to Dana. I guess she could tell how much I liked Dana by the way I talked about him the night before and how he sort of looked at me while he was sitting in the living room. There was electricity in the air whenever he and I looked at each other, and I'm sure Momma figured that one out for herself.

130

Finally, she got up from her chair and headed to the kitchen. She turned back to the living room, "Dana would you please come into the kitchen?"

Oh no, I thought, *here it comes.* I just looked at Dana helplessly and shrugged my shoulders.

He nervously looked at me, then Chris, and stood up to walk into the kitchen. "Yes ma'am, on my way," and joined her in the kitchen.

I scooted over on the sofa so I could peek around the corner to see what would happen in the kitchen.

Momma looked at him and told him, "I can tell the way you look at my daughter you want something. I ain't no fool, so while you're here there'll be no thumpin'! Now get on back in there." Momma stalked back to her room.

"Yes ma'am." Dana said, then turned and stomped back into the living room. "Thumping? Chris, what the hell is 'thumping'?" Dana asked.

I was curious to hear Chris's answer, since I knew what it meant.

"It means Aurianna's mother doesn't want you having sex with her daughter." Chris laughed.

I guess it was apparent to everyone that Dana was very attracted to me and I guess Momma didn't want the situation to get out of hand. I don't think anything would have happened anyway, I'm not that type of girl, and Dana seemed to be pretty chivalrous, so I'm sure nothing would have happened. But that was typical of Momma, jumping in and interfering in my business. I think she was afraid these guys were going to whisk me away and she would never see me again.

But I didn't care about Momma's wishes; I was determined to spend as much time with Dana as possible. In defiance of Momma's edict, I did something else she wasn't going to like.

"I'd like you guys to come to my graduation tomorrow," I said.

Chris and Dana exchanged glances. Tony and Hector also looked over at Dana. Chris stood up like he was getting ready to leave.

"Okay," Chris said, "What time and where?"

"It starts at 7 o'clock, at Fontana High School stadium."

"How do we get there?" Chris asked.

"Basically the same way you got here, just take a right on Beech instead of the left and look for the stadium lights on the right about a mile after the turn."

"Okay, that's easy enough, I guess," Chris looked at Dana.

"Yep, we'll be there." Dana looked eagerly at me, "We wouldn't miss it for the world." The other three stood up and they walked towards the front door.

I followed them out on the porch and gave each of them a hug and gave Dana a kiss on the cheek, "I can't wait to see you guys tomorrow night."

Dana stammered, "Me too," and jumped off the porch following the other three to the car.

They waved just before they got into the car in their normal stylistic manner, and drove off to the sounds of *Slide* blasting out of the windows.

I was surprised they accepted my invitation to go to graduation. I especially wanted Dana to attend. I had a secret plan to get some time with him alone and away from the rest of the guys, and I needed Latisha's help.

I ran back into the house and called Latisha from the kitchen phone. When she answered I greeted her with "Latisha, those guys were just here."

"What guys?"

I could feel her smile through the phone. "You know, the Transmanauts, from Texas."

"Your mom let them come over?"

"Yeah, but she cornered Dana in the kitchen and told him 'no thumping'"

"Really?!" she screeched, "Tell me everything."

So I told her about how the Transmanaut visit had gone, then I got to the purpose of my call. "Hey Latisha I want to have Dana go with me to 'Grad Night' at Disneyland after graduation."

High schools in the area were given tickets for their graduating seniors to get into Disneyland for free on the night of graduation, almost like a "lock-down" where the park closed except for graduating seniors from all over Southern California. Each school was only issued one ticket per graduating senior, but

I wanted Dana to go with me, so I had to get someone to give up their ticket. That someone was Latisha, my best friend, and the only person, other than Cee Cee, who knew how I felt about Dana, and how important this was to me.

"You want me to give up my ticket? For him?"

"No, for me. You know how I feel about him. I've never felt this way about anybody and I want to spend some time with him alone, away from his brother and the other guys; but especially Chris."

"Huh, okay, but how do we get him on the bus? You know they'll know he's not part of the class."

"I don't know, I'll figure something out, but I need your ticket."

"Alright, I'll give it to you when I see you tomorrow at the rehearsal."

"Thank you, thank you. I love you Latisha"

"Hmph, I think I know who you love, but who am I to stand between you and this Dana guy? I'll see you tomorrow. Bye"

"Bye." I hung up the phone.

I thought it might be difficult to separate Dana from the Transmanauts, especially his brother, Chris, but I thought I could get it done. Just thinking about getting Dana alone at Disneyland gave me the chills! My plan was to tell him right after the graduation ceremony and then he could just get on the bus and we would be whisked off to Disneyland on a dream date and hopefully in all the confusion no one would notice. I was so excited! This was going to be wonderful! I couldn't wait for Graduation Night.

South Central

After we left Aurianna's house, we sought out our friend from El Paso, Clara, who was staying with her brother in South Central LA, near Crenshaw Blvd. Clara's house is down the street from our house in El Paso. She had just graduated from high school with Dana, Hector and Tony, and had recently come to L.A. to visit her brother for the summer. At some point she had a crush on Dana, and Dana had a crush on her for a brief period of time during their seventh or eighth grade years in junior high school. She and Dana had gone to various formal affairs; and she, Dana, Melanie and I had double-dated on occasion. She had also been part of our dance group and appeared on the *Steve Crosno Show*. Clara was a cute girl with caramel-colored skin, pretty face, and nice figure. She always reminded me of Janet Jackson when she starred in *Good Times* as a little girl. We had called her earlier in the trip to arrange a time and place to meet.

Clara had given us directions to get to her brother's apartment complex, but when we got there we found there was a security gate with a guard and a booth. I drove up to the gate when this Black rent-a-cop, wearing some raggedy-looking uniform, sauntered out of the booth and put his hand up like a traffic cop to stop the car.

"Yo man, who you come to see?" he asked as I rolled down my window.

"Reggie, he's in apartment C-249." I replied.

The guard went back into his booth and he consulted a list. He came back out to the car, "Sorry bro', yo man Reggie didn't put you on the list. You ain't on the list, you don't get in."

He then pointed back to the street, "You need to pull this muthafucka back out the way you came in and get out the way of these other cars."

I looked in my rearview mirror and saw other cars stacking up behind us. It was becoming dark out and the lights were coming on in the surrounding neighborhood.

"Alright, we're going," I said. *Fuck you bitch, we'll find some other way of getting in*, I thought to myself.

Strangely, the apartment complex loomed in the dark, without many lights burning the darkness away except near the entrance and the security gate.

"What do we do now?" Hector asked.

"Let's drive around the complex, maybe there's another way in." I said.

I turned the music off as we made a U-turn out of the drive leading up to the security gate. The apartment complex took up an entire block and was surrounded on all sides by streets; but the busiest street was the one bordering the complex in the front. I turned right out of the drive and followed the chain-link hurricane fence around the complex searching for some other ingress to the complex.

"Do you guys see anything?" I asked.

"No," Dana said. "All I see is fence, no other way in."

"Okay, I'm going to drive all the way around and go back up front, and then we'll figure out what we're going to do."

We didn't think of simply calling Clara's brother to have him put us on the list at the security gate, I guess that would have been too easy. Once we got back to the front gate after traversing the entire circumference of the complex, we knew there was no other easy way into the complex. I pulled over to the curb on the street near the security gate.

"Well, what do you guys want to do? She's y'all's friend." I said over my shoulder.

"It was dark on that third street, you know at the back of the apartments," Tony said. "I bet we could jump the fence and get

136

in that way."

"Wait a minute," Dana said. "That fence is at least seven feet tall, and we could get in a lot of trouble going over the fence. Isn't that trespassing Mr. Lawyer-wannabe?"

"Yeah probably so, but I'm game if you guys are." I said.

"Uh, yeah, okay, I'll do it if everyone else does." Hector added.

"Alright then, let's do it." Tony said.

"Okay," I looked around for any cops as I pulled away from the curb into traffic. I made the two right turns to get us back to the darkest, most remote area at the rear of the apartments. There weren't any lights back there and the street was bordered by trees and an empty lot on one side, and the apartments on the other. I pulled up next to the fence and backed up the car to the fence in the combat parking method in case we needed a fast getaway. I turned off the car and the four of us got out as surreptitiously as we could, very un-Transmanautic, like we were sneaking in somewhere. Oh yeah, we *were* sneaking in somewhere.

"What now?" I whispered to Tony. The quiet was unbroken except for car sounds from the busier streets around the apartments and occasional laughter from the apartments; it was really quiet back where we were.

"Let's go over the fence." Tony whispered, and then he took a running leap towards the hurricane fence and bounded up the side and over. Thankfully, there was no barbed wire at the top, just the normal sharply-edged fencing material at the top of any chain-link fence.

"Oh shit, here we go," I said as I took a running leap at the fence. I didn't get over quite as fast as Tony, but after a few seconds, I was over as well without much damage and not too much noise from the metal fence.

"C'mon Dana," Hector said. "You're next."

"Okay" Dana took a running leap and scaled the fence in pretty good fashion with only a little jangling of the fence.

By that time I was getting a little nervous, "Hector hurry up and get over here."

"Okay." He took a running leap and showed us why he was going to college on a track scholarship. He made it look so effortless as he glided over the fence with almost no sound, and within a few seconds was standing next to the rest of us.

"Listen up, we need to run to the closest apartments and figure out which building Clara's brother lives in." I said. We took off running to the closest building under cover of the blanketing darkness.

"What's the building number Dana?" I asked.

"The apartment number is C-249. I guess that means building 'C' apartment 249."

"No shit Sherlock," I said sarcastically. "What building is this?"

Tony looked around the side of the building where the cars were parked, came back and said, "This is 'G' building. I don't know where 'C' is from here."

"Okay," I said, "let's do this. We need to stay together. We know the security gate is somewhere to our front. If the buildings are in alphabetical order then 'C' may be near the front. So, let's head that way."

"Sounds logical," Hector added. "Let's go."

The farther we got in to the complex, the more people we saw. We were wandering around trying to find the right building and probably looked like we didn't belong there. In every little nook and cranny there were guys hanging out. It was so dark I couldn't see what they were doing, but there was a lot of laughing and guys looking at us, making us nervous. I'm not sure what was going on, but I was happy when we finally found building "C." We cautiously went up the stairs to the second floor and knocked at the door of 249. We could hear someone approach from the inside and the footsteps stopped on the other side of the door.

Someone with a deep voice yelled, "Who is it?"

"The guys from El Paso," I yelled into the door, "Clara's friends."

I could hear the chain being removed and the deadbolt lock being turned as the door opened up. That was one big dude and older than us. He took up most of the doorway as he stood there in jeans and white muscle shirt, more commonly known as a "wife beater."

"Hey fellas, what's up? I'm Reggie, Clara's brother," Reggie said as he shook all our hands, "Clara's not here. She left a few hours ago when you all didn't show. She's at my auntie's house."

"Damn, okay," I said, "Where's that?"

"Not too far, I'll give you directions." And for the next few minutes he gave us directions on how to get to his aunt's house.

"I think I got it, if not we'll figure it out." I said.

"Hey, how did you all get in here? I forgot to give your names to the security guy at the gate." Reggie asked.

"We jumped the fence in back." Tony volunteered.

"Damn, it's good you guys weren't caught. They got roving security guys around here, and worse, a lot of gang members live here. You need to watch yourselves on the way out. Is your car parked out back too?"

"Yeah," I said, "Should we be worried about it being there?"

"Yo man, you need to get back to your car now, before it's not there anymore." Reggie said.

"Okay, we're out, and thanks a lot." I said.

"Yep," he said as he moved back into the apartment and closed the door.

I could hear him relocking all the locks and chains as I turned to survey our surroundings with a different eye.

"You think all those guys we saw coming in were gang members?" Hector asked.

"I don't know, and I don't want to find out," I said. "Let's get out of here."

"Yeah, great move there Chris, announcing we were from El Paso so everybody could hear," Dana said looking around as we descended the stairs.

"Too late now, we need to get back to the car." I said.

As we moved back through the apartments, it seemed like all the occupants of every building, mostly young black guys, were outside smoking weed, talking loud, and looking at us, and they all looked ominous. We must have looked like we had a target on our backs, with them the predators and we the prey. We got through that gauntlet unscathed and arrived at the last building, Building "G." I saw the fence and the Trans Am beyond it.

I knew we were just about home free when I heard someone behind us say, 'Hey motha' fuckas what you all doin'?"

Oh shit! We looked behind us and saw this really short Black guy wearing all black, with a heavy bicycle chain in his hand. He had just sort of appeared out of nowhere. He was heavily muscled in a tight, black muscle shirt.

He repeated his question, and Dana said, "Hey, uh, we're just leaving." Apparently, the guy didn't like the answer and gave a loud whistle. At the sound of his whistle, two more guys came out of the shadows, and they were huge. These guys were dressed identically to the little guy, and were big enough to play for the Los Angeles Rams. Unlike the small guy, these guys looked like they had something else in their hands.

They yelled at us, "You niggas need to get the fuck out of here before we shoot your sorry asses!"

Needless to say, we needed no further encouragement, and took off for the fence. To make sure we went over the fence and never came back, one of the big guys fired a shot over our heads! BANG!

Oh shit, they're shooting at us!! I guess we knew what these guys had in their hands! Yeah, we got over the fence faster than we had the first time, except one of us. When Tony heard the gunshot, he froze! He looked like he was having some sort of flashback.

I yelled at him, "C'mon Tony, what the fuck is wrong with you? We need to get the fuck out of here!" That seemed to snap him out of his funk and he got over the fence before the rest of us!

We jumped in the Trans as fast as we could, I started the car and we squealed out of there with our tires spinning so fast we were shooting gravel out like bullets! Damn, that was close!

I looked around the car and said, "Everybody okay?"

Everybody laughed nervously. "Yeah, we're okay."

Now we could laugh about it. I screeched around the first corner and then the second.

I looked back at Tony and asked, "What the fuck happened to you?"

Tony sheepishly admitted, "Yeah, I know, I was a little slow getting started, but once I got started, I damned near jumped the fence in one leap. I took one step back and jumped to the top of that fucking fence. I wasn't going to hang around and find out if those guys were serious about putting a cap in our asses. So yeah, I got the fuck over the fence as fast as I could."

We laughed uproariously about that and as we calmed down I popped an 8-track into the player and looked for something appropriate. The sounds of Earth, Wind and Fire, began to crash against the inside of the car, *"Getaway, leave today, getaway, yeah yeah yeah, oooh hoo."* Yeah, we got away with that one and went on to find Clara's aunt's house; hopefully, in a better neighborhood with less drama.

After about twenty minutes of careful searching and several "famous U-turns" we made it to Clara's aunt's house. We got out and rang the doorbell. The house was in a respectable residential neighborhood in South Central, significantly different than the one we'd just escaped.

When the door opened, it was Clara, looking very cute in short shorts and a tube top. A smile crossed her face. You would have thought it had been three or four years, rather than the weeks it had been. She gave us hugs all around, and of course, a special hug for Dana.

"It's great seeing you guys, but you look sort of shook up. What happened to you?" She asked.

We looked like a hot mess – our clothes were all disheveled and we were still a little out of breath from our recent run-in with the gang guys.

"Do you want to come in?" Clara continued.

"No, but we can go to that Jack-in-the-Crack we saw on our way in and we can tell you all about it." I said.

"Okay, let me tell my aunt where we're going and I'll be right back."

When Clara came back outside we were already positioned by the car. We wanted to show off a little, so at my nod, we executed our Transmanautic maneuver to get in the car.

She squealed with delight, "That's a beautiful car, can I sit up front?"

We answered, "Not only **No,** but **Hell No!** Not only **Hell No,** but **Fuck No!**" and she laughed at that too. We let her in the back seat between Hector and Tony and drove to the Jack-In-the-Crack closest to her aunt's house.

Apparently she hadn't been to that Jack-in-the-Crack, as we called it, so she was unfamiliar with the menu. We all got our normal two tacos for $.99, and she got a Jumbo Jack as we crowded into one of the booths.

"So tell me, what happened to you guys?" Clara asked.

"It's a long story," I said and proceeded to tell her what happened at Reggie's apartment complex. The other Transmanauts chimed in during the telling until we finally finished the story with our arrival at her aunt's front door.

Clara laughed and laughed throughout our recitation of our most recent adventure.

142

"You know you guys stumbled into the gang headquarters for that part of town. My brother's apartment complex is where all the gang members hang out." She continued, "I don't know which gangs, but they definitely are around because I've seen them since I've been visiting Reggie, and he told me about them. They aren't like those wannabe gangstas you have in El Paso. You don't want to mess with these guys. I had no idea you guys might run into those gang members like that or I wouldn't have sent you to my brother's apartment."

"You know, it's like when you step on an ant hill and all the ants come running out; but this time we were surrounded by a bunch of gun-toting ants. And, oh yeah, we were definitely run off the ant hill." I said.

Clara had to laugh some more. I don't think she knew we could be this much fun to be around.

"You guys are hilarious. It sounds like you've had a great visit so far with the whole Transmanautic thing, the basketball games, Hector's uncle, the college campus, Sea World, and now at my brother's apartment," she laughed. "And who is this girl you've met out here Dana? Tell me all about her."

Dana looked embarrassed.

I said, "If you've seen the *Godfather*, it's like when Michael Corleone sees Apollonia for the first time and it's described as the 'thunderbolt' hitting him. That's what happened when Dana met Aurianna. We're going to her graduation tomorrow night."

"I'm jealous," Clara said. I saw the crestfallen expression on Dana's face, and she must have too because she quickly added, "Not really, I'm just joking Dana. I hope it works out for you. What about the rest of you guys, have you all found anyone yet?"

"Maybe Thursday night," Hector laughed. "We've been invited to a graduation party and hopefully, there'll be plenty of girls for us to meet."

"Sounds like fun, I hope you guys have a good time." Clara looked at her watch, "I guess I should get back to the house, it was great seeing you guys again. I haven't laughed that hard since I've been here, and it felt really good. You all need to keep in touch, okay?"

143

"Geez, you make it sound like we'll never see you again, you know there's mail, and airplanes, and all kinds of ways to keep in touch," Dana said as we got up to leave Jack-In-The-Crack.

"Yeah, I know," Clara said. "It's just that seeing you guys made me a little homesick. I'm just so glad you were able to come by tonight."

"Our pleasure Clara." I said as we got to the car.

"Hey Clara, you think you can braid my hair tonight? I want my 'fro to look as good as possible tomorrow night." Hector asked.

"No, I don't think so," Clara said, "at least not tonight. I'm not sure my aunt would appreciate you all hanging out for the next few hours, 'cause I know from previous experience it takes a few hours to braid your tender head."

In a few minutes we got back to Clara's aunt's house and let her out of the car. We all got out and walked her to the door where she gave each of us a hug and little kiss on the cheek for her high school classmates. When she got inside, I saw her watching us get in the car Transmanaut-style, and she waved at us from the front window as we left the driveway. That was the last time we saw Clara.

The next day we went looking for a basketball game, again. We decided to go outside of Redlands and find a game elsewhere, anywhere else where we could win. We were tired of losing.

Inspired by having met with Clara the night before, we went looking for a game in South Central. We didn't think much of where we were going, except we wanted to play ball and win. It didn't cross our minds that we might run into some gang bangers on the basketball courts, so we went back into South Central to play ball. We found a playground not too far from the Jack-in-the-Crack and Clara's aunt's house. We didn't call Clara to come watch because, well, you know; in case we lost we didn't want to be embarrassed in front of her and didn't want to embarrass her either. We drove up in our car, but not as ostentatiously, so as not to draw undue attention to ourselves. Once we got out, we sought out the guys on the court. These guys didn't look like hardcore gang bangers, so we thought we would be okay. They looked at us and knew we weren't from the area. Even though we tried not to be too noticeable, we were sort of hard to miss. Not everybody drives up in a brand new, black and gold Trans Am, with Texas tags, and expects not to be noticed. Oh well, here we go again.

As before, we said we would only play four-on-four, rather than five-on-five. The guys on the court said "No problem," and figured out who would play us. Again, as before, we established the rules and got to it.

Almost from the first time we took out the ball, I knew we were in trouble. The guy I was supposed to guard, their point, looked like he had played some college ball. This guy was about 5' 11", a little taller than me, and really cut. He had a medium-sized 'fro and was a little darker than me also. And he could talk trash! But he could back it up.

He would say things like, "You know I can take you to the hole anytime and anywhere I want! It don't matter what kind of car you drive, you ain't shit!"

He would just stand there and dribble the ball in front of me, daring me to make some sort of move, and when I did, this boy would drive right past me like I was standing still. I prided myself on keeping up with just about anybody, but this guy was the best I had ever been up against. This boy had serious game! I could barely keep him in front of me. He was doing reverse lay ups, driving past me on the baseline, shooting little hook shots, and pushing the ball hard down the middle. I felt like the Washington Generals trying to keep up with Meadowlark Lemon and the Harlem Globetrotters.

After the first few baskets, I panted to Dana, "This guy is too good for me to guard by myself. When he comes down the lane for a layup we need to double him, so come off your man and make this guy pass the ball." Dana said okay. This wasn't something we had practiced much since we normally played one-on-one, but Dana was able to come off his man whenever my guy got past me. So, with me coming from behind, and Dana clogging the lane in the middle, the strategy seemed to work and we forced him to start passing off to his teammates. Luckily, Hector and Tony had pretty good games scoring on their opponents, so we were able to keep it close – 10 to 8, but we lost again.

After the game, one of the brothers on the other team told us, laughing, that the guy that I was guarding played the summer pro leagues and had a tryout coming up with the Lakers. Damn. Yeah, no wonder we got our butts kicked! At least on the bright side, we were going to Aurianna's graduation that night. That was better than losing on the courts, again.

Gettin' to Graduation

Graduation was scheduled for 7 o'clock that evening. We stopped by the same Jack-In-The-Crack we'd been the night before to get sodas to cool off after losing the last basketball game. As we came out of the drive-thru lane we put basketball behind us and started focusing on going to Aurianna's graduation that night. We had a long drive back to Redlands and we talked about what the evening might bring and our own senior years. But first, the conversation turned to Aurianna.

"Yeah man, I can't wait to see Aurianna again," Dana said. "I don't care what her mother said, I want to see her again."

"Man, you've been hit hard by the thunderbolt," I said. "As much as you've laughed at us and our trials and tribulations with girls over the years, and your vow that you'd never let a girl get to you like that, look at you now." I laughed, and Hector and Tony joined in.

"Yeah Dana." Tony started, "What's up with that? She's got you so wide open you can't stop talking about her," he laughed.

"I love it!" Hector added laughing, "There's this big ass ring in your nose and you had to come all the way to Cali to find the girl who put it there." He slapped hands with Tony. They were having a great time with Dana and his obvious infatuation with Aurianna. Tony and Hector had been on the receiving end of Dana's barbs on their ups and downs with various girls, and they were apparently taking pleasure in watching him go through the same thing.

"Okay, okay, but do you think she really likes me?" Dana

asked with a sheepish grin.

"Yeah man, she really likes you," Tony laughed. "Why else would she have invited us out to her house, you dummy."

"Yeah dummy," Hector chimed in, "Aurianna from Fontana – that even sounds sexy. She's pretty hot, I'm sure that's why her mother doesn't want you anywhere near her daughter."

"How you goin' to get around that Dana?" I asked.

"I'll figure something out. Maybe when we come back through here after San Fran, we can see her again, like with Clara, without her mom around."

"Maybe," I offered. "We'll see how it works out tonight."

"How much farther Chris?" Tony asked.

"We got a ways; we're just now getting out of the city, probably another thirty minutes or so," I said. "You in a hurry?"

"Nah, just wanted to know." Tony answered.

"Hey Chris," Hector leaned forward in his seat, "you've told us a little about your experiences at UT, what was your senior year like before graduation?"

"Oh, you want the whole story, huh?"

"We got nothin' better to do until we get back to Aunt Rose's so I thought you might tell us more about being at UT." Hector continued.

"Let's see, I've already talked about the car; that guy thinking I was a fag; us winning the Delta step show; and that one incident with the girls down in Beaumont, right?"

"Yeah, but that wasn't everything right?" Hector asked.

"Nope, there's more, just didn't think you all would be interested." I said.

"Go 'head Chris, tell us all about being at the mighty University of Texas," Tony laughed.

"Alright Negro, here you go," I started. "You guys were focused on graduating high school, and in Dana's case going to West Point, and for you two guys going to State and Tech. My agenda was a little different. I was trying to finish up my senior year at Texas so I could graduate and go to law school this year. I was a cum laude designee the fall of 76; and I was on track to be commissioned as a second lieutenant in the Army when I graduated."

"What's cum laude?" Hector asked.

"That means graduating 'with honors.'" I said.

"Congrats," Hector said.

"Didn't turn out that way. I ran into computer science and couldn't pass the course, so I made a deal with the dean of the college that if I got enough credits in the class to satisfy the professor, I would graduate, but without honors." I explained.

"Yeah, Chris was pissed at graduation," Dana said.

"At least I graduated, unlike that other motherfucker from Eastwood who didn't tell his family that he wasn't graduating until they showed up in Austin for graduation." I said.

"That's pretty fucked up, who was it?" Tony asked.

"Not important," I said. "But I did graduate and he didn't, so I'm okay with that. At least I didn't fuck my family like he did."

"Okay, so what else happened your senior year?" Hector asked.

"As you all know, I was also heavily involved in getting Kappa Alpha Psi established on my campus, as well as on other campuses within the general geographic area around Austin. Working with the fraternity took up a lot of my time during my senior year, and gave me the opportunity to be exposed to different campuses around Texas, including Southwest Texas State University in San Marcos. You already know part of the HT story and the Lamar University incident, and I also visited the University of Houston; and East Texas State. My exposure to those campuses and the different chapters of my fraternity located on those campuses taught me a lot about being a member of my fraternity. It also allowed me to interact a lot more with undergraduate members of the various sororities and little sister organizations," I said as I continued to navigate the freeway traffic.

"What's a 'little sister organization?' Hector asked.

"Organizations of women who are supposed to help the frats. Ours was called the Kappa Diamonds; the Qs had their Pearls; and the Alphas had their Angels. We had to start our own chapter of Diamonds at UT, and that helped my confidence when interacting with undergraduate women." I said.

"How?" Tony asked.

"Boy, you're an inquisitive motherfucker aren't you?"

"Just trying to learn at the feet of the master," Tony laughed.

"Yeah, okay. Anyway, the selection process, pledging them into the Diamonds, and further interaction gave me more confidence in being around college women. Talking, joking, working with them, going to their apartments, and even a pajama party at one of their apartments with all the Brothers and all the Diamonds."

"You hit any of that?" Tony asked as Dana and Hector leaned in to hear the answer.

"No, not that night. We had fun talking, dancing, listening to music, some drinking wine, and a little fooling around, but nobody got any pussy that night, but it wasn't like dick teasing. We knew it would happen sooner or later, that was like foreplay. It was a lot of fun." I added.

"So you failed again to get some pussy." Tony laughed.

"Fuck you Tony," I laughed. "We had fun and our purpose wasn't to create a pussy factory, but to actually form an organization to help us with our projects. The pussy came later."

150   "What kind of projects?" Hector asked.

"Parties, giving food baskets during the holidays, Kappa Week activities, stuff like that." I replied.

"What else did you all do this past year?" Tony asked.

"We had to establish ourselves on campus. We pledged three different lines from three different campuses at the same time in Fall '76 – a total of twelve guys, four from UT, six from HT, and two from Southwest. We also pledged twelve girls on that first

Kappa Diamond line that same fall. That was sort of tough on us, but we managed," I continued, "We also had parties, and I became the DJ for all of our Kappa parties on campus and helped organize all the parties. We worked as a team– one frat brother, Cornell, would provide the equipment; another frat brother, Ken, would provide the expertise for setting it up and advice on the music, and I would provide the music, and me and Ken would DJ the parties as well. I also became the "step master" or "pimp dog" for our fraternity when we performed at step shows."

"Pimp dog?" Hector inquired.

"Yeah, when we stepped I was the guy leading the various steps, and also the one outside the formation doing my own thing while the rest of the guys performed the routine. You know Kappas step with red and white striped canes, and they were very similar to the baton I had mastered in high school; so, I got good real quick with the canes. That was a lot of fun." I said.

"Man, you're long winded." Hector laughed.

"Shut up. You guys asked, so there you have it." I exhaled. "What about you guys, what was your senior year like? I wasn't around, so I don't know how it was at Eastwood this past year."

"I'll go first," Hector said, "My senior year was a Dow Jones industrial type year filled with many highs, and just as many lows. I gained and lost my first love. I dropped a touchdown pass in the end zone for the city championship game. I got third place in the district track meet because of a bad start when I was the favorite to win the 100 meter dash. Hell, let's be honest here shall we? It was more like the 1st and 2nd place finishers false started so badly I assumed there would be a recall gun. But there was no gun and I had to go from 0 to 60 in a hurry. I was lucky to have gotten 3rd under those circumstances."

151

"And you called me long winded?" I laughed.

"Shut up Chris. Yeah, I'm still a little bitter about it. I should have won that race, just like you should have graduated with honors. I was also one of the leading receivers in the city, and got my name in the paper a few times. And thanks to Dana, one day the notoriety wasn't so great."

"Why what happened?" I asked glancing at Dana, who was

just shaking his head.

"One Monday morning after our Friday night loss, I saw I was listed in the paper as the second leading receiver in the city. My stats were leading everyone else's except for one player. I was so excited, I showed my mother and she got excited and was calling family members. I remember going to school that morning thinking I hated that we lost the game, but something good had come out of it. Maybe I can become more of a part of the offense after this. I remember going through the halls at school and teammates were congratulating me, girls were taking notice, and it was probably the best start of the day I could have. I was feeling proud of myself until sitting there in my second period class when I heard the morning announcements. As the Student Council president, Dana made the announcements. Dana got on the mike and mentioned I was the second leading receiver in town and for everyone to give it up for me!!!! Now I guess normally this would have been a good thing, and I know Dana got excited and meant well and was happy for me. A lot of people thought I put Dana up to doing that. But it wasn't true. I hadn't even seen Dana up to that point, nor had the two of us talked yet that day."

"So what? Were they just jealous, or what?" I asked.

"It wasn't that," Tony said. "People thought Dana was trying to make his friend Hector look good even though we lost the game – like Hector was bigger than the team or something."

"That's not what I meant," Dana said.

"Yeah, needless to say the great day I was having kind of turned a little ugly after that, and it's too bad. But Dana's heart was in the right place, and he was truly excited for me and that meant a lot. I spoke with Dana later and told him to please don't do that anymore, and he understood."

"Yeah, I was pretty excited for you," Dana started, "but I didn't mean to embarrass you."

"I know, no problem. I was also one of the leading sprint champions in town. Got my name in the paper several times for that honor. My senior year our school won the district track meet when I anchored the mile relay and helped us to win the title. It was even sweeter that I was able to beat the 7th rated sprinter in

Texas, the guy from Burgess. Yeah, that was pretty cool. I was the team co-captain and the guys carried me around the track with me holding the trophy up in my hands! I'll never forget that moment in my life…I remember Dana and Tony coming over to me afterwards and the three of us were going out to celebrate the win. That was one of my proudest moments…not just for the win, but because I was with my friends as we celebrated."

"That's pretty cool. I guess that's one of the reasons you got your scholarship to New Mexico State." I said.

"Yeah, they had a scout out there and he talked to me about going to NMSU. I didn't have many scholarship opportunities and it was close to home, so I agreed to go to Las Cruces." Hector finished.

"What about you, Tony?" I asked as we hit the freeway towards Redlands.

"Oh you know, my year wasn't as exciting as Hector's, but I had fun playing football, running track and dating Greta."

"What, that's all?" I asked, "Nothing else happened?"

"Not really," Tony said, "Well, you know, I had to work a part-time job at Smuggler's Inn so I could earn money during the year, and as a result, I ended up missing out on a lot of social events because of work. But, I tried to get out as much as possible. You know one of the reasons I worked was so I could take Greta out to some of the nice places, and of course I had an employee discount at Smuggler's, so we ate there a lot. But I dated Greta all senior year and had big fun when I could. All of that paid off, because I was able to get in to Texas Tech and got an ROTC scholarship. I was a little disappointed because I didn't get any athletic scholarship offers, but I'm looking forward to the military. And who knows, maybe I'll pledge Kappa at Tech."

153

"Yeah, they've got a chapter at New Mexico State, so I'll probably pledge Kappa too. I guess that'll make my dad happy." Hector added.

"Don't pledge for someone else, pledge because that's what you want to do." I advised.

"Don't worry, I've grown up around Kappas, so I'm pretty

sure that's what I want to do." Hector said.

"I don't know if they have Kappas at Tech," Tony said. "But if not, I'll do like you at UT and start the chapter there."

"Who knows," I laughed. "Maybe I'll make it up there to take you over."

"I know there aren't any Black frats at West Point, so I'll have to pledge grad chapter." Dana said.

"Don't worry about that," I said. "What was your senior year like? I know you had some challenges with René there."

"Oh shit, that was a real pain in the ass," Dana recalled. "She really fucked up my senior year."

"How's that?" Tony asked. "I guess I don't know that whole story."

"As you all know, René was our younger cousin who came to live with us after her mother passed away," Dana pointed out. "In what should have been the pinnacle of my career at Eastwood, René came in and gravitated to the lowest denominator of Black kids at the school and hung out with the gang banger wannabes. She just ruined my reputation at school. Damn."

"What happened?" Tony asked.

"You know she's from Philly, and looked for kindred spirits at school. She was rough around the edges and liked to thumb her nose at authority. Back talking, making trouble in class, hanging out with the wrong crowd, that sort of thing. Initially she was given a pass by most of the teachers and administrators because she was my cousin, and I had a great reputation at school. But after a while Mom was spending a lot of time at the school cleaning up behind René because of all the havoc she was causing. I just think that all that shit she was doing ruined my shot at 'Mr. Blue and Gold.'" Dana lamented.

"But you still had a pretty successful year even if you weren't Mr. Blue and Gold, right? I mean you all pretty much ran the school." I said.

"Well, yeah, I was Student Council President, an Optimist Award recipient, and Cadet Colonel in ROTC, National Honor

Society, as well as top ten percent. I should have been Mr. Blue and Gold, dammit."

"Let it go, it's done," I said. "You got more going for you than anyone in your class, and you've been planning this for some time."

"You're right. At the beginning of our freshman year, me, Sonja, Melanie and these two mapped out a strategy for me to win the freshmen class presidency, and then just keep it going until I won student council. Yeah, we were an organized political machine. " Dana laughed, "Eastwood never knew what hit it."

"Yeah, it was kind of a Student Council Mafia," Tony added. "We pretty much ran the school. Dana was the most popular guy in school and he ran it the way he wanted to and the teachers and the principal couldn't do much about it." Tony laughed.

"I dated a lot, but nothing serious," Dana said, "Sonja, Diana, Clara, a bunch of girls for various formal events. You know, some of those girls from Northeast."

"Yeah, they always seemed to be finer than our girls," Hector added. "I liked going out there or on post to the Teen Center to check them out. They were cute."

"I missed all that working at Smuggler's, but I got to take Greta out." Tony said.

"And Chris, you had Melanie back home right?" Hector poked me in the shoulder.

"True, but during my senior year at UT there were a lot of opportunities to be with some of the girls at school, but I chose not to take advantage of all of them. I had Melanie, so I was okay, but if there was an opportunity thrown in my face I wasn't going to turn it down, you know. But that never quite seemed to work out, no matter how I tried to make it happen. I think sometimes I tried too hard."

"Like what?" Tony asked.

"Like when I went to the AKA's regional in Waco, Texas over Easter. This was different than when Dana and I took over the teen scene at the national AKA convention in New York last year. That was fun, but those were teenage girls. This was more on my territory – these were collegiate women and I was much more comfortable this year than last year. I have to admit that in summer 1976, I was still intimidated by pretty college women, but I got over that and had some success with women of different sororities, including the AKAs at UT."

"What happened in Waco? Did you get any pussy?" Tony asked.

"Damn Tony, is that all you think about?" I laughed as we approached the exit for Aunt Rose's house.

"Pretty much, yeah," he laughed.

"No, I didn't get any pussy. I was sharing a room with my mother and most of the girls were sharing rooms with other girls, so no real opportunity there; but I thought something might happen when we got back to school, but it never did." I said.

"What happened in Waco?" Hector persisted.

"Alright, so when I attended this regional convention of the 'oh-so-fine Ladies of Pink and Green' I was ready to participate as a college man who was both in a prominent fraternity from the flagship school of Texas, and who was getting ready to graduate college and go to law school. In addition, Dana wasn't at this convention, so I was solo in that respect. I had the opportunity to interact with all the undergraduate AKAs at the convention. I had a great time because there were only a few undergrad guys in attendance, and there were plenty of attractive AKAs with little to do in that kind of backwater city. The convention was held over a three-day weekend and there weren't many social activities outside of the convention. So, really, the only social activities were at the convention – there was a mixer Friday night, and a banquet and dance on Saturday night."

156

I took a breath and continued, "I met a lot of women at the mixer, and then had a great time at the banquet and dance the next night. I wore a brand new black three-piece suit that was an Easter gift from Aunt Eloise, and danced all night after the banquet. And since there weren't a whole lot of guys, I pretty much had my pick of who I danced with, and I danced with as many pretty women as I could in one night. Yep, I had a ball that night."

"But no pussy," Tony laughed.

"Hey, we're here," Hector exclaimed looking around, "I didn't even notice we'd made it back to Aunt Rose's."

It was about 3 o'clock and it was time to get ready to go to Aurianna's graduation.

We crowded into our bedroom and looked at the clothes we had to wear for this graduation ceremony. We had washed our dirty laundry over the past couple of days, so we had all our clothes available to us. Dana and I selected our gray window pane bell bottomed jeans with a long sleeved silk shirt and low heeled platforms. Tony and Hector both had similar shirts to Dana and selected dress slacks to wear as well to the ceremony. Getting dressed took a couple of hours because of access to only one bathroom, and the need to iron much of our clothes. Once we were done dressing, we decided to get some dinner. Aunt Rose had fried up some chicken, so we ravenously attacked her tasty fried chicken, biscuits and fixings with Uncle Rudi keeping a watchful eye on us. Around 6 o'clock we headed out to the car calling out our thanks and goodbyes to Aunt Rose as we set sail towards Fontana and Aurianna.

"Do you remember how to get to the stadium?" I asked Dana.

"Umm, yeah, I think so. You heard the directions just like I did. I've looked at the Trip Tik, so we need to head west on I-10, then north on I-15, then east on Highway 66, right instead of left on Barrier Road and we'll need to look for signs for the stadium as we get closer." Dana looked at the map.

"Okay, we'll follow your lead on this one." I said as we pulled out the driveway.

"You looking forward to seeing Aurianna again?" Hector asked Dana.

"Yeah," Dana said. "Wouldn't you?"

"Most definitely," Hector exhorted. "She's fine, and yeah, I would love to see her again."

"I know, you've said that. I've never met anybody like her," Dana smiled. "I'd like to get to know her better."

"I'll bet." Hector laughed.

"Well, maybe you'll get your chance later this trip." I said.

"I kind of liked her friend Latisha," Tony chimed in.

"She was cute, but she wasn't Aurianna," Hector said. Dana nodded his agreement.

"Okay, granted, but you never know." Tony said.

I drove the car onto the venerable I-10 and headed west. The closer we got, the more excited Dana got – he had it bad.

"You all remember your graduation night?" I asked to break up the silence.

"Duh, we just graduated a couple of weeks ago." Tony said.

"Yeah I know, but what do you remember about getting to graduation that night?" I asked as I maneuvered the car north on I-15.

"I remember being nervous," Hector said. "I just wanted to cross that stage and hear my name called and get my diploma."

"What about you Dana?" I nodded to Dana.

"I just wanted them to make sure they pronounced my name right," he said, "and to correctly announce my appointment to West Point."

"What about you Tony?" I asked.

"I was ready to get it over with and go somewhere to get something to eat with the family." Tony answered.

"So what do you think Aurianna's thinking right now as she gets ready for graduation?" I asked.

"Don't know," Dana said, "but she might be nervous because we're going to be there. Probably fussing with her hair and makeup, but I'm sure she'll look great tonight."

"She could wear a barrel and mud flaps and she would look good to you." I laughed.

"Yeah, you're right. I can't keep her out of my mind." Dana said.

As the conversation wound down, I pulled off of I-15, and onto Highway 66 and headed east but didn't recognize any of the landmarks.

I leaned over to Dana, my navigator, and asked, "You need to focus on navigating. Where are we?"

"Uh, I think we're supposed to be on Beech," he answered, while looking at the map.

"Hey, you told me Barrier, why didn't you say something? Now we're going to be late!"

"No, we're not going to be late. Take this next left and we'll take a short cut." Dana said.

Alright, I thought, *here we go again; we're going to get really lost now.* I executed another of my "famous U-turns" and started back the other direction. Luckily Dana was right, the short cut he suggested cut about five minutes off our drive, so we got there on time. Of course exceeding the posted speed limit by several miles per hour didn't hurt our chances either.

When we arrived at the stadium, we had to find Aurianna's family in all the throngs of people trying to get up in the stands. The stadium was not like the football stadiums we were used to in Texas, with the concrete stands, and the towering press box on the home side. This stadium wasn't built with concrete, but with wood, and looked very old, and was not very big or sturdy-looking. It was really just two sides of the field with wooden grandstands, and not very impressive at all. I almost felt sorry that Aurianna had to graduate in such a sorry-looking structure. I was hoping the thing wouldn't come crashing down with all the people surging up the steps. As it turned out, one of Aurianna's brothers was also graduating that night, so the whole family was out in force and they were easy to spot amongst the multitude of people.

We found them up near the top of the grandstands where Cee Cee was waving frantically to get our attention. We made that long trek up the steps to the top. That normally wouldn't have been too taxing, but we had just played a pretty tough game against that semi-pro wannabe, and we were a little tired. Once we got up there, Dana sat between Cee Cee and Aurianna's mom, and immediately started searching for Aurianna in the crowd of graduating seniors. All the seniors were seated in several rows of metal folding chairs on the football field. There was a stage with a podium on the field where there were several dignitaries, including the principal, valedictorian, salutatorian, other officials, and a whole stack of diplomas. Cee Cee pointed Aurianna out to him, and he was able to relax a little. The graduation went as most do, sort of boring with all the preliminary stuff.

Finally, they began to call the names of the graduates, and as each row of graduates stood up to make the trek across the stage to receive their diplomas, the anticipation grew. We watched anxiously as they got closer to Aurianna's name. When she finally marched across the stage, and they announced her name, Dana cheered the loudest. Yeah, okay, he had it pretty bad. Of course, right behind her was her brother, and he got a pretty big cheer from the family too. I got the impression the family had been waiting a long time for him to get out of high school. The rest of the ceremony was pretty anti-climactic. As Dana sat next to Aurianna's mom waiting for the ceremony to end, she was really bending his ear about something. I was thinking, *Uh oh, here it comes, this can't be good.* Unfortunately, my instincts were right.

During the whole ceremony, rather than concentrating on the graduation of her two children, Aurianna's mom had been staring at Dana like a vulture looks at carrion on the side of the road. Her look was a mixture of almost pure hate and disgust, and she wasn't even trying to hide it. Dana couldn't see her expressions because he was too close and focused on Aurianna and talking to Cee Cee; but a few seats away, I had a perfect vantage point to see the changing expressions on her face whenever Dana would mention Aurianna. Finally, I guess, she couldn't stand it anymore and she was going to set him straight about her daughter.

"I've seen the way you've been lookin' at my daughter and I swear you're not going to ruin her!" She scowled with a malevolent expression.

Dana, incredulously, said, "I don't know what you're talking about, I wouldn't ruin Aurianna!"

"Yes you would," she growled, "You already have!"

"What are you talking about?" Dana inquired.

She hissed, "Aurianna may invite you to Grad Night at Disneyland after graduation, and if you go with her she's going to get in trouble, and I'm not having that!"

"What!" Dana exclaimed, "I didn't know that!" He grinned as wide as Texas.

"If you get on that bus they're going to throw you off and probably throw her off too!" she continued.

"You can't tell me what to do," Dana defiantly said, "If I want to get on that bus, I will!" And he got up from his seat and started working his way past me. He looked angry and frustrated as he squeezed by me. I stuck out my leg to stop him and asked him what was wrong.

He said, "Nothing. Move your leg, I just need to get away from here!"

I pulled my leg back and jumped up to follow him. I motioned to Hector and Tony to stay seated as I rushed to catch up to Dana. He was moving quickly down those rickety steps, but I caught him at the bottom of the steps on the walkway in front of the metal railing, and said, "Okay, what's up?"

"Did you hear what that witch said to me?! I can't believe this shit."

I don't think I'd seen him this angry in a long time. As he told the tale, I also wondered what would happen if he got on the bus. I thought that if there were chaperones – which is a good bet there were – they would probably recognize that he wasn't one of their graduating seniors and might kick him off the bus. Aurianna could get in trouble, especially if she came to his defense or they found out she gave him the ticket. That wouldn't be good for either of them. I also selfishly thought of the Transmanauts. We hadn't been separated this whole trip and I didn't want to see that happen. The Transmanauts had also made a decision – we weren't going to Disneyland, so Dana was going back on our agreement to run off with some girl? What if something happened to him? What would happen to him going to West Point? What about the "Work"? What would I tell Mom if something happened to her baby?

As these thoughts rocketed through my mind I told him, "I don't think it's a real good idea for you to go. It might cause more problems than it's worth. Look, we're coming back here

161

in a few days, maybe we can see Aurianna when we come back through and spend the day with her and Latisha, and some of their friends." I continued, "You'll see her again, trust me."

"Okay, if she offers me the ticket I'll just decline and tell her we had some other plans for the night. We'll catch her on the flip side on the way back through LA," Dana agreed.

I thought that was the more mature decision and would hopefully be the best decision for everyone.

A few minutes later the graduation ceremony was over, and everyone was streaming down out of the stands to the field to find their graduate. We caught up with Aurianna's family as they got to the walkway to go find and congratulate her. She was easily one of the prettiest girls in her class, and when we got up close to her, I wondered if Dana's resolve would remain firm. Aurianna was wearing a burgundy graduation gown in contrast to the guys who were wearing gold graduation gowns. Under her gown she was wearing a cream colored dress that she had made herself, and she looked quite fetching in that dress. After graduation, we all took pictures. The Transmanauts took a picture with Aurianna, and then Dana took one by himself with her.

Following the picture taking, Aurianna called Dana off to the side. I could see her asking him something, and showing him the tickets to Grad Night. I held my breath waiting for his response, and I saw the saddest expression on his face as he, apparently, graciously declined her offer. I felt so bad because of the crestfallen expression on Aurianna's face. But I thought it was for the best. As a consolation, I knew we would be back here in a few days. After Dana declined the tickets she gave him a little hug and kiss on the cheek, and turned away to board the school bus that held her fellow graduates and their chaperones.

The last we saw of Aurianna was her getting on the bus going to Grad Night at Disneyland, and staring out the back window with a forlorn look on her face, waving goodbye.

The Party

Thursday morning dawned with a bright sun and great promise of things to come. Time for us to wipe out all the memories of losing basketball games, gangs, and Aurianna going off without Dana. We're going to have a great time at the Party tonight, and hopefully meet a lot of nice-looking women. If Brenda was any indication, we should do both.

Audrey stayed at the house the rest of that week instead of at the dorm because we were in town. That morning, she joined us at the breakfast table and I instantly knew she had an attitude because she wasn't invited to the Party.

"Do you have the Blanchard's address?" I looked directly at Audrey while taking a bite of toast.

"I thought you were going to wait for Brenda to call with directions." Audrey snapped.

"She hasn't called yet. We're not doing anything today, so we were going to do a little recon to make sure we don't get lost tonight."

Unfortunately, during this trip we tended to get misoriented at times, and we needed to make sure we could find the house in the dark.

"I think I know how to get there. I'll give you directions before you leave," she said in a calmer voice, "Have fun."

"I think we'll have a good time tonight." I laughed trying to lighten up the mood, "Maybe not as good as Dana over the last couple of days, but we should have fun."

"Yeah, how did that go with Cee Cee's sister?" Audrey looked at Dana.

"We went out to her house the other day, and then she invited us to her graduation last night. We accepted and that's where we were last night."

"I wondered where you guys were last night." Audrey said, "How was it?"

"It was cool. Aurianna looked good, then she went off to Disneyland for Grad Night." Dana looked at me with a pleading look in his eye. I'm pretty sure he didn't want Audrey to know the whole story, so I just agreed with his story. "Yep, we had a good time the last couple of days around Fontana and playing ball in South Central."

"Hector told me about that," Audrey began, "Have you guys beaten anyone yet?" She laughed.

"No, but we're not done," Tony jumped in. "We'll win a game sooner or later."

"Probably later," Audrey laughed. "I told you these boys out here were good. Bobby said anytime you guys are ready for a rematch, they're ready to run."

Yeah, well fuck that, I thought. "We'll find someone else to beat up on us." I said, "We'll be leaving in a couple days and we may find some games up in Oakland or Frisco."

"Good luck." Audrey laughed.

"You're not going to the party tonight?" I asked knowing she wasn't invited. I had to have some sort of dig at her since she laughed at our inability to win at least one basketball game.

"No, I guess I'm not good enough, or at least I'm not a guy. So, no, I'm not going." Audrey pouted.

"We'll tell you all about it later on." I grinned. "Let's go guys. Let's see if we can't find this party house." We got dressed in shorts and T-shirts. I sought out Audrey to get the directions. She was watching TV in the family room.

"You know how to get to their house?" I asked.

"They live in Riverside. Take I-10 west, then I-215, it becomes Highway 91. Then look for signs for Arlington Heights, and get off at Washington street. Make a left, then a left on Victoria; go a few blocks then turn right on Mary Street. Take a right on Sundance Trail, and that turns into Jessica Street. The address is 5117 Jessica. Got it?"

"Yeah, I got it." I wrote furiously. "Thanks. We'll see you later." I went to find the other three out front by the car.

"Okay, I got the directions, let's go." We finally got out of the house about noon to go find the Blanchard house.

The house was supposed to be about twenty minutes away based on the directions and the Trip Tik, but as usual, once we got off the freeway we got lost and misoriented for several minutes until we found the right street. After about a half an hour we found the house on Jessica.

"What's the use of the Trip Tik if we keep getting lost?" I inquired of our navigator.

"Don't blame me, Mr. Second Lieutenant, if you can't follow directions or read a map." Dana said. Hector and Tony snickered.

"Never mind, at least we made it here. Let's see if anyone's home." I pulled into the driveway behind a couple of cars.

We exited the car in our normal Transmanautic manner just in case someone was watching, and walked to the front door where I rang the bell.

Brenda came to the door and looked a little surprised to see us. "Hey guys, I was going to call you later with directions and the time." Opening the door wider, "But since you're here come on in and meet my sisters Vivian and Debbie."

"Sorry about that, but we wanted to make sure we knew how to get here so we wouldn't get lost tonight," I explained. "We saw the cars in the driveway and thought someone might be home."

"No problem, I'm glad you all came by." She turned back into the house, "Hey Vivian, Debbie, those four guys I told you about are here!"

"Which guys?" A female voice inquired from within the house.

"You know, the ones from Texas. The car."

We followed her in the house and I could hear footsteps coming from farther back inside.

Brenda did the introductions as her sisters came into the foyer. "This is Vivian," she indicated the older of the two, who was very attractive, "and this is Debbie, the graduate."

I turned to Vivian, who appeared to be in her early 20's, "It's nice to meet you; we didn't mean to interrupt. I'm Chris, this is Dana, Hector and Tony."

"Nice to meet you guys. Don't worry, we're just decorating for tonight. Debbie stopped by to help decorate. I'm glad you'll be able to make it tonight."

"We wouldn't miss it for the world," Tony said. "We're goin' to turn it out tonight, just like we do wherever we go!"

"Yeah, we like to have a good time, so we're really looking forward to tonight." I said backing up Tony's bragging. Now I was repeating myself. I seemed to be a little tongue tied in front of Debbie. I had to get my cool back.

Debbie glided over to us and offered her hand. I wanted to kiss her hand, but refrained from making an ass of myself at the first introduction to this vision of loveliness. Her complexion was sort of a caramel color that was smooth without blemish, and she looked at us with curiosity in her pretty amber eyes. She had pretty dark auburn hair that she wore down to her shoulders. She was about 5'6" with all the curves in the right proportions. She was absolutely beautiful and was wearing cut-off shorts and a pink, navel-revealing, halter top that set off her flawless skin. She had on sandals that showed off her pretty feet with matching pink-painted toenails. She was easily the prettiest girl I had seen on this trip and was the epitome of a Brickhouse. The lyrics ran through my mind, *"36-24-36, what a winning hand...Oh, she's a Brick...House!"*

"Nice to meet you guys," she said in a sexy contralto voice. "Brenda's told us so much about you. I'm really looking forward to you all coming by tonight."

Now it was my turn to stammer, "Yeah, we're looking forward to coming by tonight too. Do you live here?"

"No, I live with our parents. Brenda and Vivian live here. We wanted to have the party somewhere where our parents aren't around so we can have a really good time."

"When did you graduate?" I asked Debbie.

"Just last night," she replied, "from Riverside High School."

"We were at Fontana High School last night for a graduation." Dana said.

Way to go Dana, show that we've gotten around a little bit. "Yeah, we were at graduation last night, and played a little ball in Redlands and South Central over the past couple of days." I said.

"You guys play ball?" Debbie asked as Brenda and Vivian left the room.

"Yeah, we call ourselves the Transmanauts and we go around playing other teams four-on-four with our Texas brand of ball." I bragged.

"So you guys are pretty good, huh?"

"We like to think so." Hector finally freed his tongue.

"I'd love to see you all play one of these days," she touched my arm.

A shot of electricity ran up my arm at her touch; must have been that thunderbolt again. "The next time we play, I'll let you know." I stammered.

"Well, it was great meeting you Texas guys. I better get back and help Brenda and Vivian with the decorations since it's my party. I'll see you all tonight." She led us to the front door. "Is that your car?" She asked looking out the door.

"Yep." I said.

"It's beautiful."

"Thank you," I said. I hoped she wasn't going to ask to get in the car or ride in it or drive it; I really didn't want to have to cuss her out. I looked at the other three and they looked like they were eager to tell her "fuck no" if she wanted to get in the car. They were wearing that Cheshire Cat smile.

Luckily she said, "See you all tonight," and closed the door behind us.

Hot damn! We were definitely going to be there. She was drop-dead gorgeous! Wow, we were hitting the jackpot when it came to meeting beautiful young women on this trip. I mean, this is why we came to Cali, to meet women like her and Aurianna. Debbie had all of us salivating in anticipation of coming back that evening, hopeful for a little excitement, or something else, at the Party.

We got back into the car in our normal manner, again just in case someone was watching from the house. We weren't far down the street when the conversation turned to Debbie.

"Damn, did you see her?" Tony asked.

"Like duh. Man, she was fine." Hector agreed.

"I think she was looking at me." Dana added.

"Negro, what makes you think she was looking at you?" Tony prodded.

"She was looking right at me." Dana said.

"Yeah, well. She's not Aurianna and I think she was checking me out," Tony argued.

They continued to bicker about who Debbie was checking out, but it didn't matter what those three thought. I was going to hit that regardless. I felt the heat from that touch on my arm, and that was enough to signal me – it was on. I didn't contribute to the conversation, and just let their hopes wash over me in my certainty of how events were going to transpire that night.

This time it took us less time to get back to Aunt Rose's house and we were there in about twenty minutes.

Once we got back in, I told the other three, "Thanks to Tony, we'll need to practice a little on our moves. I refuse to fuck up on the dance floor tonight."

"That Scroller thing huh?" Tony laughed.

"Yeah, that Scroller thing." I growled.

"Any song in particular?" Dana asked changing the subject.

"Yeah, what about *Wine Flow Disco*?" I said.

"Okay, I'll go back out and get that tape." Dana volunteered.

Uncle Rudi had an 8-track player in his family room. Hector got his permission to play the music and for us to practice our dance moves. Over the next hour we practiced dancing to *Wine Flow Disco*. We practiced our synchronized moves, back and forth, with jazz splits, Locker steps, and "freeze" moves where we froze in place for four beats of the song. Uncle Rudi and Audrey watched us with bemused expressions on their faces.

"You think those moves will help?" Uncle Rudi smiled.

"This is one way we know to help turn out a party." Hector replied, "We've done this before and the girls like it."

"Is that right Audrey?" Uncle Rudi said.

"Well, they might be right. A lot of times house parties are kind of dead until someone gets it going, so, they might be right."

"Okay, I guess it's different from when I was going to parties." Uncle Rudi commented.

Yeah, when was that, the Stone Age? I thought. I couldn't picture Uncle Rudi at a party at any age.

Soon after we finished practicing, and before we started getting dressed, we were hanging out in the bedroom playing cards and talking about the party.

Audrey came to the room and got me, "I need to talk to you. Now."

"Go ahead," I said.

"No, I need to talk to you by yourself."

I stepped out of our room to talk with her. I was a little curious as to what she needed to tell me away from everyone else.

"Brenda called and said, that after you all went by their house, they decided they didn't want one of you guys to come to the party." She said in a low tone.

"Who're they talking about?" I said.

"Tony."

"Why?"

"They said he's not cute."

"What do you mean, not cute?"

"Well, to be blunt, ugly."

A lot of things can go through your mind in a split-second – images of the four of us together just doing stuff over the years; my feelings of loyalty to the guys; and then the pitiful image of Tony being left behind and the three of us going to the Party without him – unacceptable! And then I got angry. *How dare these wenches call and say my good friend Tony was ugly! Fuck them!* It was like calling all of us ugly, and I wasn't having that!

I didn't care how fine they were, I didn't hesitate, "You can tell them that if Tony isn't invited, none of us are going, period. All of us go or none of us!" I whispered fiercely.

"Alright, I'll call Brenda, and tell her. I'll let you know what she says."

"Okay," I said, and returned to the room where the other guys were hanging out. I didn't say anything to anybody about the conversation.

A few minutes later, Audrey returned and pulled me out of the room.

"They said okay. They're looking forward to all four of you guys attending the party."

170

Yeah, I'll bet. I figured they'd prefer to have all of us there rather than none of us, so I called their little bluff. The point was, we were a tight group and I wasn't going to allow these girls to break us up like that. You know, "Bro's before ho's."

When I went back in, Hector asked me, "What's up with Audrey?"

"You know how it is, the sisters called because they were

anxious for us to come to the party. They're looking forward to us being there, and were just making sure we're going to show up."

After that announcement, Tony, in particular, got loud.

"I told you. I told you guys, they can't wait for me to get there. I knew it, we're going to turn that shit out, and I'm going to hit that shit tonight."

That's ironic, I thought, but I didn't say anything; it wasn't appropriate and not necessary to tell him the truth, yet.

We had a few hours before we had to get ready, so we took our time to carefully dress the part for the Party. I pulled out my British-style terry cloth red driving cap, with a blue denim vest with no shirt – to show off my pecs and six-pack – and white "window pane" bell bottom jeans with the raised squares, and my Locker-style black and white shoes. I liked the "window pane" bell-bottom jeans, both gray and white. I don't know, I just thought they looked cool on me. Tony wore a similar hat, and so did Hector. They wore matching blue jeans and long-sleeved matching silk shirts that were a kind of teal color with floral pattern. Really pretty shirts. Dana didn't wear a hat, and he didn't wear a shirt like Hector and Tony. Instead he wore a denim jumpsuit, with no shirt, that was body-hugging and showed off his physique to the max. Oh yeah, we were ready to take over this party like we had taken over parties during the past couple of years.

While we were getting dressed, Dana and I discussed our experience from the year before at the national AKA convention in New York where we had taken over the teen parties.

"You know this is a lot like when we got ready for that first party in New York last year," I started, "We really took over."

"I remember you guys talking about that when you got back last year, but no details." Hector said.

"Chris and I went to this AKA convention at the Waldorf and saw we were probably the oldest guys at the teen parties. Those younger guys didn't stand a chance with us around." Dana laughed.

"Kind of like tonight, we practiced in Philly before going up to the Big Apple and made up a hustle to *Get Up Offa That Thing* by James Brown." I said,

"The party was kind of dead when we got there, and after a few minutes we asked the DJ to play *Get Up Offa That Thing*. He asked if we had something going on and I told him, 'Yeah, check us out.' And he put that record on and we turned it out."

"What happened?" Tony asked.

"We had hooked up with these two honeys, and when he put on that record, we got them on the floor." Dana explained, "Chris and I started to do our hustle and they picked it up pretty quick. We made it so that it matched the song perfectly, and was easy to learn. Once we started doing that, kids from all over the room got on the floor because whatever we were doing was more fun than what they were doing. In a few minutes, we had the whole dance floor full of kids doing our hustle. The DJ played the song twice in a row; he knew a good thing when he saw it and gave us a 'high five' after the song was over." Dana continued, "Then the girls we were with, one from Virginia, and one from Florida, showed us how to do the Washing Machine on *Getaway* by EWF, and again, everybody was doing what we were doing on the dance floor."

"Man, I wish I'd been there," Hector said, "But we used to turn parties out like that all last year. Is that where you got that from? New York?"

"Yeah, but mostly from being on *Crosno* and other events where we just decided to take over. It's really easy, because nobody else does it, and the girls love it." Dana looked at me.

"Yeah, that's the plan for tonight. We go in strong and we take it over." I said, "And we see what happens from there. Don't you all get it? They're having it at the older sisters' house without any parents. I think it's goin' to be wide open."

"Oh wow, I didn't think of it like that. So you think this is like a chance to maybe hit on some honeys?" Hector said.

"Definitely." I said, "Just be yourselves and you'll be fine. Look for targets of opportunity and go after it. You don't know what other opportunities we may have on this trip, so hit it if you can. I know I'm going to."

After that pep talk, we were like a football team getting ready to hit the field. We were high fiving and slapping hands getting ready for our night at the Party.

When we arrived at the Party there were a lot of girls and women there already. I say "girls" and "women" because the ages of the females ranged from friends of Debbie who had just graduated from high school, around 18 years old, in contrast to other females who were older than the high school girls, and much more mature. I didn't see any ugly girls in the house.

I also didn't see many guys. That was good for us – that meant we had a lot of women to talk to and to potentially "get with." This was what we in the military might call a "target rich" environment. Yeah I know, we all had girlfriends at home, but this was a Road Trip and what happens on the Road Trip stays on the Road Trip.

When we came in everything just stopped. Our arrival was highly anticipated by most of the girls there, and we didn't disappoint them. Brenda introduced us around to many of the girls, and as we went through the intros, we checked each one of them for availability. Some had boyfriends in attendance, including Debbie, many did not. The ones who didn't became much more available in our eyes.

The party was in slow gear when we got there, but after we arrived it went into a higher gear. We sauntered into the kitchen to get something to drink, and found that there was a large tub of beer, wine coolers, and pitchers full of Kool-Aid and alcohol. I saw why they had the party at this house, so they could serve liquor. There were even sodas and soft drinks for those of us who had to drive that night. After we got our first of many drinks, we began to assess the situation.

173

The first thing I noticed was the music sucked. The DJ wasn't doing a very good job, so I suggested to Brenda, "I have some 8-track tapes out in the car that have some jams on them that may get people up to dance. I used to DJ in college, so I think I know what people want to hear."

Plus, I had an ulterior motive, I wanted to play music that we knew because of the dance routines we had developed to those songs, like *Wine Flow Disco,* which seemed pretty appropriate for the setting.

"Anything to get this party started, I want Debbie to have a good time." Brenda said.

"Oh yeah," I said. "Me too."

I definitely had an ulterior motive when it came to Debbie, and I was willing to do what it took to look good in front of her. I went out to the car and brought in the tapes. I went over to the DJ and showed him where to set the track for *Wine Flow Disco.* He was familiar with the song, so when he put the song on, the four of us got on the floor without partners and sort of cleared the floor so we could do our little dance routine. We lined up from left to right with me on the left, then Tony, then Dana, and Hector on the far right.

Our dance routine consisted of us starting in a line facing the direction with the most girls, moving back and forth in a two-step or four-step move with synchronized turnaround moves, and stopping in a "freeze" position where we would assume either a quick "cool" pose, or just freeze in place.

At times we would go to our knees with a quick one-two move and then back up into our basic two-step front and back move. At the end of the song, we each did a signature finale move – Dana and I did jazz splits; Tony and Hector did moves that were upright and then they froze. We got an ovation from everyone there, well, the girls anyway, and the party continued in high gear.

Following our dancing demonstration, I was targeted by two women – Debbie and a woman from Denver, Colorado, Lisa, who was 24 years old. The two were a contrast in builds and looks. Debbie wore a red tube top made of that sort of clingy terry cloth material that exposed her navel along with form-fitting jeans that looked like she had been poured into them over high heeled sandals. She was easily the finest girl at the Party.

Lisa was gorgeous, but different than Debbie. She was wearing a colorful summer sun dress with flat sandals. She was a little heavier than Debbie, with that more mature woman's body and more voluptuous curves on a slightly larger frame. The additional weight looked good on her. Her coloring was slightly lighter than Debbie, and she wore her hair to one side held back with a little barrette.

Immediately after our dance routine, I saw Lisa studying me intently from across the room. Before I could explore that possibility, Debbie intercepted me and let me know she was interested in getting together.

"Hey you," she touched my vest, "that was pretty cool. I didn't know you all could dance like that."

"Yeah, we used to dance on TV, sort of like a local *Soul Train* in Texas."

"Well you all looked good, especially you."

"Uh, thank you," I was still a little tongue-tied. "You look really good tonight."

"Thank you, I've been thinking of you since I saw you this afternoon. I thought of you as I got dressed and I couldn't wait to see you again tonight."

"Yeah, I feel the same way." Well, okay! That was a boost to the old ego.

"I've got a boyfriend and he's here tonight."

"Alright. Where is he?"

"In the kitchen, I think." She didn't seem too concerned.

I decided to take a chance. "Do you want to take a walk outside?" I wanted to get her out of the house and away from her boyfriend.

"Sure, I'd like that." She started walking towards the front of the house.

As we walked toward the front door, I looked for Dana to catch his eye to let him know what was going on. He didn't seem to notice; he was occupied talking to some other girls.

When we stepped outside, Debbie asked, "I know you're from Texas, but where exactly?"

"We're here from El Paso." We started walking along the sidewalk.

"El Paso? Where's that? I've never heard of El Paso."

"It's the farthest west that you can go in Texas. It's on the border with Mexico, close to Juarez."

"I know about Big D and Houston, but I didn't think there were guys like you in some place like El Paso." She smiled.

"I know. Everybody thinks that Dallas and Houston are the only cities in Texas, but we've got it going on in El Paso too." I continued, "I went to school in Austin, at the University of Texas. Maybe you've heard of the Texas Longhorns?" I added proudly.

I've heard of the Longhorns. Football right?"

"I'll be going back to UT for law school."

"Law school? You're going to be a lawyer? Really?" she was incredulous.

"That's the plan. I was just commissioned as a second lieutenant in the Army, and at some point after I get out I want to go into politics."

"That's impressive, I've never met anyone like you," she said.

Of course she hadn't, she just graduated from high school, but she seemed so much more mature for her age; and she was so damn fine! But if I had to say so myself, I also looked pretty good that night, and I think that it was kind of a magical time for me and my effect on girls, at least during this trip. Well that, and the car, of course. Part of our conversation was next to the car and she was quite impressed with the car.

"Can I get in?"

176

"Sure." No hesitation as I unlocked the passenger side door and opened it for her.

She slid into the glove-soft velour passenger seat and looked around the interior. I stood outside the car peering down at her. She looked really good in the Trans Am. Hell, she would have looked good in a burlap bag and combat boots.

"This is really nice." She ran her hands over the velour and gripped the knob-like gear shift in the middle console. Then she leaned back in the car and let out a little sigh and closed her eyes for a moment.

"You look like you belong in the car." I observed.

"Thank you for letting me sit in here for a minute," she sat up and swung her leg out the car.

I held her hand as she swung the other leg out of the car and stood up so I could close the door.

As we were walking and holding hands, she declared, "I haven't felt this way about anybody else, I really want to get next to you."

Okay, I was in there! Now my problem was what to do about that particular declaration by this beautiful and sexy young woman. I couldn't just "jump her bones" right then, I had to be cool.

"I feel the same way. So, what do we do about it?"

We got back to the house, and stood outside the door. "I need to get rid of my boyfriend, then maybe we can get together later tonight," she said.

"Okay. Do you need my help?"

"No, I can handle it." She went inside presumably to look for her boyfriend to get rid of him.

After a few minutes I walked inside and ran smack into Lisa standing in the foyer. She had an expectant look on her face.

"Where've you been? I've been waiting on you."

I may have been the oldest guy, and certainly the only college graduate, so there weren't many prospects for her to talk to at her level. Luckily she hadn't seen me with Debbie.

"I was outside cooling off a little after our little dancing demonstration." I said.

"You all looked like you were having fun. I wish I could dance like that."

"Oh, I'm sure you can handle yourself on the dance floor," I laughed.

"I don't get out too much these days. Thankfully Vivian

invited me to this party or I would've been bored out of my mind at my apartment."

"How did you meet Vivian?" I looked for somewhere to sit.

"I work as a secretary in the same office and we've become friends, so she invited me out here."

"You're from Denver, right?"

"Yeah."

"What brought you here to sunny southern California?" I moved towards a vacant loveseat in the living room area away from all the sounds in the larger family room.

"I came out here a few years ago to break into 'the industry' like a lot of women. I work as a secretary during the day, and at night and on the weekends I make the rounds of auditions as an actress and singer."

"Oh wow! That sounds exciting," I said as we stood in front of the loveseat.

"No, it's not very exciting, but you got to pay your dues in Hollywood if you're going to make it."

"Have you been cast in anything?"

"Some commercials, but I'm waiting for my big break. Who knows, maybe it'll come soon." She took a seat on the loveseat and patted the cushion next to her.

I sat down next to her. "Enjoying yourself?"

"Now that you're back, yes. I was invited to the party so I could meet Debbie, but I really didn't think I would actually meet anybody worth talking to and I was more than pleasantly surprised to meet you."

I enjoyed hearing her describe her aspirations for Hollywood stardom and I was getting a strong vibe from her. She looked good, and just by her body language and her tone of voice I think she had more in mind than mere dancing.

She moved closer on the loveseat. I could feel the heat of her thighs against mine. Hmm, this was starting to get stimulating. "Well, you're a lot more interesting than most of these girls."

"How's that?" She cooed. We were so close I thought we were about to kiss.

"Uh, well, you're a lot more mature than these little girls around here, and I was hoping to find someone like you."

"You're so much more mature than the other guys. I can tell you're out of college."

"Oh yeah, how do you know that?" I was curious as to who gave her the 411 on me.

"You know, girls talk. Brenda told me about your car, that you're a second lieutenant in the Army, and that you're going to law school in Texas."

"All true." I laughed a little embarrassed. "I guess there aren't many secrets are there?"

"Why would you want to keep all that a secret? If I were you, I would be bragging about that to every pretty girl I saw, especially since you're so handsome." She smiled and her eyes twinkled.

Okay, this was about to get interesting. Let's be honest, that's one of the reasons we went to Cali – to have sex with pretty girls. And now, it seemed, at least one of us would have that opportunity. My advantage was having been there before. I wasn't a virgin and my experiences up to that point were not extensive; but what they lacked in notches on my gun belt, was made up in audacity and boldness. So, I was not daunted at the prospect of potentially trying to get with one or both women that night – or maybe the two of them together. After all, this was Cali!

No doubt alcohol was helping to fuel this highly-charged sexual and partying atmosphere. There was beer, which we didn't drink, and wine, which we did drink, and some sort of punch mixture with vodka, gin, Thunderbird, or some other type of clear strong alcoholic beverage that mixed well with Kool-Aid. I didn't drink because I was driving, so to the extent that my mind was not clouded by alcohol, I had a pretty clear head in observing the party and talking with folks. Tony didn't drink very much so he also remained sober throughout the party, which as it turns out, was a good thing.

I can't say the same for Dana and Hector. I don't remember their drink of choice, but whatever it was, they drank a lot of it. Dana had his eye on Debbie and made his intentions known to everyone as to what he wanted to do with her.

Tony came looking for me a few minutes after I'd sat down with Lisa.

"Chris, the sisters want us to perform some more routines. I thought we could do something to *Slide*. What do you think?"

I really didn't want to get up. I just looked at Tony like he'd grown a horn in the middle of his head. Couldn't he see I was busy? But, the hosts had made a request.

"Okay. Lisa, I don't know if you already met him, this is Tony. He's one of the guys who came with me from Texas."

"Hi Tony," she said.

"Nice to meet you," Tony said, and looked at me, "You ready?"

"Yeah." I reluctantly stood up. "You ready to see some more dancing Texas style?" I said to Lisa.

"Sure." She stood up and followed us into the family room where Dana and Hector waited. Debbie also waited by the kitchen door with some guy I assumed was her boyfriend.

The four of us lined up, and I signaled the DJ to start the music, this time to *Slide,* by Slave. We began the routine by doing our signature "slide" move. A move that involved "sliding" across the room whenever the word "slide" was sung in the song, and then freezing in a "cool" pose. After a few minutes, I "slid" over to Lisa and grabbed her hand to drag her on the dance floor.

180

She mouthed, "No," but I didn't care, I then twirled her on the floor in a sort of "swing out" move. The other three Transmanauts followed suit and grabbed a girl from the audience. Dana grabbed Debbie from under her boyfriend's watchful eyes and escorted her to the dance floor.

Hector grabbed this cute little cheerleader, who had a vivacious smile, beautiful chocolaty-brown skin, a short 'fro and looked eager to dance. Tony set his sights on another nice-looking girl that resembled Uhura from *Star Trek*. Damn she was nice. Once we finished dancing, I walked off the floor with Lisa and the other three escorted their partners off the floor to scattered applause.

The DJ wanted to keep the groove going and put on *Brickhouse* by the Commodores. We all knew the lyrics, and began singing the song to the ladies in the room. Dana was singing the lyrics to one person in particular – Debbie. No doubt in anyone's mind who Dana thought was the "Brickhouse" in the room. Apparently, her boyfriend wasn't very appreciative of Dana's attention to his girlfriend and sulked over to a sofa with two of his friends.

Over the next hour, Dana and Hector continued to drink the punch. The more they drank the less inhibited they became, especially Dana.

The DJ put on *Get Up Offa That Thing*, and Dana and I jumped on the dance floor to perform our hustle from the year before. We cleared a little area for just the two of us. Everyone let us do our thing. Hector and Tony were off talking to the two girls they had danced with previously. They didn't join us on the dance floor.

As we got into the routine, I think the alcohol began to take its effect on Dana. About halfway through the song, Dana began chanting his mantra over and over to the beat of the music.

"Gonna take that shit to bed, gonna take that shit to bed." He was keeping his eyes on Debbie while chanting his mantra. "Gonna take that shit to bed, gonna take that shit to bed."

Debbie's boyfriend was getting visibly upset from his seat across the room. Debbie hadn't joined him on the sofa, but stayed closer to the kitchen and some of her friends. Debbie looked amused by Dana's attention but didn't seem inclined to reciprocate.

I caught her eye from the dance floor and smiled. She smiled back and her eyes seemed to glow. Yep, still there. Unfortunately, Dana wasn't aware of my previous conversation with Debbie, and her expressed feelings for me. So, if anyone was "gonna take that shit to bed" it was going to be me.

After the song ended, I went over and sat next to Lisa,

who'd taken a seat in the family room to resume our previous conversation; but, as you might imagine, when you combine alcohol, pretty women, and jealous males, something is bound to happen, and it did.

We hadn't been in a fight since we'd been in Cali, although we had been threatened and shot at; it looked like now might be the time.

Dana was getting pretty obnoxious with his attention towards Debbie, and I'm sure it was obvious to Debbie's boyfriend and his two friends. This guy had been watching us all night, with his ire mainly directed at Dana. The boyfriend had been drinking and watching and getting angrier and angrier. He looked to be about 18 or 19 years old, about 6 feet tall, and fairly muscular. He had a big 'fro and a scraggly mustache. He was dressed in a silk party shirt and tight jeans; he came to party, not to fight, but that's what he seemed to have on his mind.

Obviously, he couldn't stand it any longer and leaped off the sofa and said, "Nigga' I'm tired of you fuckin' with my woman! Get the fuck out of here!"

He got in Dana's face and his two friends stood up with him. They had been drinking too, so I think that bolstered their confidence that they could take on all four of us in a fight. His two friends were not as tall as he was and they were skinny. They looked taller because they had big 'fros, but big 'fros aren't a good substitute for muscles. They didn't look very athletic, and now they were about to take us on in a fight – not very smart on their part.

Since the age of 13, my uncle, a second-degree black belt in the Korean martial art of Tae Kwon Do, had been training me off and on. I had continued that training with other instructors all the way through college. In addition, during my two stints at Fort Knox and Fort Riley, the Army had trained me in various forms of basic hand-to-hand combat, pugil stick training, and various forms of killing people with knives, bayonets, guns and other implements. I wasn't scared of these two-bit-wanna-be thugs, or whatever they were. Tony and Hector, also up to the task, were bigger than any of the three guys we faced.

The guy's anger surprised Dana. Compared to having been shot at by some **real** gang bangers, we weren't going to get pushed around by these weak-kneed looking guys. I was tired of getting threatened and shot at by California punks – I was ready to kick some California ass.

"I think we're going to have a situation here, wait for me!" I said to Lisa as I rushed over to where Dana stood facing Debbie's boyfriend.

I got in the boyfriend's face and yelled in my best parade-ground voice, "STEP THE FUCK BACK MOTHERFUCKER!" I pushed him back on his heels.

That stopped the Party. About that time, Tony and Hector hurried over from where they were and stood next to me. Tony had met this really nice-looking girl at the party. She had an exotic name like Tyanekwa Deshaun or something like that (well, it was exotic then, now the ghetto's calling and wants its name back). He had been spending most of the night with her since they danced together earlier. But when he heard my voice, he rushed right over. The same with Hector. He was talking to the same nice looking girl he had danced with earlier. But in the middle of talking with his cheerleader, Hector heard the sound of my voice and responded in true Transmanautic fashion.

All four of us faced the boyfriend and his two skinny friends, with our fists balled, and me in a martial arts back stance with knife hands up.

"Make your move motha' fucka', come on!" The adrenaline rushed through my veins and I was geared up for a fight. Cursing seemed the thing to do; and it does have a psychological effect on your potential opponent. Almost like what male gorillas do when they beat their chests before they charge, getting their courage up and giving the opponent a chance to back down.

183

The boyfriend and his friends sobered up real quick, and he said, "Fuck it, I'm out, you can have the bitch." He and his boys left the party. He didn't even say goodbye to Debbie.

If we weren't popular with the women at the Party before that confrontation, we were definitely in there now. One thing about girls, they like their men manly – you can dance and sing and do all that shit, but if you've got a little "roughneck" in you, you definitely have an advantage. And we had just proved we were not only nice looking, intelligent, sophisticated, and good dancers, but we were ready to kick some ass as well.

After the altercation Tony went back over to Tyanekwa Deshaun, who looked captivated by his courage and his dedication in coming to the aid of his friends. That definitely helped Tony's campaign for a little casual sex that night.

Our pugilistic episode also enhanced Hector's conversation with his cheerleader. He and the cheerleader continued talking after the "almost fight" and things started getting pretty hot and heavy. I could see them kind of feeling around on each other, then the two of them went outside. I think Hector ended with more play than any of us that night because he actually had an opportunity to kiss on his "fine assed" cheerleader, which could have led to a lot more; but alas, Hector's drinking caught up with him.

I returned to the loveseat to resume my conversation with Lisa, thinking that Debbie might be available later that night since her boyfriend was no longer in attendance and wondering how I could make that happen with Lisa sitting there.

Hector's cheerleader came back in the house at that moment, and walked over to me, "You need to go out and get your friend; I think he's throwing up on your car."

Oh shit! I hope not! I got up from the loveseat and rushed out the house. As it turned out, Hector had thrown up on someone else's car, but he was out there surrounded by his own vomit, what a mess! He couldn't remember much about how he got out there or who was with him. Obviously he had too much to drink.

184   At that point, I made a decision and went inside and got Tony.

"Go get Dana. No matter what he's doing, get him out to the car. We need to get him and Hector back to the house. They're both pretty fucked up."

"Okay," he complied.

I sought out Debbie who had gone into the kitchen, "We're going to take my brother and Hector home. Hopefully we'll be back in about an hour."

"Okay, I should still be here."

"Great," I then returned to Lisa, who had remained on the loveseat. "I'm running my brother and our friend back to the house. They're pretty drunk and already throwing up."

"I understand. I don't know if I'll be here, it's getting pretty late. I have to go to work in the morning."

"Well I should be back in about an hour, hopefully you'll still be here." I said.

"Without you here it's gonna be pretty dead, so I don't know if I'll hang around."

"I'd like to see you again, but I've got to go."

Debbie and Lisa looked disappointed, but I was confident they would wait for me. So, with the promise of potentially getting with one or the other, or maybe the stuff of fantasies, both of them, I took off to get Dana and Hector back to Aunt Rose's house.

Tony and I poured Dana and Hector into the car. They had a hard time getting into their assigned seats and buckling up for the trip back to the house. Yeah, they were way too drunk to stay at the Party and had started to embarrass themselves.

Within a few minutes of leaving the Party, Dana groaned, "I'm not feeling too good, you need to pull over."

Oh hell no, he's going to throw up.

"Hang on until I can pull over!" I quickly found a spot to pull over that was halfway deserted, and Dana opened his car door and leaned out and threw up. Yuck!

He apologized, "I didn't want to mess up your new car."

"You okay?" I asked.

"Yeah, I'm alright," he said. Thankfully, Dana throwing up didn't start a sympathetic reaction with Hector or we would have had a real mess on our hands.

After getting back on the highway, Dana and Hector fell asleep. After we got to the house, we woke them up, led them into the house and got them in bed.

"You want to go back to the Party" I asked Tony.

"Yeah, I think I had a chance with the girl I met, and I hate we had to leave."

"Okay, let's go back."

Tony rode shotgun – the first time he had ridden up front. We got back as quickly as we could, but over an hour had passed since we had left the first time, and it was close to 3 a.m. As I pulled up to the house, there weren't many cars out front. We got out and walked to the front door and rang the bell. Brenda came to the door looking kind of sleepy.

"You guys came back?"

"Yeah, we thought the party might still be going on." I said.

"Nope. Once you guys left, the party pretty much broke up. Just about everybody's gone. But I'm glad you stopped by, here're your 8-track tapes." She reached behind her and handed me my 8-tracks.

"Thank you. Is Debbie still here?"

"Yeah, but she's already in bed. Sorry. She really liked you, but you left." She said with a little twinkle in her eye.

"And Lisa?"

"Oh yeah, she's long gone too. Sorry."

"What about Tyanekwa?" Tony asked.

"Everybody's gone guys." Brenda said with a little irritation.

"Okay, alright, I guess we'll go home. Thanks for inviting us. We had a great time." I said.

186

"No, thank you for coming. You Texas guys really turned it out. Debbie had a great time too. Good night." She closed the door.

Once we left the first time, I guess we took the magic with us. Because we had to take Dana and Hector home, Tony and I lost out on the one chance to hook up with those nice looking women. And we didn't get any phone numbers, although Tony did get an address. We pulled back in to Aunt Rose's driveway disappointed.

I never had an opportunity to see where my "dilemma" may have led me. Damn. Damn. And double damn.

Tony and I marched into the bedroom pissed off and disappointed. On cue, Hector and Dana woke up and made a bee line to the hallway bathroom loudly throwing up several times.

Aunt Rose woke up at the noise and came out into the hallway, "Are they alright?"

"They just had a little too much to drink, they'll be okay." I said.

"Poor babies. I'm going to get them club soda and something to eat to settle their stomachs." She went into the kitchen to make Hector and Dana an early, post-hangover, breakfast.

Dana and Hector staggered out of the bathroom bleary-eyed and ashen.

"Hey, Aunt Rose is fixing you guys something to eat and drink to settle your stomachs. Your version of "Ralph Bought a Buick" woke her up and she felt sorry for your dumb asses." I laughed.

"Shut up Chris," Dana groaned, "I know you threw up in Melanie's house a couple of weeks ago, so just shut up."

"Yeah, been there done that, and got the T-shirt to prove it," I laughed. "Come on."

They stumbled into the kitchen and sank into two of the chairs at the breakfast table. Tony and I occupied the other two chairs. The frying meat and sizzling grease smelled great and made my stomach growl.

"Here guys, drink the club soda. It'll help settle your stomachs and then you can have some of the ham I fried up. The grease will coat your stomachs and help keep your food down," Aunt Rose said as she served the food and set the glasses on the table.

Hector and Dana ate and drank gratefully. We all ate like it was the last meal of condemned men. Several minutes and two helpings later, we stumbled back to our room sleepy with full stomachs and fell quickly asleep.

That morning we dragged our bodies out of bed, dressed and sluggishly made our way back into the kitchen. Uncle Rudi stood near the refrigerator waiting for us.

"Hector, I need to talk to you boys," he said in a gruff voice.

"Yes sir," Hector said. His uncle's tone brought all of us to attention."I appreciate you boys having fun and all that, but I think it's time for you boys to be moving on," he added in his stern voice, "You all can spend one more night here, then you all need to move on."

Yep, it was time for us to go. Of course, when we first got there, everyone seemed happy to see us. We hadn't yet worn out our welcome, but after several days I guess we had. That sort of became a pattern wherever we went in California.

Venice Beach

I think we had pretty much gotten whatever fun we were going to get out of LA anyway, so it was just about time to go. But we still had some unfinished business. One of the activities we were supposed to engage in while in Cali was to go to one or more of the famous beaches– Venice, Malibu, somewhere. One of the reasons we went to LA and Southern California in the first place was to see beautiful women in bikinis, and maybe a topless sun bather or two at the beach. We'd brought swim trunks, we had a little time on our hands – it was now or never. A last chance to experience some R-rated memories to brag about back in Texas. We were ready to hit the beach.

On our last day we decided to explore at least one of the "movie-set" beaches we'd heard about. The one beach that I was most curious about was "Muscle Beach" located at the world renowned Venice Beach. We were way out in Redlands, so we had to ask directions on how to get to Venice Beach.

"Hey Audrey, have you ever been to Venice Beach?" I asked as we walked out to the family room where she was lounging and watching TV.

"Nope," she said, "never wanted to go out there."

"Really?" Dana asked. "Why not?"

"Nothin' but white girls out there trying to look black with their tans. Nothing for me to see."

"What about Muscle Beach?" I asked, "Aren't there guys out there?"

"Yeah, but it's too far to go to look at some conceited guys lifting weights."

"Okay, but do you know how to get out there?" Hector asked, a little exasperated by his cousin's attitude.

"I told you no."

"Don't worry yourself, we'll figure it out." I was a little pissed off at her unwillingness to offer any help in getting to the damn beach.

"I'm sure you will, just like you figured out how to get home last night." Audrey shot back.

Okay, here we go. She's still pissed off at not being invited.

"What do you mean?" Hector asked.

"Brenda already called me this morning and told me all about the Party. Your fight; you guys getting drunk; and then trying to go back after it was all over. What were you thinking? Now you've managed to make me look bad." Audrey added.

"Damn. We were just having fun. Did she tell you it was pretty dead until we showed up and turned it out with our dance routine?" I asked.

"No, but she did tell me you tried to hit on two girls, including her younger sister Debbie. What were you thinking?"

She sounded like a broken record. The images of Debbie and Lisa flashed in my mind. No, I couldn't tell her what I'd been thinking; but yeah, I guess we made a lasting impression one way or the other.

"Well, we had a good time," I said, "and now we want to go to the beach. So, I guess we'll get there without your help."

"I'll go get the Trip Tiks." Dana volunteered and went out to the car.

Once Dana came back in we sat down at the kitchen table and pulled out our trusty map of LA. We went over the map and found what appeared to be the best route to the beach. With the traffic in LA we had no idea how long it would take to get there, but we set out on our newest adventure.

Our route to the beach was fraught with the normal turnarounds and missed turns, but eventually we got within smelling distance of the ocean. It was a beautiful day and we had the windows down. We could smell the ocean long before we could see it, and we desert-dwellers hadn't smelled anything like it in quite a while. We could hear the ocean as well, and we let our instincts guide us toward the beautiful white beaches.

As we approached the area, the first thing we saw were women. Women in bikinis, in shorts and halters, in tube tops and jeans, and other various hip-hugging, curve-revealing clothing. We were definitely in the right place. As we rolled up, one beautiful blonde in a bikini top and wrap-around sarong, was walking her Afghan hound as natural as the sky was blue. We were definitely at the beach!

The buildings were painted in pastel and bright colors, from reds to blues, yellows and oranges. Various stores were hawking their wares with loud and colorful signs, and music playing out of hidden speakers. The sound of funk, R&B, and disco music blared from various establishments. Guys and girls were roller skating by in swim wear and short shorts, moving and juking to the various beats, just having a good time. We pulled into a parking lot as close to the beach as we could, stripped down to our swim trunks and t-shirts, and got out of the car in our normal Transmanautic manner. We didn't seem to attract any attention because our routine seemed to fit right in with whatever was going on at the beach – just regular activity.

"What do we do with the towels?" Dana asked.

"Just leave them in the car. We probably won't need them. We can always dry off under the sun; and if we do need them they'll be right here." I said.

"Aren't we getting in the water?" Hector asked.

"Yeah, I mean that's why we're here, right?" I asked.

"What about our tennis shoes? We can't take them in the water, right?" Tony asked.

"Hadn't thought about that." I said, "We normally wear flip flops to the beach and just leave them with our stuff on the sand when we get in the water."

191

"I'll bet we can get some flip flops at one of these stores." Dana said.

"Good idea," Hector said, "Let's find out."

We walked towards the colorful store fronts and found a shop fairly quickly that sold swimwear, including flip flops. We strolled inside and spotted a large bin full of men's and women's flip flops.

"Yeah, these are fine." Hector said, as he pulled a pair out of the bin.

"And cheap too." Tony added. "Make sure you pull a men's pair Chris."

"Yeah, don't want to be mistaken for a girl by my flip flops." I laughed.

"Well, you're the one with experience with faggots, so we don't want you getting into trouble on the beach," Tony guffawed.

"Fuck you Tony," I was getting a little annoyed by his constant reference to my experiences with homosexuals in Austin. I never should have told them those stories. "Let's buy these things and get back to the car." I picked up a pair of flip flops and walked to the cash register.

Once we bought the flip flops we strolled back over to the car to change into them, taking in all the sights of the beach.

"We ready?" I asked as we finished changing.

"Yeah, let's hit the beach." Dana closed his door.

We walked wide-eyed along the boardwalk towards the water and beheld a sight that could only be seen at Venice "Muscle" Beach. I thought the stories of huge muscular guys doing nothing but working out with huge barbells and dumbbells was just a myth; but right there, in front of us, stood about ten guys working out and posing in an open air enclosure outfitted with the best array of free weights and weight benches I had ever seen. And the guys! Each of them looked like a Mr. Universe contestant. They were either oiled or sweat-covered and their muscles literally burst from their bodies. I had never been this close to real body builders, and these guys were impressive.

They were lifting and pumping weights beyond my

comprehension. As a guy, I know that's kind of strange to say, but I was in awe of the raw power these guys just emanated as they went through their routines and posed for the open-mouthed crowds. Beyond the weight lifters were basketball courts, short-racquet tennis courts, and handball courts. I was intrigued by the short-racquet tennis courts because it looked like a composite between tennis and racquetball. I played a pretty good game of tennis and racquetball, and looked forward to trying my hand at this new game. We briefly discussed getting on the basketball court, but thought better of it. We weren't here to play ball, but to experience the beach and see beautiful women. So we pushed on to the beach.

What a beach, I thought. I hadn't seen a beach quite like this one.

"Damn, look at all the women!" Tony exclaimed.

We just stared, awestruck at the sights before us! There were acres and acres of women in tiny bikinis arrayed like sausages on the griddle, frying in the sun and covered with suntan oil and umbrellas. Some lay on blankets on the sand, and others lay on lawn chairs. Some lay on their backs and others on their stomachs. A tantalizing few looked like they were lying on their stomachs without their tops. Oh my goodness! One thing they all seemed to have in common – they looked damned good.

The contrast in colors practically hypnotized me – the glistening white sand, the dark-tanned women with their colorful bikinis, colorful umbrellas and the cobalt blue ocean in the background. People played volleyball on the beach, some guys threw a football around, and some people had their dogs out on the beach just having fun. The crashing of the waves, the yelling and screaming of kids on the beach, dogs barking, and folks hollerin' back and forth playing their games. This was great!

Dana yelled, "Well, what are we waiting for? Let's hit the water!"

"Wait, wait, where do we drop our flip flops?" Hector asked.

"What about with some of these girls?" I looked around at some of the women sun bathing.

"Okay, go ahead." Tony said.

I walked over to the nearest two women lounging back on their beach chairs. One was blonde, of course, and wearing a daffodil yellow one piece suit, with cut outs on the side, and big butterfly-shaped shades. She looked to be in her thirties and had a blanket arrayed around her and a beach umbrella. She was reading a book under the shade of a big floppy straw hat as I walked up.

"Hi, uh, excuse me. We didn't bring a blanket, and we wondered if we could leave our T-shirts and sandals near your stuff for safekeeping." I blurted out.

She looked over her shades at me, and her companion – a younger pretty brunette who was lounging on her back in another horizontal beach chair, soaking up the rays in a turquoise bikini – sat up to look over her white-framed, oversized grasshopper shades too. She had a nice body encased in that little bit of turquoise.

"Excuse me?" The blonde asked.

"Uh, we just wanted to leave our stuff here for a few minutes while we got in the water."

She looked over at the other three and then back at me. "Okay," she said. "We'll be here for another hour or so. If you guys aren't back we'll just leave your stuff here, okay?"

"That's fine, thanks." I waved the other guys over.

"I'm Chris, this is Dana, Hector and Tony," I said. "We're visiting from Texas and came out to see your beautiful beach. We'd heard so much about Venice Beach."

"Nice to meet you. I'm Tammy and this is Suzy," indicating the other girl in her softly Southern voice. "We'll keep an eye on your stuff. Enjoy the water, I hear it's nice today." She leaned back in her chair and continued reading her book.

Suzy continued watching us with some interest. She was younger than Tammy and looked like she was in her early 20s.

"You guys really from Texas?" She finally asked. She had that unique Valley girl cadence in her voice that I'd only heard in Southern California.

"Yep," Tony said as we shucked our flip flops and T-shirts.

"Nice," she said.

Hmm, was that a comment on us being from Texas or our physiques? I wondered. Gotta love the Speedos. Well, no time to explore that possibility, Dana was already running to the water with Hector and Tony in tow. With a wave back to Suzy and Tammy, I started after the other three.

Like crazed men who had never seen water, and thought this was just a mirage, we started yelling as we ran to the water. The waves were breaking nicely against the beach in beautiful, rolling never ending patterns, with just the right amount of frothiness to remind you of surfing and having fun. As we approached the water, we dodged around several pretty women sun bathing, throwing sand on their well-oiled bodies.

"Hey you guys watch it!" A pretty young brunette in a white micro-bikini jumped up and yelled. She'd been lying on her back when we rolled by, and now stood there with her ample chest heaving in that little bit of material holding it all together.

"Sorry," I yelled back, but I didn't care; we were trying to get to the water. I didn't even stop to get a better look. We hit the water running and dove in as far out as we could. We were all good swimmers and we just struck out with strong overhand strokes towards the deeper areas.

"Yay!"

"Whoo hoo!"

"This is great!"

Watching the four of us, I couldn't help but think of the scene in *Planet of the Apes* when the sun-burnt, desert-weary, and half-starved astronauts found that oasis on the edge of the desert and dove naked into the refreshing cold water. Yep, the Transmanauts were on an alien planet full of beautiful women in itsy bitsy bikinis, and we were enjoying the respite of being in the beautiful, cool, Pacific Ocean.

We dodged through a multitude of beach-goers who were splashing and playing in the water. We got about 100 yards from the beach and started treading water, just kind of checking out the ships out there and the view back to the beach. There were a lot of people between us and the beach, but none out in the deep water with us.

We were laughing and having a good ol' time when Dana shouted, "Hey quit screwing around!"

"What are you yelling about?" Hector said.

"One of you guys pushed up against my butt!"

"No we didn't, you're just imagining that." I said.

"No, I felt something against my leg!"

"Oh c'mon...Yikes!" Tony yelped.

"What, what happened?!" Hector cried.

"Something just bumped my leg!" Tony yelled.

I thought, *oh no, don't tell me*...I said, "Did anyone see a dorsal fin?"

"You mean like a shark!?" Dana yelled.

"Yeah."

"No!" Everyone yelled.

"We need to get back to the beach right fuckin' now; we may be too far out here!" I goaded them into action.

"Oh shit, let's get out of here!" Tony started swimming quickly towards the shore.

"Don't stir up the water too much; sharks are attracted to that motion." I cautioned.

"Yeah, we've all seen *Jaws*. Nobody wants to end up in a great white." Dana gasped out between strokes.

As I looked behind us, I saw something swimming in the water, but it didn't seem to be heading our way.

"Shit. There's something back there! Fuck it, swim faster! Get the hell out the water!" I yelled.

Everybody swam as fast as they could, splashing water with arms wailing away. We got back to the beach in record time. Whew! That was a potential tragedy avoided. Well, until we got out of the water. That's when we discovered the reason the shark left us alone.

Apparently, the shark made a meal of the back of Dana's

swim trunks and Dana didn't realize it until we got out of the water.

"Aw shit!" Dana exclaimed, "What the hell? The damn shark took a bite out my trunks!"

"It's good he didn't bite your narrow ass," Tony laughed in relief, "he would never have made a meal."

"Shut up Tony," Dana yelled, "do something."

"Stay in the water, we'll get you some shorts." I laughed.

"Hold on, we'll get you something to put on, just stay in the water." Hector said.

He and Tony ran back to where Tammy and Suzy were still lounging and grabbed their flip flops. I could see them throwing them on and then continuing to the car to get Dana a pair of shorts while I stayed in the water. Dana was so embarrassed he just kept his lower body in the water. Luckily no one seemed to notice his dilemma.

"You're lucky; the shark could have bitten off your dick!" I laughed. That got us both laughing with relief, because we both knew a real disaster had been avoided.

Hector ran up to the edge of the water and yelled, "What do you want to do with the shorts?"

"I'll be over to get them." I scrambled out of the water and grabbed the shorts from Hector and returned to where Dana waited anxiously. Tony arrived back at the water's edge and waited with Hector for Dana to make the change. Dana squatted in the water so no one would see his bare behind as he changed into the wet shorts. Unfortunately, now Dana didn't have anything dry to change into, but that was better than the alternative…bare-assed and embarrassed!

Once Dana changed, we came out of the water and walked over to where Tammy and Suzy stared at us approaching.

"You guys okay? I thought I heard some yelling from the water." Tammy looked at the ruined trunks in Dana's hand.

"Yeah, we're fine. Thanks for looking out for our stuff." I started putting on my T-shirt.

"No problem guys," Tammy said, "You didn't stay in the water too long."

"Nah, we just wanted to get in and get out, just to experience being in the water." I laughed looking at Dana.

"Yeah," Dana said, "just a quick in and out."

"Sure you guys can't stay around any longer?" Suzy asked.

"Wish we could, but we're heading up to San Francisco today, so we need to get on the road." I replied.

"Too bad." Suzy murmured.

Huh, I thought, *maybe my first impression was right.* But again, we didn't have the time to explore that possibility as we finished getting dressed.

"Are you all taking the PCH to San Francisco?" Tammy asked.

"What's the PCH?" I asked.

"Pacific Coast Highway, state highway 1 and 101. Maybe the most beautiful stretch of highway in America. If you're going to drive north, you can't miss that. It'll take you through Monterrey, San Luis Obispo, and along some of the prettiest coast line in the country."

"Oh, okay, we'll take a look at that." I promised.

"You guys have a good trip." Suzy smiled. "It was nice meeting you."

"Yeah, me too. Wish we could stay longer." Tony winked at Suzy, and we walked backed to the boardwalk.

198   As we approached the wooden boardwalk near the colorful store fronts we disposed of Dana's ruined swim trunks and decided we'd had enough for one day at the beach.

"You ready to go back?" I asked.

"Yeah," Dana said, "but I'd like to get something to eat on the way home."

"Okay," I said. "You guys ready to go?" nodding at Tony and Hector.

"Yeah," Tony said. "And I'm hungry too. Let's stop at that KFC we saw coming in; I feel like some chicken."

"Yeah, *Chicken of the Sea,*" Hector laughed, "Sorry, Charlie…wasn't he a shark?"

"I think so," I said. "That's why they wouldn't put him in the can, he wasn't a tuna."

Tony started making the signature sound of the shark approaching in *Jaws,* "Duh nunt, duh nunt, dun dun dun dun dun, Aargh!" he laughed as we walked back to the car.

"Fuck you guys," Dana laughed.

"Aww, you know we're just glad you're okay," I said. "But you got to admit, it's pretty funny." Hector and Tony laughed.

Once we got back to the car we put the towels on the seats to absorb the water from our trunks and keep the seats dry. Tony, Hector and I changed into our dry shorts in the car, but poor Dana had to keep his wet shorts on. Lucky him, it could have been worse.

We found the KFC not too far from the beach and ordered a bucket in the drive-thru. We munched on the chicken as we laughed about the beach and the Party the night before. It took about an hour to get back to Redlands. It was a lot easier once we knew the route.

On the way back to Aunt Rose's house we were howling about what could have happened to Dana if the shark had better eye sight.

"Yeah, you small-dicked motherfucker," Tony laughed. "I guess this is the one time it paid to have a small dick!" He popped Dana on the back of his head.

"Maybe your dick was so small the shark couldn't see it!" Hector howled from the back seat. "I hear sharks have bad eye sight."

I looked over at Dana and grinned.

"Yeah, well you all can suck my dick." Dana didn't seem very appreciative of the jokes, but again, was grateful we could have a good laugh at his expense and him not ending up as shark food.

When we got to the house we went back to our room for the final time to shower, get dressed and pack up our stuff. Apparently, Uncle Rudi informed everyone of our imminent departure, so it was no surprise that we were leaving at that particular time.

"C'mon guys, let's load up the car first, then we can come back in and say our goodbyes." I suggested.

"Okay," Hector said, "I want to make sure we let Aunt Rose know how much we appreciate her letting us stay here this week."

"Absolutely," I said in my best Rocky Balboa imitation.

"We don't want to just run out of here without saying goodbye," Dana agreed as we walked out to the car.

"Well, let's get it over with so we can get on the road," Tony said.

"Always the sentimentalist, huh Tony?" I said opening the trunk.

"I'm not that good with goodbyes, especially when we've been thrown out." Tony tossed his bag in the trunk and started back to the house.

"I agree, let's get this over with and get on the road," Dana said.

I loaded the other three bags and the cooler Aunt Rose had filled with ice and bottles of soda.

Dana and I followed Hector back to the house where Aunt Rose, Audrey and Ronnie were waiting.

"I'm going to miss you boys," Aunt Rose started. "No matter what Rudi said, I enjoyed you being here and I'm sure Audrey and Ronnie did too. Isn't that right girls?"

We hadn't seen much of Ronnie, but she looked ready to cry at our imminent departure.

"You guys can't stay any longer?" she wailed.

"Nope," Hector said. "We're on our way to San Francisco, but we'll be back through here, and if we have the chance to come by we will, okay?"

She seemed mollified, "Okay, promise?"

I looked at Hector knowing Uncle Rudi did not want to see our happy faces again for a very long time.

"Yep, we'll do our best," Hector vaguely promised as he turned to Aunt Rose. "Thank you Aunt Rose. You don't know how much we all appreciate your hospitality." He gave her a big hug. You could see the tears in both their eyes. Pretty emotional, like they knew they'd never see each other again.

Three of us lined up to say our goodbyes and gave Aunt Rose, Audrey and Ronnie each a hug in turn. Hector was last to give Audrey and Ronnie hugs.

"Thanks cuz, we really appreciate you helping us out while we were here," he said to Audrey.

"You're always welcome, you know that. But please, bring more game the next time you come. You guys embarrassed me with your Texas brand of basketball," she laughed breaking up the somber mood.

Always the comedienne.

We turned from the door and got into the car for the last time at Aunt Rose's house – Transmanautic style. Audrey, Ronnie, and Aunt Rose stood at the front door to see us off. They looked kind of forlorn as they watched us. The brown Cadillac wasn't in the driveway. I don't know where Uncle Rudi was when we left; didn't care really.

I carefully backed out of the driveway for the last time, and we all waved as we drove off to go north to San Francisco. Our last sight of Aunt Rose was her waving from the front door.

On the 101

We didn't spend as much time at the beach as we would have liked, but that's okay, we had fun doing all those other activities. And maybe, just maybe, we met more women on land than we would have in the water or on the beach. So, we bid adieu to LA and all it offered and were now on our way to Oaktown and San Francisco on the 101, and state highway 1, a.k.a. the Pacific Coast Highway, the PCH.

Just as Tammy had described, this was maybe the most beautiful highway in the country. This was true California – driving along the coast. The other reason for taking the 101 was the lack of presence of CHiPs. On I-5, or "the 5" the CHiPs were everywhere swooping down from their perches like hawks on their unsuspecting prey. We wanted to avoid that and to have a more picturesque drive from LA to San Francisco. I don't think we saw a single CHiP the entire time we were on the PCH.

We took I-10 East from Redlands through LA proper, until we got to the 405 which we took north until we ran into the 101 going east, then north. Once we picked up the 101 east of Los Angeles we began our drive north along its picturesque roadway where it merged with California State Highway 1.

"Hey, did you see that sign back there?" Hector asked.

"Which sign?" I kept my head on a swivel and always looked at passing signs to keep up with warning signs and, more importantly, speed limits.

"The Los Angeles city limit sign." Hector replied.

"What about it?" Dana asked.

"The population. It said population two million, eight hundred thousand. That's a lot of folks."

"Yeah, and we saw about one-tenth of one percent of that total population," I laughed. "But it was a fine-assed one-tenth of one percent."

"You got that right," Tony agreed. "We saw so many honeys, it was like being on TV."

"Yeah, and we actually had a shot at some of them," Dana added.

"Some of us more so than others," I laughed.

"Yeah, what was that shit between you and Debbie, and what's her name at the Party?" Hector asked.

"Her name was Lisa, and I was trying to hit one or both," I boasted.

"You really think you could have pulled that off?" Hector persisted.

"I don't know; but I was just going with the flow and had no idea where it was leading." I continued, "You know Debbie told me she wanted me, right?"

"Wait, what?" Dana sat up in his seat, "What do you mean? I was going to hit that."

"Not hardly," I smiled. "She told me early on she 'wanted to get next to me' while we were outside by the Trans, and you know what that means. I was just looking for the right opportunity and then Lisa entered the picture, so I had my dilemma."

"And you let me fuck around thinking I was going to hit that?" Dana wasn't happy with this revelation.

"Well, you were a good diversion for Debbie's boyfriend, from the real attack on Debbie – me."

"Damn Chris, that's fucked up." Tony leaned forward, "But I got to give you some on that. That was pretty cool." We slapped hands between the seats.

"Hey Dana, I don't know what you're crying about, you have Aurianna," I laughed as I drew out the "R" in Aurianna.

"Yeah, Dana, what about Aurianna?" Hector asked.

"I know, I know. She was great wasn't she?" Dana was moonstruck.

"Yeah, she was pretty special. Don't worry, we'll see her on the way back," I assured him.

"What did you think about that white girl on the beach?" Hector changed the subject.

"Which one?" I asked.

"What's her name, Suzy." Hector said.

"What about her?" Dana still bristled.

"You think she was interested?" Hector asked.

"Yeah, I think so," Tony said, "I think if we could have stayed around we could have hit that."

We?" I asked.

"Yeah, all of us." Tony replied laughing.

"Damn Tony. You wanted to run a train?" I asked.

"What's a 'train'?" Dana asked.

I looked over at him incredulous; then I remembered these guys just graduated high school, and weren't as worldly as me, no matter how they acted.

"A train is when we screw a girl in succession. Maybe you've heard the term 'sloppy seconds' that's kind of where that comes from."

"That's just nasty! You ever done that?" Dana asked.

"No, and really don't want to." I said.

"What about three or four of us at the same time?" Tony interjected laughing.

"What have you been reading Tony?" I asked. *"Penthouse Forum?"*

"Something like that," he admitted.

"Huh. Well, it's called 'making them airtight' because you've plugged all the holes." I explained.

"Ewww," Dana said. "Really?"

"Yes, really," I said. "And no, I haven't done that either." Closing the conversation on that subject.

The car got silent as everyone digested the most recent conversation. In the background I played my *EWF Greatest Hits* tape and let the sounds of *Africano* and *That's the Way of the World* drift over us in our contemplative moods.

I drove north wrapped in my own thoughts about the trip. Looking around the car and in my rearview mirror, everyone seemed occupied by his own thoughts; but as we drove north along the Pacific Coast Highway, we saw such scenery on the other side of the highway that we just had to pull over to admire the view.

"Where are we?" Dana asked.

"You're the navigator, don't you know?" I snickered.

"The signs say Pismo Beach," Dana offered, "but I'm not sure."

"I've heard of Pismo Beach," I said. "It's supposed to be beautiful."

"Chris, can you get over to the other side so we can get a better look?" Hector asked.

"Yeah, I was just thinking that, but I need to find some place to turn around."

"No shit, we've got a rock wall on our right on this two-lane highway, and no place to make a U-turn." Dana observed.

"Thanks," I said. "Maybe there's some place up ahead where we can make a U."

"What's that over to the left" Tony pointed.

"Looks like a viewing area," Dana said. "Pull over there Chris."

"Hold on." I slowed down enough to make one of my famous

U-turns and screeched into the viewing area before we could be hit by oncoming traffic.

We piled out of the car in a helter-skelter motion. Nothing Transmanautic about our exit, we were trying to avoid being hit by oncoming traffic. At this juncture, not only was the PCH a two-lane highway, but the viewing area was at a blind curve on the southbound side and we didn't want to get hit. There was only a narrow strip of gravel separating the car and the tarmac, and the smallest miscalculation by a southbound car could be disastrous.

We stood on the precipice of a cliff overlooking the Pacific Ocean. The sight that greeted us to the west was a cluster of vegetation-covered rock formations, jutting out of the ice-blue water in a beautiful insulated cove. White frothy waves washed over the rock formations with a rhythmic pounding beat announcing the power of Mother Nature; the power of water and pressures of the Earth. I could see ships and other water-borne traffic far out in the distance on this beautiful cloudless day. An impressive sight for sure.

We stood there for several minutes admiring the view, and after we'd gotten our fill of the scenery, got back in the car to continue our trek north on the PCH.

"You know, this is a lot like the poster I had in my room." I said.

"What do you mean?" Hector asked.

"Well, I had this poster of the Trans-Am on my wall this past year. And in the poster, was this white guy driving a special edition Trans-Am along what appeared to be the Pacific Ocean with the sunset in the background, and rocks jutting out of the water and waves splashing against a beach in the foreground." I paused as I thought about the poster in my room. I continued, "And just now, I realized I'm actually driving my dream car on this highway – just as I had always imagined sitting there in my dorm room. I mean, wow, this is almost a transcendental existentialist out-of-body experience. This feels surreal." There was silence in the car.

"Boy, they teach you some big fuckin' words in college don't they?" Tony laughed breaking the silence.

"Yeah, well fuck you. Maybe you'll learn a couple of words

with more than one syllable Tony."

"No, I think that's cool." Dana reverted to his baby voice, "Widdle Cwis is living out his widdle dweam in his widdle dweam car." He and Hector laughed.

"Okay, fuck all y'all. You're just jealous."

"You know, you're right," Hector laughed. "Are we still going to stop in San Luis Obispo to check out my cousin Bev?"

"That's fine with me. Is that where we stop for the night?" I asked.

"Yeah, that's probably a good idea," Dana checked the Trip Tik, "It's about another hour up the road, and by the time we find Bev we might as well stay in the area."

"Sounds like a plan." I said.

We took our time driving up the 101. As we approached the San Luis Obispo area we looked for signs for the college campus where Bev attended classes during the summer.

"What's the campus?" I asked.

"She goes to Cal Poly San Luis Obispo." Hector replied.

"What's Cal Poly?" Tony asked.

"California Polytechnic State University at San Luis Obispo." Hector said.

"Boy, that's a long-assed name," Tony laughed. "Is she into something technical?"

"I don't know what her major is," Hector said, "but I know she's a junior or senior this year."

"Does she stay on campus?" I asked.

"Yeah, like Audrey down in San Bernardino." Hector said.

"Huh, this is where we came in." I chortled.

"I found it on the Trip Tik," Dana said, "We need to find either the California Boulevard exit or the Grand Avenue exit. They're both off 101."

"Okay," I said and looked for one of the two exits. Within a few minutes of entering the San Luis Obispo city limits I saw the California Boulevard exit for Cal Poly.

"There it is. Where are we going on campus Hector?" I pulled off the highway onto the California Boulevard exit and made the left towards campus.

"I'm not sure. When we get on campus I'll give her a call and see if she's in."

When we got to the entrance to the campus there were signs directing us to the University Union where we figured we'd find pay phones.

As we wound through the beautifully appointed campus we saw some guys on the basketball courts outside the Recreation Center. Uh oh, this is where we came in.

"Did y'all want to play ball?" I asked.

"Not me," Dana said. "I don't feel like it. I just want to find Bev and get some sleep, I'm pretty tired after the beach today."

Yeah, I guess so since you dodged a shark attack. "What about you guys? You up for some ball?" I turned to look in the back.

"Nah," Tony said. "I agree with Dana. Maybe some other time."

"Agreed," Hector said. "Let's just give Bev a call and get somewhere for the night."

We were also probably tired of losing. "Okay, just a thought." I drove up to the University Union façade and pulled to the curb. I opened my door, and Hector got out on my side, ran around the back of the car, and bounded up the steps to find a phone, as we idled at the curb.

209

A few minutes later, Hector came back out. "She didn't answer her phone at the dorm," he said as he got back in the car.

"You got any idea where she might be?" Dana asked as we pulled away from the curb.

"Nope. I even looked around the Union. If she wasn't in the dorm and she wasn't anywhere in there, I have no idea where she might be." Hector replied.

"No problem not hooking up with her?" I asked.

"Naw. You know, if we saw her we saw her, if not, it's fine."

"Okay, lets find a place to stay for the night," I said. "Any preferences?"

"No, just somewhere cheap, I don't feel like staying in a Howard Johnson's or a Holiday Inn," Tony chimed in. "Plus I don't know if this little town has any large hotels. One of those little motels is fine with me."

"Sounds good to me," Dana agreed. Hector met my eyes in the rearview mirror and nodded.

"Okay." I said.

I drove back through campus to California Boulevard, and back onto the 101 heading north. After a few exits we saw signs that indicated lodging and food.

"Get off at the next exit Chris. Looks like it might be a good place to find a motel," Dana said.

"Alright, here goes." I slowed down to get off the short exit ramp and saw several motels along the main drag.

"What about that place over there?" Hector pointed to the left.

"Looks okay." Dana said, "Let's pull in there."

I slowed down to make a left turn into the courtyard of the Oceanside Motel and pulled over inside the parking lot.

"This okay?" I asked.

"Yeah, this should work." Dana said.

"Yeah, this is fine." Tony and Hector chorused.

The motel overlooked the highway and was in a good location with easy access on and off the highway. I drove farther into the motel courtyard where I parked the car in front of the window facing out from the lobby. The Vacancy sign was lit so we knew there were rooms available.

As usual, I got out to get the room. There were twenty units in a U-shape, with a few cars parked in front of some of the units. The motel was definitely showing its age – a faded turquoise paint job over a weathered wood facade. Maybe in its heyday the color scheme evoked visions of the ocean; but now it only evoked feelings of better days gone by.

I thought twice about staying there but it seemed clean, and based on the sign, "19.99 a Night," the price was right. To the right of the bleak-looking door of the lobby was a wooden sign "Owned and Operated by John and Mabel Smithson." *Hmm, a privately-owned establishment. Oh well, can't be all bad,* I thought as I opened the rough-looking door.

The lobby was fairly small – to the left was the counter, and to the right was a small table and two wooden chairs with faded cushions; and the sun streamed in from a window covered by faded floral curtains. Behind the counter was an older white couple. There was a small black and white TV playing behind them, next to the myriad of wooden cubbyholes filled with keys to each of the twenty units. To the right of the counter was a door that may have led to the proprietors' living quarters.

The man, who appeared to be older than the woman, was fairly tall, and balding with wisps of white hair around his ears; a bulbous nose in the middle of a craggy face reminiscent of Dick Tracy's evil character Prune Face. He was wearing a plaid shirt tucked into gray, sagging trousers, held up by suspenders and a black belt. The woman was only as tall as his shoulders. She had a head of white hair with a little gray in a Lois Lane hairdo from the old *Superman* TV series. She wore a plain gray dress, with a white collar, somewhat covered by a frilly flowered apron with a large pocket in front. Both wore frameless glasses. *You know,* I thought, *with a pitchfork and a farm in the background, they would have been great models for Grant Wood's* **American Gothic** painting.

"May I help you?" the older man asked with a deep voice.

"Yes, we wanted to get a room with two beds for one night."

"We?" the woman peeked out the window.

"Yes, there're four of us," I said, "and we'll need two beds."

She again looked out the window. "Is that your car out

there?"

"Yes," I said, "is there a problem?"

"No, no," she said in an irritating school-marm voice. "We require the full night's rent plus a $50 deposit for incidentals and to cover any damage to the room."

Neither one looked very happy renting a room to a bunch of Black guys, but the money was right, so they couldn't stop us from getting a room. Somehow, though, I don't think they charged everyone this bogus deposit.

"Okay," I forked over the seventy bucks as I filled out the registration form. "Are there any fast food restaurants nearby?"

"Yes, if you go back out the front and make a left down the street you'll see a lot of places a few blocks down."

"Thank you."

"Do you plan on bringing the food back to your room?" The old man asked as he handed me the key to the room.

"Yes, is that a problem?"

"Well, we do have some rules – if you bring any food to your room you have to clean it up yourselves; you can't have the TV on past ten o'clock because that might disturb other guests; and you can't make a lot of noise or we'll have to call the police. We live right here, so we'll know if you all are acting up."

What kind of bullshit was this? His comments were totally fucked up, but I didn't let on how I felt. "Okay, any other rules I need to be aware of?"

"No, that's pretty much it. Make sure your friends know. Just behave and there won't be any problems." The woman reiterated.

Fuck you. "There won't be any problems." I assured them and strode back out to the car.

"What's up?" Dana asked, "You look pissed."

"It's these cracker motherfuckers putting rules and shit on us and charging us this bullshit deposit." I related what had happened in the lobby.

"Do we still want to stay here?" Hector asked.

"Fuck them. I've already paid the money." I said. Dana and Tony nodded their concurrence. "Let's get something to eat."

I pulled out of the motel courtyard into the street and screeched my tires in the direction of the fast food restaurants.

There's just something about the smell of Kentucky Fried Chicken. Maybe it's the 11 herbs and spices, but when that aroma wafted through the vents the car just steered itself into the KFC drive-thru. We ordered a bucket of chicken – original recipe, sodas, corn on the cob, and headed back to the motel.

Once we got back to the room, I parked in front of the room in combat parking position, just in case. We unloaded our bags and went into the room. The room was okay. It had the two queen-sized beds, a tiny bathroom with the toilet and bathtub behind the door, and the sink area situated on a vanity by the bathroom door. The TV was a decent size with a remote to power it on. Each of us spread out our food on the plastic trays in the room, and sat down on our respective beds to eat and watch TV. Once we finished eating, I pulled out the X-rated cards I'd bought in New York the year before to play spades.

Our spades battles are legendary in their enthusiasm and decibel levels. We'd divide up into different teams and play for hours. It didn't matter who your partner was, we'd talk big shit and try to back it up by embarrassing the other team.

"How many books you callin' Chris?" Tony asked as my first partner.

"I've only got three I can see, maybe four."

"Okay, I got your back, I've got at least four." Tony wrote it down on the notepad.

"Bullshit," Hector said. "I've got five by my damn self, and I know Dana's got at least three. That don't add up to thirteen, someone's bullshitting."

"I guess we'll see bitch," I laughed as I threw down the first card, a deuce of diamonds. Diamonds are Kappa symbols and my number on line was two. "Take that motherfucker."

We were sitting on one of the beds, away from the TV so all of us could see the screen. If we wanted the cards to make some noise we had to slap them hard on the bedspread.

The next card was from Hector to my left. "Uh!" he slapped down an ace of diamonds, "take that yourself, bitch!"

I had thrown down a low card to smoke out Hector's hand early. Tony followed my play by throwing in a low card when it was his turn. Dana tried to keep his card low, but threw out a ten of diamonds, which told me he was almost out of that suit.

Hector won that hand, and followed with the king of diamonds. "Uh! Take that!" He yelled.

Okay, he's probably got a few in that suit, but Dana's going to have to either throw out another high card in that suit or go out of suit.

Tony threw out another low card in that suit, and Dana followed with the queen of diamonds. Oh yeah, that suit's about played out for them.

Hector again won that hand and threw down the jack. "Take that!"

Tony smiled, and threw down a low spade, "Kiss my ass motherfucker, you ain't got shit!"

Dana followed but couldn't beat Tony's spade. He probably didn't have any, because he threw down a card from a different suit, but not the suit Hector led with.

"Yeah baby!" I was emphatic as I threw down a card in the lead suit. I knew we were going to win this set just based on that one hand.

Tony won that hand and threw out the spades starting with the ace and working through all the face cards.

Each time he threw down a spade, "Take that, and that, and that!" he crowed -- slapping the cards down as hard as he could.

The poor cards were bent at the middle from the unbridled slapping and abuse. The people on the X-rated cards were screaming in protest.

I got up to increase the volume of the TV so we could hear over our own noise – cussing, encouraging each other, and insulting each other's playing ability.

"Nigga where'd you learn to play?"

"Damn, my momma plays better than you."

"Yo momma invented the damn game."

"Yeah, well yo momma's so old she's got a wooden kickstand for a leg."

And on it went. For hours.

Around nine o'clock, there was a loud banging at the door. I went to the door and the old guy was standing there looking pissed off.

"We've had complaints from other guests about the noise in here. I warned you earlier about the rules. If you can't keep it quiet I'm gonna call the police and have you thrown out."

I just stared at him. He looked like he was going to blow a gasket he was so angry. "Alright, we'll keep it down."

"Make sure you do." He turned away; and I closed the door.

"Ah, fuck him." Tony said. We all laughed and continued our card game.

A little later, about 9:30, we heard a sharp knock on the door, and when I went to answer the door, there were two white police officers standing there. *Oh shit! Here we go.*

"Is your name Chris?" The taller cop referred to the registration form I filled out earlier.

"Yes."

"Mr. Smithson called us because he had complaints about the noise. He said he warned you but you refused to settle down. Is that true?"

"It's true he told us that, but I didn't think we were bothering anybody." I said. I was tired of this bullshit and it showed.

"Well sir," he began, "If we get another complaint about you guys we'll haul all of you off to jail and arrest you for disturbing the peace. So I suggest if you don't want to go to jail tonight you need to quiet down. Got it?"

I immediately went into "submissive black man" mode. "Yes sir, I think we understand. There won't be any more problems tonight."

They looked into the room at the other guys – who had been silent and still during the entire exchange – nodded and left.

Fuck them and fuck the owners. There seemed to be an obvious bias against us by this owner and his wife that started the moment we showed up. We were angry about the officer's threat, but we weren't going to risk getting thrown out or arrested for just being loud at a motel. So, yeah, we quieted down. We continued to play spades, but much more muted; and as we played, we continued to get angrier and angrier.

While we played, Tony spoke up, "Hey, screw them! We weren't doing anything wrong. We need to do something to pay them back for treating us like dirt."

"Oh yeah?" I said, "What do you want to do about it?"

Tony's idea was pretty nasty, but we had been treated badly by this older white couple. We were tired of being treated poorly because of their perceptions and prejudices. I really didn't agree with his plan, but that was about to change.

The next morning I went to the office to settle the bill and both Smithsons were in the office behind the counter.

Mr. Smithson looked up at my entrance. "I see you boys didn't go to jail last night."

Fuck you, I thought, *no thanks to your old dumb ass.* "No, we didn't. You made your point by calling the police."

"I told you boys if you didn't behave that would happen," he chortled.

This motherfucker was not my father, and I really didn't need to take this shit. Let me get my money back and get the fuck out of here.

"I came in to settle the bill and get my deposit back." I said.

"Oh, I'm sorry young fella, you don't get your deposit back."

Mrs. Smithson spoke up.

"What are you talking about? We didn't cause any damage to the room and we didn't use the phone." I said in disbelief.

"We had to call the police and you disturbed the peace of the other guests, so you don't deserve your deposit back." Mr. Smithson said smugly.

Damn these crackers! "Look, you give me my deposit or I'll call the police and tell them you charged us a deposit unnecessarily and that you are now going to keep it illegally when there wasn't any damage to the room." I wasn't going to law school for nothing.

"There were complaints, and we're going to keep the deposit," Mrs. Smithson added with a note of finality.

"I think you're lying about the complaints and I think you just tried to get us arrested; and if you don't want more trouble than it's worth you'd better give me back my deposit. That's theft and I *will* report it to the police." I locked eyes with Mr. Smithson.

They exchanged looks, and he nodded. "Alright sonny, you've got some fire, I'll give you that. Just don't come back here any more."

"You can depend on that," I said as he handed me the fifty dollars. I stalked out of the office without another word and slammed the office door without a backward glance at those two rednecks.

When I got back to the room I told the guys what had happened – that they tried to screw us out of our money adding insult to injury from the night before.

Tony looked at me with a questioning look in his eyes. "Well?"

I looked back at all three of them. "You guys do what you think is appropriate. I'm tired of this shit, I'm out." I walked out the room with the bags while they remained in the room.

I began to load the bags in the car when Hector came out and said, "You need to get the car started, because if they come by while we're still here, they're going to call the police."

Oh shit. "Okay," I said, "Tell everyone to hurry up so we can *vamanos* out of here."

I finished loading the car and got it started. Luckily it was parked in combat mode ready for a quick escape.

In the next sixty seconds, all three came running out of the room with Tony slamming the door behind him. They jumped in the car gasping with laughter and I put the car in Drive and shot out of the motel courtyard. The last image I had of the motel in my rearview mirror was the owner and his wife walking out of the lobby in the direction of our room.

As I accelerated towards the entrance ramp for the 101, I asked them what happened in the room.

"You don't want to know," Dana laughed.

"Yeah I do. What did y'all do? Did you follow through with Tony's idea?"

"Tony did," Hector laughed. "Me and Dana just pissed in the toilet and didn't flush it, but Tony left a little present on the bed for those racist owners to clean up."

"Tony, did you shit on the bed? I laughed.

"Well let's say I didn't quite make it to the bathroom and I really had to go, so I pinched a loaf on the bed. Oh well, they shouldn't have treated us like shit. That's what they get – shit." He was gasping with laughter. We all were.

"Man, I wish I could see their faces when they go in that room. It's good we have a really fast getaway car." Hector gasped.

"Yeah, we need to get the hell outta Dodge." Dana laughed.

I thought about what we had done as I entered the 101 heading north. And yeah, no matter who did what, we were all involved. But I didn't feel any remorse. Was it the right thing to do? Maybe not, but it seemed the right thing to do at the time – to leave some sort of message of outrage directed at these mini-oppressors. To see the expressions on that couple's faces when they found the little presents left behind would have been priceless. I'm sure it didn't help with race relations in San Luis Obispo, but they shouldn't have treated us like second-class citizens. Fuck 'em.

Oh well, on to the next adventure.

218

Oaktown

Once I hit the 101, I put the pedal to the metal and if I'd gone any faster we would have taken flight. I was determined to put some distance between the motel and us. I didn't stop driving for a full hour. No telling what the old couple might do once they saw Tony's "little present." No doubt they called the police on us. There was probably an "all-points bulletin" on a black and gold Trans-Am with Texas dealer plates being driven by four armed and dangerous black guys. Hell, every cop in California would have been drooling to make that arrest.

Even though the scenery was beautiful, we couldn't afford to stop and admire it. The only sounds in the car for that first hour were the sounds of *KC and the Sunshine Band; the Temptations; and Kool and the Gang.* We were all somewhat subdued after our high-speed getaway from the motel.

When we finally got to Salina, I figured it was safe to gas up. I took the exit ramp and headed toward an Exxon station at the corner.

"You pullin' over for gas?" Tony asked.

"Yeah, and to give you a chance to wipe your ass. I know you didn't at the motel and I've been smelling you for the past hour. You need to get in there and clean yourself up." I said as I pulled into the station and stopped next to a pump.

"Thank God," Hector laughed, "He was getting ripe back here."

"Yeah, the AC doesn't work that good," Dana agreed. "The

funk was getting pretty bad."

"Yeah, jet funk," I chuckled.

"Shut the fuck up," Tony laughed as we stopped in front of a gas pump, "Let me out so I can go take care of business."

"Yes, *please* let him out," Hector said still chuckling.

Dana opened his door and Tony slipped out to the gas station convenience store and bathroom. Dana and Hector followed him to buy some snacks. We'd taken off without eating and everyone was hungry.

I got out and pumped the gas. After a few minutes, the tank was full and I drove the car up to the little store.

"You guys ready?" I asked when they all came back to the car. "Any problems in the store?"

"What sort of problems?" Tony asked as he got in.

"I don't know. I had visions of Wanted posters with our pictures on it and police hiding behind every bush and combing the stores along the PHC looking for us."

"We're good, nothing like that happened." Dana said, "Let's roll."

"Okay." I let Hector in. "How much farther to San Fran navigator?" I called over to Dana as he got in.

"Hold on, let me check the Trip Tik."

"Well?"

"Hold on, I said." Dana looked over the map. "Looks like about another hour or so and we'll be in the vicinity."

"We're going to the Wittens first, right?"

"Yeah, in Oakland." Dana replied.

I pulled out of the gas station and merged back on the highway as I placed another tape in the player. Almost an hour later, Highway 101 led us along the west side of the San Francisco Bay. As we approached San Francisco, we could see the vista of the city below us. The downtown area, with its unique skyline and hilly topography, beckoned to us on our left.

San Francisco may be the most beautiful major city in America – The City by the Bay. Certain things come to mind when you think of San Francisco: China Town, steep hills, Lombard Street "the Crookedest Street in the World," Rice-A-Roni, cable cars, the Golden Gate Bridge, San Francisco Bay, Fisherman's Wharf, Alcatraz Island, and the Bay Bridge into Oakland. San Francisco is a great, diverse metropolis, from the gay population to one of the largest Chinese communities outside of the People's Republic of China or Taiwan. This was a great place for four young guys to experience a once-in-a-lifetime road trip.

As we approached the city, I asked Dana, "What's the best way to get through San Francisco to get to Oakland?"

"Keep on 101 until we see signs for I-80 north. That should lead us to the San Francisco-Oakland Bay Bridge."

"Not the Golden Gate?"

"No, San Francisco-Oakland Bay Bridge."

"Huh, okay. Where's the Golden Gate?" I asked

"It's farther north and west on the 101," Dana said. "Maybe we'll see it on our way back."

"Yeah, okay. Maybe we can put that on our list of things to see."

"Where we going first?" Hector tapped me on my shoulder.

"Going to see our parents' friends, the Wittens."

"Who are they?" Tony asked.

"A family we knew in Missouri," Dana answered.

"Yeah, he's a doctor and he has a daughter, Michaela, who should be about 15 by now I'd guess," I replied.

"I think he got remarried." Dana added looking over at me.

"Oh, divorced?" Hector asked.

"No, his first wife died," I looked back at Dana.

"Yeah, she died while we were in Missouri." Dana shared another look with me.

"What kind of doctor?" Tony asked.

221

"OB-GYN. You know, a baby doctor." I answered.

"Yeah, but I bet he see's a lot of pussies." Tony laughed.

"I guess I never thought about it like that, but I guess you're right." I laughed.

"Is that all you think about Tony?" Dana asked.

"Yeah, pretty much."

"Just checking." Dana said.

I pulled up to the toll booth and paid the toll and drove on the lower of two levels. The bridge itself is a wonder of engineering and the entire San Francisco Bay was open to us.

"Hey, isn't that Alcatraz?" Hector pointed off to the left.

"Yeah, I think it is," Dana consulted his map.

"Wow, 'The Rock'!" Tony craned his head for a better view. "I hope I don't ever end up in there." Tony laughed.

"If anybody ended up in there, it would be you." I snickered.

"Fuck you Chris," Tony scowled.

"I don't think it's open anymore," Dana said. "I think I read that somewhere."

"Huh," I said, "I wonder what they do there now?"

"Think we can go out there?" Hector asked.

"Fuck no. And why would you?" Tony said.

"I don't know, just to take a look." Hector replied.

"Maybe we could sail by on a boat or something." Dana chimed in.

"Maybe. We'll see." I left it pretty vague. But I didn't see us wasting time trying to find a way to get to Alcatraz. Just the name evoked images of dark, dank cells, and I wanted nothing to do with that place. We continued across the bridge, exiting into Oakland.

Oakland is depressing when compared to San Francisco, its richer, and more cosmopolitan sister city. The city just didn't have the same vibe as San Francisco. Not as alive.

"You know where we're going?" I asked Dana.

"Yeah, Mom gave me the directions before we left home."

"Okay, call them out and we'll get there."

Dana fed me the directions as we made our way through the various neighborhoods of the home of the Oakland Raiders; my only real reference to this other city by the Bay.

We skirted the downtown area, staying more in the business and residential areas of the city. We saw a lot more people of color as we got closer to Dr. Witten's neighborhood. Oakland appeared to be much more "blue collar" than San Francisco, and had kind of a mean feel to its streets.

After several turns and U-turns, I finally closed in on Dr. Witten's block. His choice of neighborhood was interesting. It was kind of a rough looking area as we drove through. When we pulled up to Dr. Witten's house there was a beautiful black Porsche Carrera 911 parked in the driveway, you know, the kind with the "whale tail" on the back. The sort of car you'd expect a doctor to drive. Dr. Witten had a nice looking house, but not ostentatious, in this heavily African-American neighborhood.

"Good job getting us here Dana," I said as I pulled up next to the Porsche, "We didn't have to make too many U-turns."

"That's a nice ride," Hector commented. "Think it could outrun you?"

"Fuck if I know. I only know Porsches are supposed to be some of the fastest cars in the world, so, yeah, he can probably blow my doors off." I said.

"Hopefully, we won't find out." Dana asked, "You guys ready to get out?"

"Yeah, let's do this." Tony said.

We got out in our normal Transmanautic manner and pimp walked to the front door. We had to affect a cool aura – you never knew who might be watching.

The doorbell rang with the tune from "Beautiful Dreamer." That was pure class. I wondered how Dr. Witten managed that when the door opened.

"Hey guys, come on in!" he bellowed. He'd put on a little weight over the years, but he was the same handsome guy I remembered. He was about six feet tall, wearing fashionable wire-rimmed glasses over his brown eyes. He was dressed in a dark blue polo shirt tucked into light brown slacks with his bare feet tucked into penny loafers. The light shined off his balding head, but he still had thick brown, wavy hair styled around most of his head. He was a lighter caramel color and carried himself well. He was probably a few years younger than our parents, and always struck me as a "cool jazz" sort of guy.

He led us into his spacious family room where I saw a full stereo system with reel to reel tape system, 8-track player, a top of the line turntable and tuner, and speakers everywhere. I had a little knowledge of stereo systems and I was impressed by the array of electronic equipment.

I was more impressed by his wife as she stepped forward from the kitchen to greet us.

"Honey, this is Chris and Dana, and their two friends..." he started.

"Hector and Tony," I finished for him, transfixed by his wife.

"Yep, Hector and Tony. I told you I've known these guys since they were little boys in Missouri," Dr. Witten continued. "And they've definitely grown up to be handsome young men." He beamed at us.

"My name is Teresa," she said. "Welcome to our home." She shook our hands. "Our two boys are around here somewhere, you'll see them at dinner."

"Looking forward to it ma'am," I said still staring at her. I don't know how Dr. Witten did it, but he definitely pulled a star. She was fine. She appeared to be several years younger than he, and looked like Vonetta McGee, a Black actress who starred in *Blacula* and the *Eiger Sanction*. She was wearing hip-hugging white jeans and a red and white horizontally striped short-sleeved top that clung to her figure in desperation of being thrown off. She wore golden sandals encasing long feet with perfectly painted toes. Her hair was kind of short, and done up in waves which framed her face perfectly.

"Please sit down, make yourselves comfortable," she said. "I would think you guys are thirsty after your long drive. I'll be right out with some nice cold lemonade."

"Thank you ma'am," I intoned still staring at her retreating figure.

As we settled down on the closest sofa and love seat, and waited for her to return, Michaela was ushered into the room by her father.

"Hey guys, you remember Michaela don't you?"

We stood up to greet the young lady who stood before us. Michaela, her father's namesake, had grown up to be a very attractive young lady. She was light-skinned like her mother with large hazel eyes. Her finely-textured long ginger-colored hair was pulled back into a pony tail held in place with a blue ribbon. She was wearing a T-shirt and blue jeans, also over sandals.

"Hi Michaela," Dana and I said in unison. We both gave her a hug.

"These are their two friends, Hector and Tony," her father completed the introductions.

"Hi," Michaela said shyly to Hector and Tony. She took a seat opposite us on a leather recliner.

The room was well appointed in all dark leather. Sofas, love seats and two recliners in front of a large 25-inch color TV console. There were several paintings and other objects d'art around the room of an Afro-centric nature. The artwork depicted African scenes; consisted of the works of prominent Black artists; and statuettes with the images of Black women and men. This was a very comfortable room that expressed a pride in our shared African-American culture and heritage.

Teresa returned with chilled glasses of lemonade on a serving tray and coasters for the glass-topped coffee table.

"Here you go," she said as she set the tray down.

"Thank you," we chorused and reached for the sweaty cold glasses.

Dr. Witten settled into the other leather recliner with a glass of something of a golden pale color with a frothy top. He took a few sips of the beverage watching us over the lip of the glass.

His first question after the obligatory questions about our parents showed his pride in his car. "How fast is that Trans-Am out there?"

"I don't know," I said. "I know the speedometer tops out at 120, but I don't know how fast it will go."

"What are the specs on the car?"

"What do you mean?" I asked.

The other guys looked interested in this conversation. Maybe he was going to challenge me to a race.

"You spent all that money on your car and you don't know its specs?" He guffawed at my expense.

This was looking like a dick-comparing contest, where he thought he was going to win. I needed to squash that notion right away.

"It's got a TA 6.6 liter V-8 engine with 200 horses under the hood." I answered proudly.

"Yeah, but what's its torque ratio? What will it do in the quarter? And how fast from 0 to 60?" he laughed figuring I didn't know the answers.

Fuck him, he was right, I didn't know. I just knew it was really fast.

Reluctantly, I said, "I don't know those specs, but we haven't lost any races since we've been in Cali." I added.

226

"Uh huh. I've only had my car a few months. It's my second Porsche 911. I had another 911 in 1974, and then when they came out with the '77 turbo Carrera, I had to have one. Let me tell you a little about that 911 you parked next to." He paused as if waiting for a reaction, and when he didn't get one he started bragging about his Porsche.

"That's a turbocharged Carrera 911 with a four-cylinder 3.0 liter engine that produces up to 290 horses. It can do 0-60 in less than seven seconds, the quarter mile in less than fifteen seconds, and will blow the doors off any American-built sports car, including the Vette."

Yeah, okay, his car was bad. His Porsche could probably blow the doors off my car in a race. That wasn't going to happen, but I think he made his point. I was driving an American piece of shit compared to his wonder of German engineering.

"Wow, that's impressive," I said. "I don't know those performance numbers for my car, but I know it runs and I would put it up against anybody's car." I added weakly.

He just laughed. "You all ready to eat?" he asked changing the subject. "Why don't you get your stuff out of your car, and Michaela will show you where you'll be staying. You guys are staying for a couple of days, right?"

"Yes sir," I answered. "We planned on spending a few days in the Bay area."

"Okay, you can stay as long as you want," he offered. "Maybe I can show you around Oakland."

"That would be great Dr. Witten," Dana said as we got up to get our stuff.

We went out to the car and unloaded our bags and dragged them where Michaela was up and beckoning to us.

"Follow me guys," she said, "I'll show you to your room."

Room? Singular? Here we go again.

She led us to a back bedroom that had been fixed up for us. It was pretty spacious and had two full sized beds, each big enough for two of us to squeeze onto. Each bed had two towels and washcloths displayed at the foot. This time all of us would be in a bed and Hector wouldn't have to sleep on the floor.

"You can put your stuff in the closet." She pointed at one of the two doors to the left of the beds. "The bathroom is right here off the bedroom," she walked to the other door, and opened it to reveal a full pass-through bathroom with a second door that opened up to the hallway.

Great, this was like a dorm suite with our own bathroom. We wouldn't have to disrupt the rest of the house when we got cleaned

227

up in the morning.

She came out of the bathroom. "Teresa will have dinner ready in a few minutes. You all need to get cleaned up."

"Okay," I said. *What,* I thought, *we smelled that bad?* I guess every house has its rules.

She turned and left the room leaving the door open. We put our bags on the bed to dig out our toiletries and clean shirts.

"Teresa's a babe isn't she?" Tony whispered.

"Yeah," I whispered as I went to close the door. "Now we can talk."

"She's fine," Hector commented. "You see the way she was checking us out?"

"Now you're dreaming," Dana said pulling out a clean shirt. "She's married to our parents' friend, we can't be thinking like that."

"Fuck that," Tony said. "We can at least dream about it."

"What, you gonna try to hit on that while we're here?" I laughed.

"No, but you know, if the shoe fits…" Tony started.

Dana cut him off. "No, fuck that, we don't go after our host's wife. What the hell is wrong with you?"

"Yeah, yeah, you're right," Tony conceded. "But it would have been fun."

I started towards the bathroom to get cleaned up and change.

"Heyyy, wait a minute. Do you think she was one of his patients before they got married and he liked what he saw?" Tony joked.

"Tony, shut up." I said and closed the bathroom door.

We took our time getting cleaned up and dressed; we wanted to look good for dinner. Fifteen minutes later we ambled back into the family room.

The whole Witten family was waiting on us. Dr. Witten looked mildly irritated.

"Okay, honey, we can eat now." He turned and led us all to the dining room.

The dining room was well thought out with the centerpiece being the 10-seat marble and glass table with matching marble chairs covered in gold and green striped cushions. The room reeked of expensive taste from the matching green and gold-striped heavy drapes over the large picture window, to the ornate crystal chandelier hanging over the table, and the huge glass-encased china cabinet filled with bright silver serving sets and china. The table was set with gold-rimmed china pieces including a soup bowl set on a dinner plate, cut crystal glasses, gold-plated silverware and matching gold candlesticks with pear-green candles. It was almost too ostentatious. If the intent was to impress, it succeeded.

"This is beautiful," Dana said as he looked around the room. We all echoed his sentiments.

"Thank you, I decorated it myself." Teresa announced. She seemed appreciative of our comments about the loveliness of the room.

She had also changed her clothes. She was now wearing white hip-hugger bell-bottom slacks, again with gold sandals, but this time with a sleeveless red top with flared collars showing off her well-formed arms and midriff, with a deep plunging V-neck exposing a good amount of cleavage to our young eyes. Maybe that's why Dr. Witten seemed a little irritated.

Dang, I thought, *she's beautiful. When did she have time to fix dinner?*

The two boys, five and seven, wearing matching shorts and short-sleeved blue shirts went straight to two chairs adjacent to each other on one side of the table close to the head of the table. Michaela found her seat directly across from them. Dr. Witten sauntered to the throne-like chair at the head of the table as we found seats closer to the other end of the table. Dana and Hector sat on the same side as the boys, while Tony and I sat with a chair separating us from Michaela. I sat closest to where I thought Teresa would be seated.

Teresa was the last one in the room, and stood behind her chair without sitting. Once she was in position, Dr. Witten asked

229

us to bow our heads. The family held hands as a part of the blessing and included us in their circle.

"Lord bless the food that has been prepared for the nourishment of our bodies, so that it may strengthen us and allow us to serve you. Bless the hands that have prepared the food we are about to partake and bless those who have come from such a distance to break bread with us on this day and keep them safe in their continued travels. In Jesus Christ's name we pray. Amen."

"Amen," everyone intoned in unison. He sounded like he put some thought into that blessing.

"I hope you all like cold cucumber soup as your first course," Teresa began, "followed by a mixed salad, a main course of grilled salmon, red potatoes and chocolate cake for dessert. How does that sound?"

Damn. It sounded like a restaurant menu. I'd never had cold cucumber soup, but if she prepared it, I was going to eat it. I looked at the other guys to gauge their reactions. They looked back at me expectantly.

"Wow that sounds great." I said. "You really outdid yourself Teresa."

"She's a great cook. I think you'll really enjoy the meal," Dr. Witten called down from his end of the table.

"Thank you," Teresa said. "I'll be right back with the soup tureen."

"Hey guys," Dr. Witten looked at me and Dana, "your mom told me a little about your career plans. Very impressive. Who would've thought little Dana would be going to West Point, and you Chris, already a second lieutenant going to law school. Very impressive."

"Thank you sir," Dana said. "We've come a long way from those two little boys you remember."

I could tell Dana didn't like that "little Dana" remark, especially in front of Michaela. He had been kind of checking her out ever since she walked in the room that first time.

"Oh yeah. I want my two boys to see some young men who

are moving forward in life. You guys are great role models."

"Thank you sir," I said. I guess being in this more formal atmosphere brought out the more formal manner of speaking.

Teresa walked back in with a silver soup tureen and ladle. She went to each place and ladled soup into the bowl. When done, she set the tureen on the table.

"Eat up guys. I hope you enjoy it. I made it from scratch."

"Thank you," we said in unison as she walked back to the kitchen. I again watched that view with interest. Down the table, Dr. Witten also watched his wife leave the room.

I grabbed the green linen napkin from its gold-plated napkin holder lying on to the side of the dinner plate, and flapped it out to the side and laid it on my lap. I then picked up the soup spoon from the right side of the place setting where it resided next to the knife. I made eye contact with Dana and Hector to make sure they picked up the right spoon. There was a dessert spoon located above the dinner plate, and I didn't want them to embarrass themselves by picking up the wrong one. That was the NMMI formal dinner training kicking in. Tony looked over and followed my lead.

"What about you two," Dr. Witten waved his hand towards Hector, then Tony. "What are your plans for the future? You guys can't hang around these two without having something going for yourselves." He grinned at us.

I was glad I didn't have to answer any questions about my future plans. I was getting this weird kind of competitive vibe from Witten, and it seemed he was going out of his way to belittle or embarrass us. Really strange from someone as accomplished as he and so much older.

"I'm going to New Mexico State University on a track scholarship, and plan on majoring in history with an eye on teaching at some point." Hector caught in mid slurp had the litany down pretty well by now since we'd been asked the same question numerous times on this trip.

"I'm going to Texas Tech University on a ROTC scholarship, and plan on majoring in political science," Tony put his spoon down and grinned back.

"You hear that Michaela? These guys are going places. You might want to watch out for them one of these days." He guffawed.

"Sure Daddy."

Michaela didn't seem too impressed with us. She really hadn't reacted well to us from the moment we walked into the house. I don't know, maybe we were reminders of memories she'd rather forget. Whatever it was, she wasn't very responsive, and certainly hadn't responded to Dana in the least.

The two little boys just watched in fascination. They seemed enthralled by us and hung on every word. At least we impressed somebody at the table.

Teresa walked back in at that time with a platter of salad bowls and several bottles of dressing perched precariously in her arms.

"Next course. How was the soup?"

"It was great," Dana offered. "I've never had cucumber soup. It was great," he reiterated.

The rest of us chorused our agreement.

"Michaela, please take the bottles," she directed. She put the platter of bowls on the table where there was an open chair and began distributing the bowls while Michaela put the bottles of salad dressing on the table in easy reach.

"The unmarked bottle with the cork is my own raspberry-flavored olive oil vinaigrette. Try it if you're feeling adventurous. We also have thousand island, french and blue cheese dressing." She said with a twinkle in her voice.

232

"I'll take you up on that," I said watching Witten's reaction to his wife's comment. "I love being adventurous."

"I thought you did," she smiled and picked up the unmarked bottle. She walked around to her chair and leaned over to serve the salad dressing, out of Tony's field of vision. As she leaned over she gave me an unfettered view of her cleavage.

Click. Something went off in my brain. *What the hell is going on here?* I wondered. This whole situation bore watching.

I wasn't sure what to expect anymore. I looked at Dana to see if he noticed anything, but he was still looking over at Michaela; Hector seemed to be focused on putting dressing on his salad; and I knew Tony had been blocked by my body. I seemed to be the only one that caught that exchange. Looking down the table, it was obvious Dr. Witten's keen eyes missed nothing, and there were storm signals flying.

Teresa cleared the soup bowls, putting them on the platter and returned to the kitchen.

We dug in to our salads, with sliced tomatoes, cucumbers, fresh iceberg lettuce, and croutons. The salad was great and was a perfectly cool follow-on course to the cucumber soup.

Teresa sat down and ate her salad as we finished ours. Occasionally she would glance around the table watching us eat.

"Everything okay?" She asked.

"Oh yeah," I said, "the raspberry vinaigrette was delicious."

"Glad you enjoyed it," she said. "And you guys?"

"So far so good," Hector said. Tony and Dana echoed his remarks.

"Great," she got up. "I'll go get the next course. Michaela can you please clear the salad bowls?"

"Sure Teresa." Michaela got up to comply and began stacking salad bowls.

"Can I help?" Dana offered.

"No thanks, I got it," Michaela replied as she finished stacking the bowls. She carried the bowls in the kitchen as Teresa walked back in with a plate of food in each hand. Each plate was full with grilled salmon and grilled red potatoes.

She first served Dr. Witten, then made her way down the table serving her guests, then her boys. Michaela came back in with her own plate as we plowed into the mounds of food on our plates.

Teresa then brought out dessert plates with slices of chocolate cake and set them before each of us.

The room was silent except for the sounds of everyone

scarfing down the delicious grilled salmon and gorging on the chocolate cake. Teresa glowed as she watched our obvious enjoyment of her gourmet meal.

I pushed back my chair after cleaning the dessert plate of every crumb of chocolate cake. "That was great Teresa. Thank you very much. I'm stuffed." I groaned.

"Thank you. What are you all's plans for the night?"

"Probably just hang out, and maybe get an early start tomorrow," I said looking at the other three.

"Okay, sounds like a plan," she said.

She began clearing the table, and Dana jumped up in his best Super Cadet voice, "Can we help?"

"Sure, why don't you all grab the dirty dishes and bring them in the kitchen. Rinse them off and put them in the dishwasher."

Thanks Super Cadet, I thought as I got up from my chair and made my way into the kitchen. I harkened back to my days doing KP duty at Fort Knox and got to work in their wonderfully appointed kitchen. The kitchen was decorated in black and white. The floor tiles and the counter tops were made of black and white matching tiles, and the appliances were all black. We spent the next few minutes rinsing and putting the dirty dishes in the dishwasher.

Once we finished that chore we convened to the family room, and joined the two boys, Damien and Louis, Michaela and her dad as they watched some movie on TV.

When Teresa came in she changed the entire dynamic of the situation. She asked, "Do you guys like to dance?"

"Sure," we said in unison.

"We've got some music, but if you all have some recent stuff you'd like to dance to, I'd like to see you dance."

Dr. Witten looked irritated, but didn't say anything to disrupt the offer.

"Okay," I said, "I'll go out and get my 8-tracks." I went out to the car to get my favorite mix tapes and wondered what

234

we were getting into. One way or the other, this was going to be interesting.

I returned to the family room with my tapes and asked Dr. Witten if I could play them.

"Sure, go ahead. You do know how to work the 8-track right?"

"Yes sir, it's pretty simple." I put the first tape in and the first song was *Wine Flow Disco*. The four of us lined up and did our routine to the song ending with Dana and I doing jazz splits and Hector and Tony in their upright freeze poses.

The boys clapped with glee, Michaela looked bored, and Teresa stood up and clapped enthusiastically. "That was great guys! I guess you've worked on that routine huh?"

"Yep," I said, "we've performed it a few times at parties."

"Can I get in on it?" she asked.

"Sure, what do you want to hear?" I offered.

"Anything by Earth, Wind and Fire?"

"Yep, got just the thing." I said and stuck their *Greatest Hits* in the player.

"You're a shining star, no matter who you are…shining bright to see what you can truly be, what you can truly be…" flowed out of the speakers arrayed around the room.

"I love *Shining Star*!" Teresa exclaimed and jumped up to dance by herself. Well, I couldn't just let a beautiful woman dance by herself, so I got up to dance with her. She seemed to enjoy dancing with me as she moved her hips and twirled around the family room floor.

Dr. Witten sat up in his chair across the room and just glared at his wife. His first reaction since I put the first tape in the player.

"Boys, you all need to go to bed. Say goodnight to the fellas and off you go. Michaela, you make sure they get to bed," he directed.

He sounded like he didn't want them in the family room to witness anything that might happen.

235

"Okay Daddy," they all chorused. Michaela marched the boys off to their bedrooms.

Freed by the absence of her children, Teresa danced with me, Dana, Hector and Tony, in turn, to the sounds of *Brickhouse, Getaway*, and *Get Down Tonight*. Teresa seemed to be somewhat taken by us.

"This is great guys. I haven't danced this much in years." She was breathing pretty hard after her exertions on the dance floor, and a little sheen had appeared on her forehead.

We were eager to accommodate a beautiful woman. I put *Slide* in the player, and turned to Teresa, "You ready for some more?"

"Yes," she panted.

"Okay, we'll do this one a little differently." I winked at Hector.

I started dancing with Teresa, keeping my body fairly close to hers as we danced, but not quite touching. As the lyrics got more seductive, I began closing in to where I was dancing almost chest to breasts. "You ain't got to speak, everyone knows you're a freak…Slide…" When I heard those lyrics I winked at Hector signaling for him to join us on the floor.

When he joined us on the floor, I said, "Lock it up!" Which meant one of us was facing her and one of us behind her, and both of us in contact with her breasts and buttocks.

She seemed to enjoy the attention, as she didn't back away from the contact.

Dr. Witten shifted his weight in the recliner so his chin was resting on his right hand, and started drumming the fingers of his left hand on the arm of the chair. He continued to glare at his wife, but didn't say a word. His expression spoke volumes.

Michaela, who had come back in the room, had a smirk on her face as she watched the attention we were paying her stepmother and her dad's reaction.

"That was great," Teresa said as the song faded out. She glanced over at Dr. Witten who was frozen in place, "But I think we should probably wrap up our little dance session for the night boys."

"Sure," I was flushed from dancing with her and Hector. Hector was just grinning from ear to ear. Dana and Tony were looking on in amazement from the sofa opposite Dr. Witten's recliner.

"Yes, I think it's time you boys retired for the evening." Dr. Witten snarled.

Uh oh. Dana and Tony got up from the sofa, and Hector and I began walking towards the back bedroom when Teresa stopped us.

"You're not going to bed without a good night kiss are you?" She then walked over to each of us and pecked us on the cheek and murmured "Good night boys, see you in the morning."

I thought Dr. Witten was going to blow a vein in his forehead. He remained silent and just stared at us as we trooped out of the family room. I did not want to be in their bedroom to hear that discussion. On second thought, maybe I did.

Once the bedroom door closed behind us, Hector asked, "What was that all about?"

"I told you she was hot for us," Tony whispered.

"You know, you may be right," I said, "that was kind of weird." I started changing for bed.

"Dr. Witten didn't look very happy about his wife," Dana added as he walked into the bathroom. "He looked pissed."

"Yeah, I thought he was going to blow a gasket when she kissed us good night." Hector giggled.

"That was pretty funny," Tony snickered. "He looked like he could've killed you, Chris."

"I didn't see all this coming," I said. "Maybe under other circumstances...but this is our parents' friend, and we can't be hitting on his wife. Not after he invited us in his home."

"I know, I know," Hector said, "but he's been playing us all day, so what's wrong with a little payback?"

"Yeah, fuck it," Tony said. "We didn't do anything wrong. Fuck him if he can't take a joke." He laughed.

"Shh, keep it down. I could hear you guys in the bathroom. We don't want them to hear us." Dana whispered returning into the room.

"What now?" Hector asked.

"We'll play it by ear," I said, "and see what happens tomorrow."

"We going over to San Francisco tomorrow?" Tony asked.

"Yeah, I think that sounds good." I said and got into bed.

Dana turned out the lights and we settled in for the night.

The next morning, we got up, dressed and followed the aroma of frying bacon into the kitchen. Teresa was at the stove frying bacon dressed in a plain white robe, pinky curlers in her hair, and fuzzy pink slippers on her feet.

"Good morning boys. Hungry?"

"Yes, ma'am," we chorused as we took seats at the six-person white kitchen table. The chairs were a black-lacquered wood with cushions matching the table.

Dr. Witten sat at the head of the kitchen table drinking his morning coffee and reading the newspaper. He looked like he was ready for the day in a long sleeved plain white shirt with paisley green tie and light brown slacks.

"You guys sleep alright?" He asked.

"Yes sir," I said looking between him and Teresa.

"Good," he said and put down his coffee and paper, "Look fellas, I don't think this is going to work out."

"What do you mean?" I asked.

"I just think you guys need to find lodging somewhere else tonight."

I looked at Dana sitting across from me. He didn't have any expression on his face. Tony and Hector looked stunned.

"When do you want us to leave?" I asked.

"You can eat breakfast, but then you have to go."

Damn. My throat constricted making it difficult to speak, "Okay sir."

"I'm going in to the office, I have a full day, so this is good bye. Enjoy the rest of your trip to California." He stood up, came around and shook each of our hands, and walked out the kitchen.

A few minutes later, I heard the front door slam, and a powerful engine growl as he started up his Porsche. The next sound was it screeching down the street.

We had remained quiet during the interim, until he'd left the house. We just looked at each other dumbfounded.

"I'm sorry boys," Teresa stammered, "I got a little carried away last night and Witten didn't like it."

"Okay," I said. I didn't think we did anything to Michaela, so it had to be something else. I guess Dr. Witten didn't like the attention we paid his wife.

"Please eat your breakfast," she served us our plates. "You need to leave as soon as possible."

Damn, that must have been some discussion last night. Sounds like Dr. Witten was not happy, and didn't trust his wife to be around us. We were a pretty virile looking bunch of guys, and certainly between the four of us, would have been an interesting collection of young manhood for an older woman.

"Can we say goodbye to Michaela and the boys?" Dana asked.

"No, they're already gone, so it's just us in the house."

Huh. This would've really been interesting had she not been so scared. But we wolfed down our breakfast, and went back to our room to pack our bags.

Teresa was waiting in the family room for us to come out. When we made our appearance, she stood up from the sofa and gave each of us a hug goodbye.

"You guys take care. I really had a good time, and I'm sorry Witten kicked you out."

"Me too," I said. I gathered up my 8-tracks and walked out the front door. Dana, Hector and Tony said their goodbyes and followed me out to the Trans Am. I was surprised Dr. Witten hadn't "keyed" it or something, but it looked pristine.

I loaded the bags in the trunk and we took our positions by the doors. I looked back at the house and Teresa was standing in the door watching our imminent departure. I decided we were going to give Teresa a final Transmanautic show as we entered the car. I nodded to everyone and we went through our Transmanautic entry.

Once the doors closed, I put in *Slide*, rolled down the windows and let the sounds of Slave blast out through the neighborhood. I backed out of the driveway, and with a final wave, we were gone.

San Francisco and Star Wars

We were a lot more muted as we crossed the Bay Bridge on our way back into San Francisco.

"What the hell was that all about?" Hector finally broke the silence, "Why did we have to leave?"

"Yeah, what did we do wrong?" Tony joined in.

Dana and I looked at each other in silent agreement.

"Not sure what happened," I replied looking in the rearview mirror.

"You heard her, I guess Dr. Witten didn't appreciate our behavior with his wife." Dana added.

"You think he'll call our parents?" I wondered aloud.

"I hope not," Dana said tiredly. "Dad might understand, but I don't know about Mom."

"Yeah I'm sure Dad would understand if we described her to him. Man, she was fine." I said.

"Yeah, you're right. She was fine." Dana agreed.

"I'm getting tired of being thrown out of people's houses or asked to leave or having the police called on us," Hector leaned forward. "What's up with that anyway?"

"Well let's see. Your family threw us out first." I laughed. "Then let me see, we ignored the rules at the Oceanside Motel and they called the police on us, and now we're on the run for destroying private property; and oh yeah, we tried to hit on a married man's wife with him sitting there. Gee, you think it's anything we did?"

"Yeah, okay, point made," Hector chuckled.

"That's pretty funny," Tony laughed.

Dana was the only one not laughing. "I hope that shit doesn't catch up with us."

"Quit worrying. We'll be fine. Why don't you tell us how to get to downtown San Fran?" I asked.

"Okay," Dana consulted the Trip Tik. "Once we come off I-80 we need to head north towards Columbus Avenue and that'll get us in the vicinity of most of the stuff we want to see."

"Okay, what about Chinatown?" I asked.

"If we go towards Columbus we should pass right by Chinatown. We can always take a cable car to go down there."

"That's fine. Where do you all want to stay?" I asked.

"Either Howard Johnson's or Holiday Inn," Tony offered.

"Okay by me," Hector chimed in.

"Yeah, either's fine by me too," Dana agreed.

"Alright, keep a look out as we go through downtown." I said as I navigated through the dense downtown of San Francisco and tried to keep from staring at various sights. The hustle and bustle of this vibrant city was mesmerizing.

"Hey, what's that over there?" Dana pointed.

"It's not a Howard Johnson's or Holiday Inn," Hector said, "but I've never seen anything like that."

"Man, that's weird looking. You all want to stay there?" I asked.

"Yeah, that's pretty cool." Tony stared out his window. "I can't believe it's still standing."

"Okay," I said. "Hang on." I made a U-turn to get back to the hotel Dana had spotted and pulled up underneath the main building.

The hotel sat on several pillars with the parking lot underneath the building. The hotel was painted in colorful pastels of aqua, pinks and blues. I got hungry looking at it because it reminded me of a huge Popsicle.

"Wow, this is pretty cool," Dana said as we got out of the car.

"Think it's stable enough?" Hector asked.

"I hope so, since we're parked under here. I'm sure it's been around for a while, so it's probably stable." I said.

"What about earthquakes?" Tony asked looking around.

"Don't think there's been a major one here since 1906, so we should be okay for the next few days. But if you're worried, we'll keep 'widdle' Tony safe." I laughed.

"Shut up Chris," Tony also laughed, still looking around.

"How do you get up there?" Dana asked as he looked for the entrance.

"Those spiral stairs over there I'd guess." I pointed to the stairs near one corner of the building.

We trooped over to the stairs that wound up to the main building and walked into the spacious lobby. The lobby was much bigger than it appeared from the outside. It was airy with bright colors and murals of seascapes on the walls. This was very nice.

"How can I help you gentlemen?" The middle-aged guy inquired from behind the counter. He was dressed in a long-sleeved blue shirt with khaki pants. His name tag read "Jonathan."

"Hi Jonathan," I answered, "We'd like to check in for tonight. Do you have any double queen-size vacancies?"

"Let me check," he consulted his registry, "Yes sir, we have several. The rate is $45 per night. Will that be cash or credit card?"

"Cash," I looked at the other three and they all looked back in agreement.

"That'll be fine. I'll need a $50 deposit for incidentals which will be returned to you minus any incurred costs," he said crisply.

Now this was a professional who showed no signs of caring who we were. This was a big change from the Oceanside Motel.

I handed him $100 and asked, "How does this building stay up on the stilts?"

"I asked that myself," he laughed, "And they gave me some complicated engineering explanation that I didn't understand. All I know is it works and it's been here for a while."

"Okay. We'll take your word for it." I smiled.

"There's an elevator back down to the parking lot. I noticed you came up the stairs." Jonathan said.

"Thanks," I said, and picked up a map of downtown San Francisco from a stand by the counter as we went down the elevator to get our bags.

We brought our bags up to the lobby and then took another elevator to our room on the third floor. The room was decorated in the same motif as the rest of the hotel. We unloaded our stuff and just fell back on the beds.

"What do you all want to do?" I asked.

"Ride a cable car," Hector said.

"What about you Tony?" I asked.

"I don't know much about this city, so I'm just here for the ride."

"Dana?"

"You know we talked about this before we left. What about seeing Star Wars while we're out here?"

"That's a great idea," I said. I'd completely forgotten about seeing that movie.

"Yeah, let's do that," Hector said.

"Good idea Dana," Tony concurred.

The year before, as we were watching more mundane and forgettable movies such as *King Kong*, the one with Jessica Lang and Jeff Bridges, we would see these trailers of this movie called *Star Wars*. We had no idea what it was about, but the trailers looked so exciting and different that we made a promise that we would see that movie the following year.

When we were planning the trip, we found out that *Star Wars* was going to premier in San Francisco sometime in late May or early June. We weren't sure of the date, but we knew we would be close to the opening of the movie and the worldwide premier. *Star Wars* had a limited release, so it was not yet showing in El Paso at the time it was showing in San Francisco, so we would be able to see it ahead of our friends back home.

Once that was settled, we piled out of the room to make our way back down to the car.

"Where to first?" I asked once we were ensconced in the car. I gave Dana the map I'd picked up from the lobby.

"Let's just drive around and see what we can see," Dana suggested.

"Okay with you guys?" I looked to the back seat.

"Yep."

"Cool."

"Okay, here we go." I pulled out into the mid-morning traffic.

We drove around town looking at various sights that one always looked for in San Francisco – cable cars, Lombard Street, Chinatown and all the hills on the streets of San Francisco.

"You guys ready to get something to eat?" I asked after a couple hours of sightseeing.

"Yeah, that sounds good," Hector said. "Where?"

"You mentioned Chinatown right?" Dana glanced at me.

"Yep, I'd like to get some authentic Chinese food. It's been a while."

"Cool with me," Tony chimed in from the back.

"Let's go," Hector said. "Where's Chinatown from here?"

"Let me see," Dana again consulted the map of downtown. "A little south of where we are now."

"You give me directions and I'll get us there," I said, and

aimed the beak of the Trans Am south towards the middle of the city.

I piloted the car through the various neighborhoods following Dana's directions until the language on the signs began to change to Chinese pictographs. The race of the people on the streets also changed from a more diverse demographic to more homogenous Asian-appearing pedestrians. We knew we were in Chinatown.

I pulled into a public parking lot with the little slots for the fee. We alighted from the car in our normal Transmanautic manner, much to the amusement of less-than inscrutable Asian persons walking past the parking lot. Maybe we looked like a clown show.

"Where to?" Hector asked looking around.

"I don't know, but I do know I want to go to an authentic restaurant." I said.

"Okay, you said that before. What makes it 'authentic'?" Tony asked.

I looked up and down the street and saw what appeared to be an authentic Chinese restaurant.

"I tend to grade the authenticity of an ethnic restaurant by who eats there. So, if there're a lot of Chinese people speaking Chinese in the restaurant, then it's probably authentic," I explained. "Let's go over there to that little hole-in-the-wall place, there're a lot of Chinese-looking people coming in and out."

We headed across the street to the restaurant and found just a red door on the street. People were coming in and out, so I opened the door and almost stumbled on the stairs leading down into the restaurant.

The delicious aromas of ginger, garlic, peanut and chili oil, and frying meats wafted up the stairs. Yeah, this was the right place, I thought, as we started down the stairs.

When we got to the bottom of the stairs, we were met by a pretty young Chinese woman who led us to a table and set menus in front of each of us. I glanced around the room and noticed the Chinese folks in the restaurant seemed to order from a completely different menu than us, because their menus were all in Chinese characters. I was pretty sure the food was as authentic as you could get. Our menus were in Chinese with an English translation. I guess she could tell we weren't Chinese.

"Any recommendations, Chris?" Hector asked.

"Yeah, this was your idea, what's good?" Tony asked.

"Look, since you guys aren't real familiar with Chinese food, I'd recommend sweet and sour pork or chicken. I think I'll have the triple delight of sautéed squid, scallops and shrimp, Szechuan style."

"Damn, that sounds good. Is it spicy?" Hector asked.

"Yeah. Szechuan is a Chinese province and food from that province is famous for its fiery flavor." I explained.

"Is it good?" Tony asked again.

"Yeah, if you like spicy beef, then order the Szechuan beef."

"Okay, I'll do that," Tony put down his menu.

"What about you Hector," I said.

"I think I'll just stick with the sweet and sour pork. I've had that before and I know that's pretty good."

"Dana?" I looked at his eyes over the menu.

"I'm still looking."

"Okay." Dana had never been adventurous in his eating habits. He took after our dad in that respect.

The waiter, a slender Chinese man in black pants and white shirt, approached our table and stood behind my left shoulder.

"Are you gentlemen ready to order?" He said in a thick Chinese accent.

I looked around the table and decided I would go first. "Yes, I'd like the Szechuan triple delight please."

"Very good sir, something to drink?"

"A coke please."

"Royal Crown okay?"

Hmm, I'd never had Royal Crown, but what the hell, "Yeah, that'll be fine."

"Very good sir." He turned to Tony on my left, "And you sir?"

"I'd like the Szechuan beef, and lemonade please"

"Very good sir, and you sir?" He nodded to Hector to my right.

"Uh, I think I'll have…um…the sweet and sour pork."

"Very good sir, something to drink sir?"

"Yes, Sprite please."

"Is 7-UP okay?"

"Yes, that's fine," Hector nodded.

The waiter turned to Dana who was still looking at his menu. I could hear crickets singing – the silence was deafening as we waited.

"Okay, I'm ready. I'll have the deep fried whole fish stuffed with ginger, mushrooms, pork and shrimp."

Whoa, that was quite a mouthful. I hope it wasn't too much for him, but it sure sounded interesting.

In the next few minutes as we chattered about the food, we saw several exotic dishes brought out on sizzling hot plates to tables around us, to the delight of the patrons. The smells were indescribably good. We were salivating waiting on our dishes.

Our waiter approached the table carrying a serving table with our dishes piled up, the delicious aromas blanketing our table were punctuated with the sounds of the sizzle. As soon as we were all served, we dug in voraciously.

The food was extremely good. We didn't say much, but the sounds of fork and knives hitting plates were the loudest sounds at the table.

"This is really good," Tony exclaimed, "Thanks for the recommendation."

"What about you Hector? How's your food?" I asked.

"Great. Best Chinese food I've ever had."

"Dana?"

Dana's mouth was full, "This is really good. Good choice."

"Hey, I don't want to ruin your meals, but I didn't see many dogs around the area, so don't ask many questions about what the meat is." I laughed.

Tony dropped his fork with a loud clang on his plate. "You don't think…?"

"Naw, I'm just bullshitting Tony," I smirked with a wink.

"Damn, I don't want to be eating no dog," he said.

"I'm sure that's 100% real beef Tony," I laughed even harder.

"Yeah Tony," Hector joined in, "I'm sure that's real beef."

"Thanks guys, why don't I feel better?" Tony finished his meal, but maybe without the same gusto as before.

Once we finished, we paid our bill and went back out on the street. After leaving the restaurant, we did a little sightseeing and then Dana gave me directions to the theater we thought was showing Star Wars.

As we were driving around San Fran, getting a feel for the city, we came to a stop light, near the base of this steep hill when this car pulls up next to us and starts revving his engine – the sign of an offer to race. I was in the left lane and he was in the right lane, and looking to race up this steep hill. I was a little daunted – I had never tried to race up a steep hill before, but this guy was really revving his engine. He was driving a white Trans-Am, the first I had seen. The car was trimmed in blue with a blue firebird on the front. It was sort of ugly. I wouldn't be caught dead driving it, and, of course, it was driven by a white guy, so there was the obvious metaphor.

"C'mon Chris, you can take this guy." Hector tapped me on the head.

"Damn, he's driving a fucking Trans-Am, a white one at that… you can't let that shit go," Tony challenged me.

I looked at Dana, and he looked back, "Take the bitch and

shut him the fuck up," he said.

I could tell that it wasn't a TA-6.6 liter engine, but probably the smaller 5.7 liter engine, which could still run, but not like mine. The TA 6.6 wasn't written on the engine cowl sticking up in the middle of the hood. When I didn't see the telltale "TA 6.6 Liter" on his hood, I thought I would have a speed advantage, and it was up to me to turn my speed advantage into a quickness advantage and beat this guy off the mark. Once I beat him off the mark, then I was pretty sure I could beat him, even going up that steep-ass hill.

All these thoughts raced through my mind in a split second, and I made my decision. We were going to run against this guy and I was going to kick his ass!

"Okay, here we go." I put my car in Neutral, revved my engine once – agreeing to the race, put it back in Drive and waited for the light to turn green.

In watching the light and traffic pattern, I timed my jackrabbit start perfectly. As the light turned green I hit the accelerator without any hesitation. This caught the other guy by surprise. From the get-go he was behind. He never recovered. I was up that hill and to the next light before he was even out of third gear.

"Yeah! Fuck that mother fucker!" Tony yelled.

"You kicked that ass Chris!" Hector shouted, and the two of them slapped hands.

"Fuck him," Dana said and put out his hand for a high-five.

"Yes!" I said, and we slapped hands as the white Trans-Am pulled up next to me. The white guy revved his engine again, in sort of a salute, and turned right to drive away.

Yeah, drive off bitch and remember – Don't Mess with Texas!

The race occurred a few blocks from where our navigator said we could find the theater showing *Star Wars*. Dana had torn out an advertisement from a newspaper that showed the times at the one theater in town that was showing Star Wars – the Coronet. The Coronet was advertised as the largest movie theater in San Francisco showing the movie in 70mm, with the new Dolby surround sound theater system. We decided that this was going to be the highlight of our trip to San Francisco, and eventually found the theater at the top of one of San Francisco's famous hilly streets. I drove past the theater to make sure it was the right one and saw the crowd.

"Wow, people are already lining up," Hector observed. "I guess we need to get in line too."

"But damn, the movie doesn't start for almost three hours," Tony protested.

"Yeah, but if we want to get in and get good seats, now's the time." I said.

"Alright, me and Hector will jump out now, and you park the car." Dana said. I drove forward and found a place to make another famous U-turn to get us in front of the theater. I pulled to the curb to let them out.

"See you in a few." I said as they jumped out. When the door closed I pulled away moving down the hill.

"Shit, what are we going to do for three hours in line?" Tony complained as we looked for parking close by.

"I don't know, we'll figure it out. Damn, there's no parking around here. I'll have to go farther down the hill."

I finally found a parking lot a few blocks down the hill. Tony and I got out and trudged back up the hill to where Dana and Hector waited in line.

We were all dressed in T-shirts and jeans, which seemed appropriate at the time.

I walked up to the front of the line to do a short recon of the theater and surrounding area. I got a good look at the theater; it was huge. Of course, we didn't see the inside for quite a while. The outside was impressive in its size, but somewhat ordinary in its façade.

As I walked back down the line, I asked a guy waiting in line, "Are you in line to buy tickets?"

He said, "No, you can buy tickets right now, we're in line to get in the door."

"Okay, thanks." I walked back to the box office and bought our tickets.

I walked back past where the other Transmanauts waited and saw the line was down the block and around the corner. It looked like we were going to be here for a while. We had to figure out what we were going to do for the next two and half hours.

Most of the people around us were white, mostly guys, some women, some kids and teenagers, but mostly guys who were kind of geeky looking…nerds. The kind of folks you'd expect to see at a sci-fi movie like *Star Wars*. Not like us.

"I went ahead and got our tickets." I began, "Man, do you see these people out here? These are some nerdy-looking mother fuckers." I laughed.

"Well, look at us, we're in line with the rest of them." Dana observed, "So, we're just as nerdy."

"Bullshit, speak for yourself," Tony jabbed Dana. "I'm too cool to be a nerd."

"Yeah, but you're in line with the rest of us," Hector laughed.

"Fuck you," Tony laughed looking around.

We were drawing attention from some of the other, closer, line dwellers, with our loud talking and joking around. They had nothing better to do, so some of them watched us. I did my best, entertaining them and the other Transmanauts.

"You guys were really fucked up at Debbie's house," Tony laughed.

"RALPH BOUGHT A BUICK," I made loud barfing sounds with my finger in my mouth, "RALPH," I laughed with Tony.

"Take that shit to bed, I'm gonna take that shit to bed," Tony laughed doing that little back and forth dance Dana did at the Party, "How did that shit work out for you Dana?"

"Shut up Tony, at least I didn't take a shit on the bed like you did," Dana retorted.

"Got you on that one Tony," Hector laughed.

"Yeah, you really did 'take that shit to bed' didn't you," I joined in laughing.

"Did you get any pussy from anybody at the Party, Chris?" Tony shot back at me, "And what was the name of your cheerleader, Hector? Oh yeah, that's right, you can't remember," Tony fired off at Hector.

The bantering went on for the next half hour. Finally, as our humor started to peter out we needed something else to occupy our time and attention.

"Damn, standing in this line is getting old quick," Dana complained.

"Yeah but what else can we do?" Hector asked.

"We could play a game or something," Tony offered.

"Not cards and especially not the deck we brought with us." I said.

"Yeah, plus the car is way down the hill," Tony said, "So, what else?"

"How about chess?" Dana suggested. "We've got these little folding chess sets at home. Maybe we can get one up here."

"Okay Sherlock, where do we get a chess set?" Tony asked.

I looked up and down the street, and saw a Woolworth's across the street and down a block.

"What about the Woolworth's over there?"

"Okay, I'll go take a look. C'mon Hector, let's go." Dana said.

"Can't cross the street by yourself?" Tony taunted.

"Shut up Tony," Hector jumped in before Dana could answer. "Let's go."

The two of them took off across the street dodging afternoon traffic and running in and out of the crowds on the sidewalk. They looked like broken-field runners on a football field, as they maneuvered their way against the current of people on the sidewalk. I watched until they got to the Woolworth's and disappeared inside.

"You hungry?" I asked Tony.

"Yeah, I could eat," he said.

"I didn't see any fast food places coming up the street," I said. I turned to the guys in front of us in line, "Do you all know where there's a McDonald's or something around here?"

"Yeah, if you go farther up the block and around to the left, you'll see a McDonald's," one of the guys said.

"Hey thanks," I said. "You guys want something if we go?"

"That's pretty swell of you, but no thanks, we're good," The older guy said.

"Speak for yourself," his younger companion chimed in. "Yeah, if you guys go to Mickey D's I'd like some fries."

"You got it," I said. "As soon as our friends get back, we're going to get something."

"Cool," he said, "I'm Rick, and my reluctant friend here is Ronnie."

"I'm Chris, this is Tony, and my brother Dana and friend Hector went to get a chess set."

"Yeah, we couldn't help but overhear," Rick said. "That's a pretty cool idea. You guys can't be from here are you?"

"Nope, you're right. We're from Texas, just taking a road trip to Cali." I smiled.

"That's pretty cool," Ronnie spoke up again. "Where you guys from in Texas?"

"El Paso." I said, expecting them not know where that was.

"I've been through El Paso," Rick said. "Right there with Juarez, right?"

"Yeah, that's right. We call it Wazoo." I laughed.

Rick and Ronnie both laughed. They had a kind of closeness I'd observed before in Austin amongst many of the gay guys I'd met. Well, this was the gay capital of the world, so it shouldn't have been a surprise. Didn't matter, we were all in line together, so no reason not to hang out.

Dana and Hector arrived back a little out of breath with a big shopping bag.

"What did you guys get?" I asked reaching for the bag.

"You guys owe us $15 each," Dana said.

"For what?" Tony challenged.

"We bought jackets for all of us," Hector said, "They were having a sale on these nice light jackets. I don't know about you, but I was getting cold in line and I figured it would get colder the longer we were out here."

Actually, that was a pretty good idea. I hadn't noticed until they brought it up, but my arms were covered in goose bumps, and I had been shivering a little.

"Okay, thanks," I said and looked at Tony.

"Yeah, okay, thanks," he said as he reached in his pocket to give Dana the money.

I gave Dana my money, then turned to Rick and Ronnie and made the introductions.

Dana shook Rick and Ronnie's hands, and then glanced at me with a little smirk in his eyes. Yeah, I said with my eyes, they're sweet, but it doesn't matter. He nodded and continued the conversation.

"You guys from here?" Dana asked Rick and Ronnie.

"Yep, born and raised," Ronnie said with Rick nodding his agreement.

"Cool," Dana said as he pulled on his jacket.

"Tony and me are going to Mickey D's around the corner, you guys hungry?" I said to Dana and Hector.

"Yeah, Big Mac and fries," Dana said.

"Same here, thanks," Hector agreed.

I turned to Rick and Ronnie, "Large fries for you?" I nodded to Rick.

"Yep, and bring some fries for Ronnie too. He's going to want some once you guys come back." He reached in his pocket and gave me a five.

"We'll be back in a few," Tony and I wrestled our jackets on and began walking up the street towards the corner.

Once we were out of earshot, "Faggots?" Tony glanced back.

"Yeah." I said, "My 'gaydar' was up when they started talking and touching each other on the arm, but they're harmless."

"Yeah, plus what're they going to do, try to fuck us?" Tony laughed, "I don't think so."

"Nah, they're here to see the movie, just like us," I said. "Plus, I don't think we're they're type." I laughed too.

"Huh, you're probably right," Tony grinned.

We turned the corner to the left as Rick had directed and espied the McDonald's right where he said it would be.

The Mickey D's was nice and warm and we unzipped our jackets as we stood in line.

"These jackets were a good idea," Tony said. "It is starting to get a little chilly."

Looking around the restaurant, I saw most of the people had on light jackets or sweaters. "Yeah, a lot of people are kind of bundled up."

"May I help you sir?" The little white girl behind the counter asked.

"Yeah, two Big Macs with large fries and cokes," I turned to Tony. "What do you want?"

"How about a Quarter Pounder with cheese, large fries and a coke."

I turned back to the counter girl, "And two Quarter Pounders with cheese and two cokes."

"Yes sir, thank you sir," She cocked her McDonald's hat and took our order to the cooks to meet their standard of one minute for each order.

Since being in San Fran, I hadn't detected an ounce of racism or discriminatory attitude from anyone. Not anyone. I knew of

256

the whole Berkeley ultra-liberal movement right across the Bay; the whole Haight-Ashbury hippie thing and of course the gay rights movement. But I just didn't really appreciate how much real bigotry we'd experienced, until I experienced the utter lack of it. This experience was definitely refreshing after some of our other encounters on this trip.

"You forgot the two large fries for the homos." Tony reminded me.

"Stop saying that," I scolded him, "I'll tell her when she gets back with our order."

"Okay," Tony looked chagrined.

The counter girl called the number on our receipt and when I went to get our order with the bags of food and Styrofoam drink carrier, I said, "I'd like to order an additional two large fries. Sorry."

"No problem, that'll be two dollars." She walked right over to the rack of fries in their colorful cardboard packaging, and pulled off two large fries, placed them in another bag and handed it to me.

I gave her the money, and turned back to Tony, "Get some straws and napkins."

"Okay." He complied.

We walked back out and retraced our steps to the theater. By this time, the line from the theater had actually stretched past the entrance to the Mickey D's. Wow, this was going to be some crowd.

When we got back, Dana and Hector were playing chess while Rick and Ronnie looked on, kibitzing on the moves.

We interrupted all the action with our advent and the food. By this time, we'd been in line for about two hours with about another half hour to go. I distributed the food accordingly, and gave Rick his change.

"Hector that was a good idea to get the jackets, it's getting chilly out here," I said as I started on my fries.

"I remember that line from Mark Twain, 'the coldest winter I ever spent was a summer in San Francisco.' And yeah, he wasn't ever lying when he said that." Hector finished.

257

"How erudite you are. I guess you learned something at Eastwood. You're not as dumb as I thought." I chuckled.

"Screw you. What's 'erudite' mean?" Hector asked.

"That's another big assed word Chris learned in college," Tony laughed.

"It means 'smart' or 'well read'" I said.

"In other words, 'youse knows what's youse talkin' 'bout suh," Dana said in his best Stepin Fetchit voice.

We all laughed, and even Rick and Ronnie joined in as they finished off their fries.

"Thanks guys that really hit the spot," Ronnie said. "Thanks for going to get the fries."

"No problem," I said. "Thanks for the directions."

"You guys *Star Wars* fans?" Ronnie was becoming chatty.

"Not really," I said not wanting to be associated with the geeks in line, "But, I am a fan of *Star Trek*, and this movie looked really cool."

"Yeah, 'I Grok Spock'" Rick laughed.

The other three Transmanauts had puzzled looks on their faces, as if to say, "What the fuck is he talking about?"

"Heinlein, *Stranger in a Strange Land,* the concept of Grok," I answered their unspoken question.

"You Grok?" Rick laughed.

"I Grok," I said, "I'm into Heinlein, Edgar Rice Burroughs and the Mars series, Clarke, Asimov, Philip K. Dick, Bradbury, H.G. Wells, and Frank Herbert. I just finished *Dune* not too long ago. It took me a while to get through it, but I loved it."

"Oh yeah, I loved *Dune*. You're really into sci-fi aren't you?" Rick said.

"Yep, in fact, my brother and I saw *2001: A Space Odyssey* at this very theater in 1969. Coming here to see *Star Wars* is almost like a homage to 2001." I looked at Dana who shrugged his shoulders. This could have been the theater back then, who knows? It made for a good story.

"Wow, that's pretty cool." Rick said.

Ronnie tapped Rick on the shoulder, "I think the line is starting to move."

He was right. We gathered all our trash and Dana ran it over to the nearest garbage can as the line began to move.

There was a palpable electric shock that ran through the crowd as the line began to move. The chatter got louder and louder as we got closer to the box office and the front doors.

The theater workers in their purple pants and gold jackets looked like they were bracing themselves for the onslaught. When the main doors swung open, people stormed in to get their seats.

"Over here!" Hector yelled over the din, pointing at seats about halfway from the front of the theater and slightly to the left of center.

"Got it," I yelled back. I gestured to Tony and Dana to follow Hector as we ran to our seats.

We didn't see Rick and Ronnie again; presumably they ended up somewhere closer to the front.

People ran into the theater like they were looking for gold; it was all pretty exciting. The excitement had built up while all these people were waiting in line and it just exploded when they let us in.

We didn't waste our money on popcorn or drinks because we had just eaten dinner in line. Once we got settled in our seats and got our jackets off, we could feel the buildup of excitement in the air. The chatter of voices in the theater rose as the anticipation increased to see this futuristic and "once-in-a-lifetime" movie.

We were going to be the first ones to see the movie of anyone we knew in El Paso. A movie we hoped lived up to all the hype.

A hushed silence moved across the audience when the theater got dark in anticipation of the start of the movie. We suffered through whatever teasers or trailers were shown, but it really didn't matter because we were there to see *Star Wars*. And then, on the screen, maybe one of the largest movie screens I've ever seen, "**A long time ago, in a galaxy far far away…**" And then – DUN, DUN DUN DUN DUN! And the signature *Star Wars* logo filled the screen with the signature music, blasting out of the Dolby Sound and surround-sound speakers, filling the theater with a cacophony of music.

As my mind was grasping the music, the story began to scroll from the front of the screen into the distance. I'd never seen anything like this, and the best was yet to come.

The very first scene of *Star Wars* blew my mind! Across the screen was this huge "Star Destroyer" firing energy weapons at a smaller ship. As a fan of *Star Trek* I had seen all the *Star Trek* episodes, and I was very familiar with the Klingon War Birds, the Romulan Birds of Prey, and all the other alien space craft from the various episodes. Of course, the Enterprise, NCC-1701, was like my very own vehicle; but what I saw on the screen, the detail, the sheer scope of it, was almost mind boggling. I was captivated. I looked at the other three guys and they were mesmerized as well.

Stunning sounds of space battles and the soaring musical score reverberated throughout the theater. The only sounds we made as we sat and watched the action unfolding on the screen were sounds of awe:

"Damn!"

"Whoa!"

"Wow!"

"Did you see that?"

"What is that?"

"Is this for real?"

"Yes!"

Alien space craft, light sabers, ships going into hyper-drive, alien creatures, alien beings, and various other-worldly scenes shot across the screen and stretched our imaginations beyond previous limits. We were fans of The Force and instantly sided with the Rebel Alliance, Luke Skywalker, Princess Leia, and Obi-Wan Kenobi. We hated the Empire and the malignant malevolence of Darth Vader, and laughed at the antics of R2-D2 and C-3PO.

We were devastated when the Death Star destroyed Alderaan, the home planet of Princess Leia. We were Luke Skywalker, and we wanted to be Jedi Knights. And when Luke made the "kill shot" that destroyed the Death Star after the miraculous and improbable counter-attack by Han Solo, we cheered and clapped as did the whole audience. And when the beautiful Princess Leia presented medals of valor to Luke, Han and Chewbacca, the Wookie, the audience again cheered and clapped as the scene cut away to the credits and the rousing chorus of the *Star Wars* theme music.

As the lights came on, we sat glued to our seats, exhausted from all the excitement. What a movie experience.

I looked around the theater and we weren't the only ones still sitting in our seats. It was almost as if no one wanted to leave the theater and lose the magic of the moment.

"Damn guys, that was a hell of a movie!" I turned to the other three.

"Yeah, and I'm not even a sci-fi guy and that was a great movie," Tony agreed.

"Well worth the wait," Hector said. "What'd you think Dana?"

"One of the best movies I've ever seen. I wouldn't mind seeing it again, like right now."

"Only if you want to stand in line another three hours." I laughed. "You guys ready to leave?"

"Yeah, let's go," Dana said as we started to file out of our row towards the exit.

Outside, the line again snaked around the block for the next showing. I was glad we had seen the earlier showing, it was even colder than it was earlier. A lot of people were bundled up in coats and jackets, and there seemed to be more adults in the line than when we stood there.

"Where'd you park?" Dana asked.

"Down the block this way." I started walking down the block to the parking lot where Tony and I had left the car.

As we got into the Trans Am, I looked around the car. "You

know, this could be like the "land speeder" that Luke piloted on Tatooine."

"And who are you, Luke Skywalker?" Tony asked.

"Yeah, and you're Chewbacca the Wookie," I shot back.

"Fuck you Chris," Tony laughed with Dana and Hector.

I pulled out of the parking lot, and aimed the Trans-Am down the hill to the hotel.

"So who's Princess Leia?" Dana asked continuing the conversation.

"Aurianna?" Hector suggested. "'Help me Obi-Won, you're my only hope.'" He mimicked Princess Leia in a falsetto voice.

Dana chuckled. "So that would make me Luke Skywalker. Maybe Chris is Obi-Won Kenobi, and Uncle Rudi is Darth Vader?"

We all laughed at that comparison.

"So who am I?" Hector asked, "That only leaves Han Solo. I'm down with that, he saves the day at the end."

"Tony can you make that Wookie sound? Aargh awoo!" I howled.

"Shut up Chris." Tony poked me in the side.

We rolled up to a stoplight.

"Watch, I'll go into hyper-drive like Han Solo in the Millennium Falcon," I said, and I took off with a screech of the tires trying to hit 0-60 in less than seven seconds.

"Yeah!" Everyone cheered.

"Do it Chris, do it!" Dana yelled.

And I did it, and we went into hyper-space all the way down the street to the hotel.

Obviously we knew it was just a movie, but it changed our perception of how movies were made, how they could look, how they could sound, and just the sheer fun of watching this type of movie. It was a great movie, and it was great fun.

May The Force be with us.

Arrested

The next morning we put San Francisco in our rearview mirror. The City by the Bay had met all our expectations for a cosmopolitan city offering a plethora of experiences and diversity in cultures and people.

I consulted with Dana on the drive away from the hotel, "What's the best way back to LA?"

"I-5," Dana said as he looked at the Trip Tik.

"Yeah, maybe we don't want to use the PHC," Tony chirped from the back.

"Uh huh, I'm sure you're still a little nervous about that APB that's probably out on your sorry ass." I laughed.

"That's no joke," Hector chortled, "Thanks to Tony we're probably all wanted men."

"I-5," Dana reiterated, "But we gotta take 101 to 580, then towards I-5. We're going to bypass San Jose this time."

"Good idea," I said as I steered the sleek black and gold land speeder towards the red, white and blue signs for I-580 via the 101. We were on our way to Los Angeles and Universal Studios.

We covered the almost four hundred miles to Los Angeles in a little over six hours speeding along with the mid-day interstate traffic along I-5.

As we approached the outskirts of LA we saw signs for I-210, which ran through Fontana.

Our navigator recognized that fact. "You think we can go by

Aurianna's house?" Dana asked, "It's right down 210, not too far away."

"Aurianna, Aurianna, Aurianna, that's all you've talked about as we got closer to LA," Hector needled Dana. "She's really got your nose wide open, doesn't she?"

"Yeah, the guy who swore he wouldn't let any girl get to him, has been got," Tony piled on.

"What about that Dana?" I asked, "Aurianna got your nose wide open?"

"I don't even know what that means," Dana said defensively. "I just know I haven't met anyone like her before and I want to see her again before we leave California."

"Or what, you gonna die?" Tony mocked in an Italian accent.

"Poor Dana," Hector said as he ran his thumb over his index finger in the universal sign of the "smallest violin." He and Tony laughed.

"Oh woe is me," Hector played his finger violin.

"Okay, okay," Dana said. "I knew I shouldn't have said shit to you guys."

I laughed. "But you did, so your secret is out. I tell you what, we can go by Aurianna's house and see if she's there. And if she's not, you can leave her a note."

"Okay," Dana seemed appeased.

"Then," I continued, "we can go by the Blanchard sisters' house and see if Debbie is around," I looked in the rearview mirror at Hector. "That okay with you guys?"

"Yeah baby." Tony was all for it.

"Definitely," Hector said, "I wouldn't mind seeing any of the sisters again."

"Alright, that's what we'll do," I said, and took the next exit to I-210 East towards Fontana.

I headed towards Fontana, flowing with the afternoon traffic. Dana kept consulting his Trip Tik for the route to Aurianna's

264

house.

"Okay, get off at this next exit," he barked.

"Hey man, calm down," I said. "I know you're anxious, but be cool, okay?"

"Okay. Turn here, left."

I missed the turn.

"No, no, left, I said," Dana hissed.

"I got it Dana," I was getting a little annoyed at his anxiousness. He was fidgeting with the map and constantly looking out the window like he might catch a glimpse of Aurianna walking along the street or something.

I made another famous U-turn to get us back on track.

"Okay, get ready to make a right at the next light," Dana ordered.

"Damn Dana, don't have a heart attack. She'll be there." Hector poked Dana in the back.

"Shut up Hector," Dana said.

Whoa, I thought, *He's really got it bad. He's never like this, especially not about some girl he barely met.*

"How much farther?" I asked.

"Not too much," Dana said. "We should recognize some of the landmarks pretty soon."

"Yeah, okay, I think I remember that turn up there," I said peering down the street.

"Make a right up there and follow that street to its end, then make a left, and we should see her house." Dana directed.

"You mean her farm, right?" Tony joked.

"Shut up Tony." Dana snarled.

Huh, I thought, *What happened to 'bros before ho's'?*

"Okay Dana, almost there." I tried to pacify him a little after his outburst. I looked over at him and he was straining against his seatbelt looking for Aurianna's house.

"There it is!" Dana exclaimed, "Hurry up!"

I pulled the car into the familiar yard and noticed a distinct lack of activity. Nothing moved, not even any of the livestock on the grounds.

"I don't think anyone's home," I said to Dana's back as he leapt out of the barely stationary car. I rolled down the windows to watch him in action.

He raced up the steps to the front door as the three of us watched open-mouthed. This was not the Dana we knew; he had it bad for Aurianna.

"No one's home," he wailed after knocking several times.

"Alright, leave a note with your address and phone number." I yelled from my open window.

"I already gave her my address in El Paso and at West Point," Dana yelled.

"Then leave her a note letting her know we came by," I said.

"Okay," Dana said contritely. He came back to the car to get a piece of paper and a pen to write out a short note to Aurianna.

"Make sure you sign it 'Love Dana.'" Tony snickered.

"Shut up Tony," Dana said as he wrote. "Are we coming back this way?" he asked.

"No, I don't see it," I said. "Universal Studios is way on the other side of LA and we're only supposed to be here a couple of days before heading back. Sorry."

"Hopefully, she'll write." Dana said resignedly.

"I'm sure she will," I said. *Anyone who tried to get him to go to Disneyland at the expense of her best friend is going to write,* I thought. *She had it just as bad for him as he had for her. Maybe it wasn't so bad she wasn't home. No telling what her mother might have done if she saw Dana again.*

Dana placed the note in the crack of the door with the frame and walked dejectedly back to the car. "Let's go," he said once he was belted in.

I backed out of the yard as Dana looked forlornly back at the house. He kept his eyes on the house until we turned the corner and it was no longer in view.

We took I-15 to 215 to get to Riverside. I was fairly familiar with the route and didn't need Dana's navigation skills. He wasn't much help anyway, as he sat silently immersed in his own thoughts.

The trip to the Blanchard house took almost an hour because of rush hour traffic. As I turned onto their block Tony and Hector woke up from their stupor and got a little excited at the prospect of seeing the Blanchards.

"Who gets to ring the doorbell?" Tony asked.

"You can do it," I said. "Since Hector lost his privileges when he lost his cookies at the party." I chuckled.

"Okay, okay, rub it in Chris. Fuck you Tony, I should ring the doorbell," Hector argued.

"Nope, I'm going," Tony said, and pushed my seat up as I put the car in Park.

"Hold on dammit, let me get out first, damn," I scowled.

"Hurry up," Tony said.

"You've got it as bad as Dana," Hector said.

"No one's got it that bad," Tony said as he wormed his way out the door.

"You're probably right," I said as I glanced over at Dana.

Dana just sat in his seat and didn't rise to the bait as we talked about him. I knew then, he was really upset because he didn't see Aurianna and I wasn't going to tease him anymore.

Tony reached the front door and I could see him ringing the bell repeatedly, but no one came to the door. Tony looked back with a questioning look.

"Don't worry about it," I yelled.

"You want to leave a note?" Tony called back.

"Nah, let's just go," I said.

267

Tony returned to the car and got in slowly. "Damn, no one here, Aurianna wasn't home, I guess we're just shit out of luck."

Couldn't have said it better myself. Yeah, the magic of LA was gone.

On our way out of Riverside we were stopped at a light when a Camaro pulled up next to us. It was an older version, but it looked like it had been "souped up" with its raised back end and larger, drag racing tires.

The driver, a young white guy, looked over and revved up his engine, the normal sign of wanting to race. That was part of that California drag racing culture. Well, you know I had to step up to that challenge. I revved my engine, and we prepared ourselves for another race.

We were in a somewhat populated area, near Riverside, where there was traffic on the road. But there wasn't much traffic in front of us, and no police in the area, so it looked clear to go. The light changed to green and we took off. I hit 80 miles per hour in seconds and was ahead of the other car when an older gray-haired lady, driving a Ford Pinto or some such car pulled out of an intersection directly in front of us.

"Oh shit!" Hector yelled from the back seat. "Watch out Chris!"

Damn, even without the warning, I was already reacting to this car pulling out in front of us. She was coming out from my right going across to my left. I made a lightning decision to swerve to my right in front of the car we were racing, with the pedal pushed all the way down to keep us accelerating past the Camaro and to avoid the Pinto. There was no light at that intersection, only a stop sign for cross-traffic which the Pinto driver either ignored or completely misjudged our speed coming down the street. Thank goodness for quick responses and my philosophy of defensive driving – "Anticipate the most stupid thing a driver will do, because they will probably do it, and that way you won't be surprised."

Whenever we raced, I always kept an eye out for cross-traffic and luckily, this time I was able to react. Whew! After that race, my heartbeat was racing – Dana just looked relieved.

I looked back at Tony and Hector and asked, "You guys okay?"

They looked a little shaken, but they started laughing and high-fiving because we had avoided death and destruction on that day, and we would live to race again.

I don't even remember what happened to the Camaro, we left him so far behind. Everyone in the car was just glad that one was over.

Later that day, as we drove towards Universal City to buy our tickets for Universal Studios, a cool red Corvette pulled up next to us at a stop light. The car was nice. It was a convertible and just looked ridiculously fast. The white guy behind the wheel wearing his obligatory cool shades, looked at us over his shades and honked his horn. He looked like he could have been an actor with his chiseled good looks and perfectly coiffed brown hair. His hair didn't seem to move, even in the convertible.

Dana turned to look at me, "I think he wants to race."

"Yeah, but I don't know if I can beat a 'Vette."

Tony and Hector both said, "Hey, c'mon man, let's take him!"

Right at that time, the light changed and I still hadn't decided. The 'Vette took off in a squeal of tires and smoke from his jackrabbit start, but I played it cool and did not take off immediately. I cruised up to the next light and politely waved at the guy. Yep, I chickened out on that one. I knew he could blow my doors off, and I wasn't going to give him the satisfaction of beating the "flavor of the month" in American cars – my black and gold special edition Trans Am.

"Man, you should have raced him," Hector chided me.

"Forget about it, there'll be other opportunities to race," I said. And, yes there were other opportunities.

After we bought our tickets for Universal Studios, we decided to hang out in Van Nuys, and cruise that most celebrated of Boulevards. We stayed in a hotel, this time, the Holiday Inn, of course, because we had overstayed our welcome at Aunt Rose's house. We had resigned ourselves to the fact that nothing exciting was going to happen between buying the tickets and going to

Universal Studios, and we looked forward to ending the trip on a good note before heading back to El Paso. Little did we know, we were in for the longest night of the entire road trip.

We cruised down Van Nuys Boulevard early in the evening on that day before we went to Universal Studios, that first day back in LA. There were a lot of cars driving up and down the Boulevard, mostly being driven by white guys with their girlfriends. Not many people of color driving, and certainly not anyone driving a car like mine. So we cruised a little, then we went off to dinner and drove around to pass the time. It was a nice night out and we were driving with our windows down, taking in the sights and sounds of the street.

When we came back down the Boulevard, it was pretty late because there weren't many cars out, and the Boulevard seemed almost deserted. We were returning back in the direction of the hotel when we came to a stoplight where an older white car was waiting on the light to turn green. The car was either an Oldsmobile Special or GTO, or a Pontiac Grand Prix. The driver was a young white guy with some Asian-looking guy in the passenger side.

He yelled out his window. "You wanna run?!" I didn't immediately respond, so he yelled again. "I'm gonna kick your ass!"

A definite challenge. But I wasn't really looking for any action, so initially I declined by shaking my head.

"C'mon Chris, you can take this guy," Hector implored.

"Yeah, don't wimp out. Damn you're on Van Nuys Boulevard, it doesn't get any better than this," Tony poked me in the side.

"Naw, I really don't feel like racing," I said, and was ready to move on to the hotel.

Then the white guy yelled, "You're a pussy and your car ain't shit, you candy-assed motherfucker!"

Dana looked at me expectantly.

Okay, I couldn't back away from that challenge, because I wasn't a pussy and I wasn't a "candy-assed motherfucker."

Oh yeah, it was on! "Fuck you," I yelled. "Let's run!"

"Yes!" Everybody cheered. "Let's do this!"

When the light turned green, I went into hyperspace. I took off faster than ever before. The tires squealed in a cloud of black smoke as I hit 100 in this 40 mile zone. I was going to show this numb-nuts white boy my rear end lights in a hurry.

All I saw was white lines and green lights whizzing by. I was so focused on driving that the whole world telescoped into a tunnel down the Boulevard. The effect in my mind was just like the effect of the space cruisers in Star Wars, when they went into hyperspace, and about as fast. At least in my mind, anyway.

The traffic lights were synchronized because they were all green and there weren't any cars in the way. I zoomed about a mile down the Boulevard before I slowed down and came out of hyper space to make the left turn for the hotel located right off the Boulevard. Everybody cheered. It had been a wild ride, but we had beaten the blowhard and it was time to go back to the hotel and get some sleep.

I didn't even see the other car, and that's when I noticed that we seemed to be the stars in a high speed police chase right out of *Adam-12*. As we came to a stop at the stoplight to make the left turn to the hotel, I heard the amplified voice of a police officer from the grill of the police car that had come up directly behind us, **"GET OUT OF THE CAR WITH YOUR HANDS UP!"**

OHHH! SHIT! I thought. This was for real, and yeah, they actually say that shit in real life.

Dana looked wildly around at all the police cars, "Oh shit, we're in big fucking trouble Chris!"

Yeah, no shit!

Tony and Hector were both looking through the rear window at what looked like half the Van Nuys police force.

"What the fuck is going on Chris?" Hector yelled.

"I don't want to be arrested," Tony wailed.

"Shut up," I hissed. "Everybody just be cool. I'm going to get out and find out what's going on."

I looked around the car and made a mental inventory of what

we had in the car and my mind locked on the machete I had under my seat. *Oh shit,* I thought, *if they find that we'll really be in trouble.*

I put the car in park and slowly got out with my hands up. Damn, there were a lot of cops surrounding my car! There were all these police cars with their lights flashing, and several police officers with their handguns drawn and they all seemed to be pointing at me! They had also pulled over the white car and I saw the driver already in handcuffs. Apparently they had caught him before me, I mean, you know, I had outraced him.

The first white officer who approached with his gun in his right hand said, "Put your hands behind your back." He pushed me forward with his free hand so that my torso was bent over the hood of my car, and my face was smooshed against that big beautiful gold firebird on the hood. I heard another cop yell at the other Transmanauts to put their hands up, and I saw him point a gun at the passenger side window.

In my defenseless position another officer searched me, while the first one covered me with his revolver in the normal combat firing stance. I observed all this coolly as I took inventory of my situation.

About that time a bottle crashed on the sidewalk next to my car.

"Who threw that bottle?" The first cop yelled.

"I don't know," I shouted. All the Transmanauts were in the car and the other guy was in cuffs. Shit, I didn't know who could have thrown the damn bottle.

All the police now went to a heightened state after the bottle-throwing incident. That didn't bode well for me and the other Transmanauts.

The second cop roughly pulled my wallet, with my driver's license, out of my back pocket. My license identified me as an upstanding citizen of the great State of Texas from El Paso. I wonder if that somehow kept them from really getting ugly with us. You know, since we weren't their garden variety thugs from the Hood. I'm sure it could have been a lot worse, but it was bad enough as it was.

Once the second cop took my wallet and handed it to another cop – who went to Dana's side of the car to join the policeman who had his gun trained on the three Transmanauts, another cop slapped a pair of cuffs on me, and kept my head down on the hood where I could watch what happened in the car.

Hector and Tony were petrified – with their hands high in the air for all the cops to see. They were hyperventilating and wild-eyed, staring at all the guns pointing at them. This whole scene was surreal. Maybe the cops thought they had a bunch of fleeing felons or something. Or maybe they were just bored on a slow night, because it seemed like every cop within miles was at the scene of a fairly minor traffic stop.

The cop who had approached Dana's window commanded, "Keep your hands where I can see them and give me the registration."

Dana kept his hands in plain view as required, and when he complied with the police officer's demand for the registration Dana loudly said, "I AM GOING TO OPEN THE GLOVE COMPARTMENT TO GET THE REGISTRATION." He slowly moved his hands towards the glove compartment on the passenger side of the dashboard.

He opened up the glove compartment and stated, "I AM LOOKING FOR THE REGISTRATION IN THE GLOVE COMPARTMENT." After looking in the glove compartment he said, "I CAN'T FIND THE REGISTRATION; IT'S NOT IN THE GLOVE COMPARTMENT."

Oh shit! We're all going to jail now! I thought, and pictured all of us behind bars calling our parents in Texas. Shit.

Dana looked at the two cops at his window, "I'M GOING TO LOOK UNDER MY SEAT TO SEE IF THE REGISTRATION IS THERE." Dana definitely did not want to be shot, and I'm sure visions of his early and untimely demise danced in his head. If this wasn't so serious, and if this cop didn't have a .357 Magnum pointed at Dana's head, this would have been pretty funny.

Actually, it *was* pretty funny. We were all fans of Richard Pryor, the undisputed king of comedy. In one of his routines, he describes a police stop while he was driving his car, and he describes how he was looking for his wallet for identification. In his routine, he describes how he loudly announces his actions before he moves his hands because the police have their guns drawn and pointed at him. This was sort of the bible for black men on how to deal with police during a traffic stop.

I almost laughed as I watched Dana go through his version of a Richard Pryor routine. Sometimes, life imitates art.

As Dana slowly moved his hands under his seat, I saw the cop with the gun at his window tighten up a little. He looked concerned because he couldn't see what Dana was going to pull from under his seat.

Dana tried to allay his fears by saying with relief in his voice, and again in a loud voice, "I FOUND THE REGISTRATION UNDER THE SEAT. I AM NOW TAKING THE REGISTRATION OUT FROM UNDER THE SEAT."

This was the moment of truth – I saw the cop tensing because anything could come up from under the seat, either a gun or a piece of paper. Lucky for all of us, it was a piece of paper. Yeah, real lucky, because had the cops decided to search the vehicle they would have found my famous machete under the driver's seat.

Dana handed the registration to the police officer who compared the name on the registration with my confiscated driver's license. Whew! Another catastrophe had been avoided.

There was no field sobriety test. I guess they were able to determine pretty quickly that I wasn't drunk or under the influence of drugs or alcohol.

"Alright, it looks like the car belongs to you," the police officer said to me.

274

He handed Dana the registration. "You need to get behind the wheel and follow us to the police station," he directed Dana.

That police officer gave my wallet to the police officer who'd handcuffed me, then he got into another car while the other police officer grabbed me by the scruff of my T-shirt and pulled me up from the hood.

"Let's go." He led me over the police car directly behind the Trans Am. He opened the driver's side car door and pushed my head down as I got in the back seat.

He slammed the door behind me and walked around to the passenger side as his partner, the first cop to get me out of the Trans Am, got in behind the wheel. He made a quick U-turn as only cops can and proceeded to drive to the police station.

I turned around and saw the Trans Am dutifully following the police car. I looked around the inside of the police car and was blocked from a clear view of the police officers because of the steel grate dividing the cops from the perps – like me. The inside of the police car wasn't as bad as I thought it would be. I thought it might be full of piss or vomit, or worse.

During the ride to the police station, the guy who'd handcuffed me tried to engage me in conversation.

He turned a little to his left as he spoke, "You all were going pretty fast down Van Nuys," he looked at his partner for confirmation. "About 100 in a 40 mile zone. The only reason we caught you was you slowed down to make the left turn, otherwise we might not have caught you." He laughed.

The driver spoke up, "The other guy had been drinking and this was his second time, so he's going to jail for awhile. You're lucky you don't have a record or you'd be joining him." He laughed too.

Yeah, yuk it up motherfuckers.

The passenger side cop took up the conversation, "You guys from Texas, right?"

"Yes," I said looking forward.

"What are you guys doing in LA?"

"Sightseeing. We've been to LA and San Francisco and now LA again. This was a graduation road trip for the four of us." I wondered if somehow my *Miranda* rights were being violated. I was definitely in a custodial situation and no one had read me my rights and now this soft interrogation.

"Oh yeah? Where did you graduate from?"

"The University of Texas. I'm a newly commissioned second lieutenant in the Army, and I'm starting law school in the fall at

Texas."

"Really? That's pretty impressive…huh." He turned back around and stopped pumping me for information.

I think he was surprised by what I told him, but I'm pretty sure he believed me because he seemed to accord me some respect, probably more than he would have had I been your typical drug dealer or gang banger.

Undaunted, I asked, "What's the best way to get to Universal Studios?" Obviously I was pretty naïve; I figured we were still going to Universal Studios the next day.

"Why do you want to know?" Passenger side cop asked.

"We've got tickets for tomorrow, and we're looking forward to going."

"Yeah, well, you may want to rethink those plans. You may be our guests for a couple of days if your friends can't post bail for you." He laughed.

I guess this shit was just too funny for this motherfucker. Sumba bitch. I thought.

We finally drove into the police station parking lot. As the police officer pulled me out of the car, I saw the Trans Am parked to the side with the Transmanauts watching me with horrified expressions. The two police officers escorted me in the station and began the booking process.

The images were a kaleidoscope in my mind. The first stop was the front desk. A tall monolithic piece of furniture with a balding, fat, police sergeant entrenched in a high-backed chair who looked at me like he was a deity pronouncing judgment on me down below.

"What's your name?" He asked reaching for my driver's license from the booking officer.

"Chris," I said.

"It says Robert on here," he countered.

"Middle name is Christan, like it says on there," I shot back.

"I'm going to keep your wallet until they let you out of here.

Awright, take him on back," he scowled down at me.

This was starting to piss me off. There wasn't anything I could do about it, but endure the process of being treated like some common criminal.

The next stop in this kaleidoscope was the photo booth. The booking officer, the first police officer on the scene, said, "Stand over there, in front of the lined wall."   He uncuffed me for the obligatory mug shots.

I rubbed my wrists and looked at the wall he indicated and saw where there were lines on the wall depicting heights from 5' 0" all the way to 7' 0" – damn, who were they expecting Wilt the Stilt?

I walked over and stood in front of the wall looking forward.

"Hold on," the officer said. He was putting my name on a little board with a black felt background with white letters one at a time.

"That's two 'T's," I said, watching as he misspelled my last name.

"Okay." He looked a little miffed that I had pointed out his mistake. "Hold this up under your chin," he directed.

I took the board from him and saw my name and a number in white letters. I placed it under my chin holding it with both hands and waited.

"Face front," he ordered.

I complied as he snapped the picture.

"Turn right," he again ordered, "and keep the board facing forward."

I turned to my right, executing a perfect right face maneuver. *Damn*, I thought, *I'm really being booked. This isn't some sort of dream I'm going to wake up from; this is for real.* It took taking my picture to make that fact sink in to my stunned brain.

The booking officer strode over and took the board from my hands, "Now we're going to get your fingerprints. Ever been fingerprinted?"

"Yeah, when I got commissioned."

"Oh, yeah, you're supposed to be an Army second lieutenant." He snickered.

Fuck you, I thought, *I am a motherfuckin' second lieutenant, and one of these fuckin' days you're going to know all about it, sumba bitch.* I didn't say anything, and endured the fingerprinting process in silence.

"Give me your right hand." The officer took my hand and put each finger and thumb on a black ink pad, then rolled it on the fingerprint paper to give five perfect finger prints.

"Other hand," he ordered. He took my left hand and repeated the process. I was now in the California criminal justice system.

He handed me a bottle with some sort of fluid and a rag, "Clean your hands."

I wiped off my hands and once I was finished, he said, "Put your hands behind your back."

I complied and he handcuffed me again. He grabbed me by the left arm as he "perp walked" me farther back into the station.

Initially, I hadn't paid much attention to my environment, but now that the kaleidoscope had slowed down, I began to focus on my surroundings.

The first thing I noticed was the noise – the cacophony of police officers screaming at prisoners and the yelling of prisoners and newly arrested suspects. A close second to assault my senses was the smell – the pungent vomitus smell of drunken guys unable to hold it all in, to the sharp, sour pissy smell of guys who couldn't wait, and the smell of fear, sweat and anger that permeated every foot of this place. Damn.

The booking officer led me past several holding cells where temporary prisoners were pacing or holding on to the bars or sitting morosely on benches. I thought, *Oh hell no, I do not want to be in that motherfucker with those guys.*

I think the booking officer was fucking with me a little bit because he hesitated in front of one of those zoo-like cages, smiled at me, then led me to a six-foot long bench where there were three sets of manacles.

Two of the sets of manacles, one on each end of the bench, were occupied. The one in the middle was available, and that looked like my place for the foreseeable future.

The officer said, "You sit there, in the middle." He pushed me down to the bench. "This is temporary. Your friends indicated they'll be back soon to bail you out, so you don't need to be in one of the holding cells."

Thank God, I thought and said a little prayer of thanks.

Then he snatched up one of the chains attached to the bench and snapped it on my handcuffs so that I was sitting on the edge of the bench with my hands handcuffed behind me with the chain holding my hands in place so I couldn't move very far in any direction. Shit.

"There you go," he said. "Enjoy yourself." He looked at the other two guys. "Leave him alone guys." He walked off laughing.

"Fuck him," I whispered tugging on my manacles. I felt like Charlton Heston on the Roman warship chained to his oars – with hate in his eyes.

I again focused on my surroundings. The noise seemed to increase, as, I guess, the police were making their rounds of the less law abiding citizens of the night. Unfortunately, two of those less law abiding night people were chained to the bench next to me. The guy to my right was a white guy and a drug dealer; and to my left, another white guy, who was a pimp. I glanced over at the drug dealer, this scrawny-looking, pale-faced white guy with dark hair. He was wearing a faded T-shirt with some sports logo, grungy jeans, and black Converse tennis shoes. The pimp was dressed better than the drug dealer – he was a pimp after all. He was slender, also with dark hair, and was wearing a pair of black slacks with matching black vest over a white dress shirt; black dress shoes and white socks. He looked like he should have been wearing a bowler on his head or something similar, like Malcolm McDowell in *A Clockwork Orange.*

The pimp turned and looked at me, "What are you in for?" he asked

"Reckless driving. I was doing 100 in a 40-mile zone, and the cops pulled me over."

They both laughed. I guess they thought that was pretty funny. Maybe I should have told them I had shot someone for a little more respect. Unlike them, I wasn't a hardened criminal, nor had I ever seen the inside of a jail, at least not like this.

I guess I had been influenced by too many movies about drug dealers and pimps, and these guys did not fit the bill. Well for one thing, they were white; and second, they weren't flamboyant and flashy like Super Fly or pimps in the movies like *Magnum Force* with their garish clothes and ridiculous cars. I didn't know if they really were in for what they said, but I played along with them. Regardless of why they were there, they had a good time laughing at me because I was chained to the same bench as them, two self-proclaimed hardened criminals. I did wonder, though, why they weren't in one of the holding cells. At least they seemed to have significantly more extensive criminal histories than me, and there I was, looking like I had robbed a 7-11, but in reality was there for speeding. Yeah, hardy har har!

As the leader of the Transmanauts, it was my responsibility to keep us safe and out of trouble. Yet here I was, in jail, waiting to get bailed out. This was definitely not one of the experiences we had anticipated for this road trip. As I sat there chained to that bench, a couple of things happened while I contemplated my fate. The first was my decision to practice criminal law once I graduated law school. Now that I knew what it was like to be treated as a criminal, I figured I would make an effective criminal defense attorney and defend guys who found themselves in the position that I found myself. The second thing that happened was an encounter with this red-haired cop.

As I was sitting there, the red-haired cop stopped in front of me. He was a pretty big white guy, festooned in all his law enforcement regalia, and was sporting a shotgun on his shoulder.

He looked down at me, "So this is the guy who had half the police force chasing him down the Boulevard!" He started laughing as he walked away.

The supposed drug dealer looked at me with a new-found

respect, "So how many pigs were after you?"

"About twelve cars," I said, "and when they busted me there were about five guys around my car." I bragged.

"Damn, that's a lot of motherfuckers," he said.

"That's nothing," the pimp said, "I had that many fuckin' with me when they hauled my ass in here."

"How'd they bust you?" The drug dealer asked.

"Ah man, they came knockin' down my door last night talkin' some shit about me pimpin' and shit, and they had an arrest warrant and shit."

"Any of yo' ho's with you?" The drug dealer seemed interested in how the pimp got busted. I just listened to this exchange thinking, maybe I didn't want to defend these kinds of guys.

"Naw man, I was by myself. I think one of my bitches turned me in. If I find her, I'm gonna kill that bitch."

"Shit man, they gonna get you out?" The pusher asked.

"Yeah, they should be postin' bail anytime now," the pimp replied.

That got me to thinking, while I languished on that bench. I hoped Dana, Hector and Tony were desperately trying to raise bail to get me out of here.

I was on that bench for about an hour when the cop who booked me came back, "Your friends posted the $125 bail, and you're free to go. You and your friends need to leave Van Nuys tomorrow." He unchained me from the bench, and then uncuffed my hands as I stood there.

"Uh, okay," I said as I rubbed my wrists. "But remember, I told you we have non-refundable tickets to Universal Studios tomorrow, or I guess today, so can we leave like the day after?"

He looked at the other two guys sitting there, and said, "Since your crime was reckless driving, and not drugs or pimping, you can go to Universal Studios. But you guys have to leave town after that."

"Okay," I said as I followed him out to the waiting area. Standing out there were the other Transmanauts. I was so happy to see Dana, Tony and Hector waiting for me I almost cried. I knew that the $125 they paid to get me out was a good chunk of the money we had left. So the cop's edict about leaving soon didn't matter, we didn't have much money to hang around anyway.

The sergeant at the desk returned my wallet to me, and then I turned to my relieved friends. We all hugged and hurried out of the police station before they changed their minds about letting me out. I walked back out to the car and nothing looked as beautiful as the Trans Am at 2 o'clock in the morning in the Van Nuys police department parking lot. We didn't get in using our normal Transmanautic style; we just got in with an air of weariness from the long day.

When we finally got back to the hotel, we had a lot to talk about and to laugh about. That's when I got their version of what happened in the car and why it took so long to get me out.

"Man, we were so scared when they pulled you out of the car and when I saw all those cops and cars and guns…man!" Hector spit out.

"Yo man, when you were ordered out of the car, you know they ordered the rest of us to hold our hands up. That was scary with all the guns and shit." Tony said.

"This was just like one of Richard Pryor's old comedy albums," Hector laughed.

"Yeah except it was for real." Dana laughed.

Tony was pretty silent through all this. "What's wrong with you Tony?" I asked.

282

"Man, I thought we were dead with all the police around like that," he stammered.

"Tony was crying like a little girl next to me in the back seat, but none of us were laughing." Hector explained.

"This was some serious shit," Dana began, "I was thinking about you going to jail, and what was I going to tell Mom, and law school and going to West Point, and all that. And when they put you in handcuffs and I couldn't find the registration and that guy had his gun on me…damn, I just knew our shit was over." Dana laughed in relief. "After they booked you they told us your bail would be $125. We didn't have it in cash so we had to go find some place that would cash our traveler's checks this late at night."

Hector picked up the story, "Thank goodness we finally found a little store a few miles away open this late at night that could cash our traveler's checks so we could bail your ass out. But it took a while to find the place."

"Yeah man, I was so happy to see you finally walk out of there I wanted to shout," Tony said.

"It's good you didn't, they may have put us all in there," I said.

"What was that shit like Chris?" Hector asked.

I described to them all about the sights, smells and sounds of being incarcerated. I also told them about the supposed drug dealer and pimp chained to me on the bench and our conversation about how the pimp got busted.

"Damn, that's some serious shit Chris," Hector said.

"Yeah, but kind of funny too." Tony laughed.

"You know what was funny? Dana going through his Richard Pryor routine." I laughed.

We laughed at that, mostly out of relief that we'd survived the ordeal.

"You know this whole thing just about broke us. We've probably got about $150 left for the rest of the trip." Dana said changing the subject back to more serious issues.

"Okay," I said, "That may be enough to get us back home, but we'll probably have to drive straight through to El Paso."

"Straight through? But that's like a thousand miles!" Tony exclaimed.

"Well, we don't have much choice – we're out of funds and I was told to get the hell out of Dodge after we go to Universal Studios."

"Fuck 'em, they won't know," Tony said defiantly.

"Well, then we're back to square one with no funds, so regardless, we need to hit the road after Universal Studios. Me and Dana will do most of the driving. If we get tired, then you guys get a shot. You got a better idea?"

"What happened to that other motherfucker?" Hector asked changing the subject.

"What 'other motherfucker'?" I asked.

"The other driver, the white guy who lost the race?" Hector asked again.

"Oh him. He was arrested for his second DUI, so I don't think he'll be out for a while," I said.

Dana laughed, "So we did our civic duty by getting his sorry ass off the streets huh?"

"Yep," I replied laughing.

Tony yawned, "Hey man, it's been a long night, let's get some sleep."

"Good idea," I said. "We need to get up around 8 o'clock to get to Universal Studios when they open."

"Why's that important?" Hector asked.

"It'll be cooler in the morning, and if we can get through by early afternoon, we can get on the road a little earlier with a little more daylight."

"Okay," Hector said, also yawning.

284

Yeah, it was time to get some sleep. We all looked beat from our experience with the police. By this time it was three in the morning, and we were going to go to Universal Studios in a few hours. It was time to rest and then have some fun before our long drive back to Texas.

We got ready for bed and turned out the lights. Damn, what a day!

Universal Studios and Home to El Paso

I woke up with a start to the morning light streaming through the windows indicating the sun had been up for a while. I looked over at the digital clock on the nightstand, Eight o'clock, I thought, We need to get on up outta here.

"Hey guys, time to get up," I yelled on my way to the bathroom.

I saw some stirring from Tony and Hector's bed, while Dana continued to sleep soundly. When I came out of the bathroom, Tony was sitting on the side of his bed, and Hector was sitting up.

Tony got into the bathroom next as Hector began gathering up his clothes to pack one last time.

"C'mon Dana, get up, it's getting late." I leaned over and shook his shoulder.

"Hmm," he muttered. "Time to get up?"

"Yeah, we've got a long day ahead of us, so we need to get going."

"Okay, I'm up," Dana said as he got up and began to pack his bag while waiting his turn to get to the bathroom.

"Universal Studios, then we hit the road, right?" Hector asked.

"Yep, that's the plan," I said as I pulled on my jeans.

"Okay, we'll be ready in a few." Hector said.

But as Tony emerged, Hector jumped into the bathroom to

take care of business.

"Hey, my turn," Dana called out.

"Sorry, I've got to go," Hector said over his shoulder as he closed the door.

A short time later, Dana stood over the sink brushing his teeth and washing his face while Hector showered. After several days together, we'd gotten this routine down pretty well, but this was the last morning we would be together like this. The last day of a pretty long road trip. I was sort of sad to see it end.

Thirty minutes later we were all dressed with bags packed. We checked the room, and dragged our bags out to the car. The morning sun looked so much brighter after my stint in the local hoosegow, and the air was cool and fresh – the air of freedom from incarceration.

"I'll load up the car, you guys go on to the lobby and get some breakfast." I said.

"Okay." They chorused, and began walking towards the lobby.

I finished loading the car on this final morning in California, looked around, and slammed the trunk closed. *This is it, we won't be coming back here for a long time, certainly not together,* I thought, and slid into the driver's seat.

I drove around and parked in front of the hotel where inside they served a complimentary "continental breakfast" of fruit, cereal, milk, juices, bagels, toast, and coffee for the weary travelers. Dana, Tony and Hector were sitting at a table when I strode in after having checked us out of our room.

286

"Looks good," I said as I picked out some fruit, juice and toast.

"It is," Tony said. "I really like the bagels."

"Yeah, you like anything with a hole in it." Hector chuckled.

There were other patrons in the little dining area. We couldn't be our normal boisterous selves, but we had to laugh at that one.

A few minutes later we finished up our morning victuals and

left the hotel; ready for a fun time at Universal Studios.

We drove the route to Universal Studios we had reconned the day before, and parked outside the theme park. We got out of the car, one last time in our uniquely Transmanautic style. All sorts of persons were gathering at the entrance to the Studios speaking several different languages and dressed in garb from their respective countries. I recognized Spanish, German, and Italian, and some eastern European languages. This was truly an international attraction.

There was a buzz and a frenzied level of activity going on around us. I was just trying to get a feel for the vibe of the place.

"Hey, this is really cool," Tony said. "What do we want to do first?"

"What about taking the tour bus over there?" Dana suggested.

I looked where he was pointing and saw several cable car-like tram cars where visitors were lining up to get on for the Studios tour.

"Why don't we do that first, then we can figure out what else to do after we finish the tour." I said.

"Sounds like a plan," Hector said. He consulted the brochures they handed us upon entering the Studios, "I'd like to do the stunt man set, and maybe the make-up stuff."

"We can do that, maybe on the tour." I said.

"Okay," Hector said as we walked to the closest tram car.

One by one we got on the tram car and took over two rows of seats. The tram cars were colorfully decorated with the Universal Studios logo of the blue globe circled with the words "Universal" in gold with rainbow-like colors on the front and back of the tram car. It was open on each side for easy viewing of the various attractions, and allowed us to hang out the sides.

"Hey Hector," I yelled from my side of the tram car, "you finally got to ride on a cable car."

"Yeah, yeah," Hector said. He had wanted to ride the San Francisco cable cars, but never had the chance. This was probably the closest he was going to get on this trip.

The tram lurched to a start and a pretty young woman with a pleasing British lilt to her voice had a microphone at the front of the tram.

"Welcome to Universal Studios, the premier studio attraction in the world. Hundreds of thousands of visitors come from all over the world to see a working Hollywood studio and to experience the thrill of making movies. My name is Heather and I will be your guide through the world of Hollywood and the mysteries of movie-making magic."

This sounded like it was going to be fun, I thought.

Heather continued her spiel, "On your left is one of the many sound stages where crews film various movies and television shows. The red light signifies that filming is going on inside the sound stage and no visitors are allowed. As you might imagine, visitors aren't allowed to just walk in on live sets where the red light is on outside the sound stage. Later on there will be opportunities for many of you to actually get on some of those live sound stages through various contests or other ticket giveaways. A lucky few of you may have the opportunity to actually act on some of the sets of current television shows."

We looked at each other and smiled.

As the tour moved on we saw several city scenes including frontier or western towns, New York City from the 1930's, Chicago from the Roaring 20's, and a generic modern city façade.

Heather continued, "Each of these sets can be modified to simulate any city or town in the world or in history. In addition to these more generic sets, there are more specific and recognizable sets from various television shows and movies."

The tram rolled along through an area surrounded by hills.

"Above us to the right is the 'generic haunted house on the hill,' which you see in many horror movies; and to your left, is the more recognizable house from the movie *Psycho,* where Norman Bates lived as the duo-personality of himself and his mother," Heather said with an exaggerated shiver.

"Wow," I said to the other guys. "That movie may have had the scariest scene in the history of filmdom when Janet Leigh was butchered in the shower."

"I don't think I ever saw that movie," Tony said.

"Yeah," Dana said. "That scene kept moviegoers from taking showers in small motels for years."

"Oh shit, maybe I need to check it out." Tony laughed.

"Hey, what's that?" Hector pointed to the left.

"What?" We all turned to follow his finger.

There was an incredible rumbling sound and the top of the hill we were passing seemed to explode out towards us.

"Damn!" I yelled, amidst the clamor from other passengers on the tram.

The side of the hill was covered in an avalanche of rolling boulders rushing towards us at breakneck speed.

Everyone in the tram was transfixed, and then the boulders vanished into a opening in the side of the hill.

"That was a simulated rock slide." Heather laughed. "Sorry to startle you, but we wanted you to have the full effect of the avalanche special effect from the movies. The 'boulders' only weigh a few pounds, but they do look real don't they?"

"Yeah that was some funny shit," Hector chuckled.

"And kinda scary," Dana added.

The tram turned the corner and began to cross a bridge leading to another collection of faux buildings. The tram rocked and rolled from one side to the next, and then there was a loud rushing sound.

"Shit, what's going on?" Tony yelled.

289

A wall of water passed in front of the tram and seemingly washed out the bridge.

"Ladies and gentleman, welcome to the flood." Heather announced. "This is how floods are shown in the movies. And the bridge appears to have been washed away, but as you can see, it is perfectly restored in its rightful place."

We looked again to where the water had swirled by and there

was the bridge.

"Wow, that's pretty neat," Dana said.

"What else is on this tour?" Tony wondered aloud.

At that precise second, the houses on our right erupted in bright red and yellow flames, bathing us in their intense light and heat.

"Oh shit!" I yelled. "I guess that answers your question."

The flames burned out almost instantly. "That is how we do the special effects of burning buildings in Hollywood." Heather said.

"How do you do that?" A lady near the front asked.

"I'm sorry ma'am, that's a trade secret; but I wouldn't try that at home," Heather giggled into the microphone.

The tram turned another corner and we saw a body of water and a pier with a small boat house perched on its edge.As we approached the pier, a huge shark jumped out of the water towards the tram, and landed on the beach with its jaws snapping and then slipped back into the water.

My heart beat jumped several levels when I saw the shark. I didn't need Heather's after-the-fact explanation to know we'd just seen the mechanical shark from the movie *Jaws*; the movie that scared the swimming public out of the water in the summer of '75.

"Hey Dana," Tony laughed, "did that bring back memories of Venice Beach?"

Hector and I also laughed.

"Fuck you Tony," Dana replied smiling.

"We're almost at the end of the tour. Make sure you keep your hands in the car," she warned as the tram turned another corner.

What the hell is next? I thought.

A few minutes later, the tram rolled through a street on the side of one of the sets, and glided to a stop. That's when we heard another loud rumbling sound.

"Can't be another avalanche," Hector said.

The tram and the street began to shake violently and the buildings began to sway. I grabbed onto the edge of the tram.

"Earthquake!" I yelled, "Hold on!" Then it stopped as suddenly as it started.

"This is the set from the movie *Earthquake*," Heather belatedly said. "I hope you weren't too startled." She smiled.

Damn, I thought, *We almost shit our pants.* I looked over at Tony and Hector, and they looked ashen. Well, as ashen as they could look.

"Damn, that was fucked up," Tony said.

"But still, pretty funny," Hector laughed.

The tram continued to roll through a façade of a western town that was reminiscent of *High Noon,* and other western favorites.

"On your left you can see two stunt men who are about to engage in a gunfight." Heather pointed.

Yep, sure enough, two white guys were dressed in period costumes with six-guns strapped to their hips and were walking towards each other. There was a crowd of tourists surrounding the simulated gunfight.

"Draw!" One of them yelled, and they simultaneously drew their weapons and fired.

"Bang!" One of them fell to the ground with simulated blood spurting from his chest. The crowd cheered the simulated death of one of the gunfighters. Hopefully the bad guy.

The tram started with a lurch and Heather said, "As usual the good guy wins. We are now at the end of the Universal Studios tour. I hope you enjoyed the tour as much as I enjoyed being your guide. There are several other attractions as you walk around the Studios. You may want to see the new King Kong ride, or do the '1000 Faces' make up artist attraction, and there's always the various sets you can visit, such as *Adam-12* and the stunt man show. Thank you and enjoy the rest of your visit here at Universal Studios."

We got off the tram and went looking for more to do at the Studios. Our first stop was the set for *Adam-12*. We took our seats and listened to the narrator.

"The set of *Adam-12*, the long running television show set right here in Los Angeles, was a series based on the day-to-day life of Los Angeles' finest and starred Martin Milner and Kent McCord. The show ran from 1968 to 1975, and was the brainchild of producer, director and actor Jack Webb, the creator of the long-running series *Dragnet,* where he starred as Sergeant Joe Friday. So, sit back, relax, and enjoy the show."

I stared at the several police cars, policemen, the police station, and simulated residential streets, and it all looked eerily familiar. Hoo boy! Did that bring back memories from last night.

"Chris, this is just like last night." Tony laughed as we watched car chases, police stops, and fleeing felons being placed over the hood and handcuffed by the television heroes.

Dana and Hector laughed throughout the show, at my expense. Oh well, it's interesting how life imitates art imitating life.

Our next stop after the *Adam-12* set was the stunt man show where studio audience members were selected to participate and be filmed for the performance of the show. They selected Hector to play a fireman. His role was to pretend that he had just climbed down off a 2-story ladder from a burning building, having saved lives. He did pretty well, but when they ran the film of the action sequence, the video showed a white firefighter going up the ladder to save the woman in the burning building, but showed Hector, a young black man coming down the ladder with the lady in distress. I wondered how they would explain the fact that a white man went up the ladder and a black man came down – soot from the fire? Too funny.

292

Our last stop was on the set of *Emergency!*, a new show written, produced and directed by Jack Webb, and starring, once again, Kent McCord.

This time, when they picked people from the audience, Dana was picked for a speaking part. He and a white woman were to actually participate in a screen test for the series, and if they did well they might get a shot at appearing on the show as an extra.

We were rooting for Dana to do well.

A few minutes later, Dana came running out, dressed as an older-looking emergency medical tech, with a black bag. He rushed to the side of the woman who was laying on the ground covered in blood, injured from a car accident.

"Don't worry ma'am, you'll be alright," he said in a very officious tone.

We cracked up.

I fell over laughing so hard. Tony and Hector were both doubled over with mirth as they tried not to fall to the ground where I was rolling.

The audience gave Dana a great ovation as the scene ended and he stood up and took a bow. What a ham.

After the scene was over, Dana went back to the make up area. We joined him back there as he changed into his overalls and sat back into the make up chair as they removed the make up.

"You were great Dana," I said, chortling at the memory.

"Yeah Dana, you were great, but you may want to keep your day job," Hector chimed in giggling.

"I thought you sucked." Tony laughed.

"Shut up you guys." Dana also laughed. "Look what they gave me." He proffered an envelope.

"What?" I asked.

"Four tickets to *Family Feud*."

"Really? With Richard Dawson? When?" Hector asked.

"Tomorrow!" Dana said.

293

Damn, I thought, *We can't go. We have to leave town.* "You know we can't go right?" I said bursting everyone's bubble.

"Oh c'mon man, one more day," Tony pleaded.

Dana and Hector both looked at me with sad, puppy dog eyes, entreating me to change my mind.

"Sorry guys, we don't have any money. We've checked out

of the hotel and we've been told to get out of town."

"Damn, okay," Dana said. "I understand, but it would've been great fun."

"I'm sorry guys." I hoped to make it up to them at some point, because it was my fault we couldn't stay an extra day.

As we were leaving Universal Studios we wanted to get souvenirs. There was all kinds of stuff to buy, and of course, because of the escapade from the night before, we were sort of low on cash and had a limited budget for souvenirs. But we all wanted something to remember Universal Studios and our trip.

"Hey look at all the *Star Wars* stuff." Hector pointed at the array of *Star Wars* T-shirts.

"This is great!" I said, and thought these might be perfect souvenirs for all of us.

Each of us picked out a different T-shirt. Mine was the actual *Star Wars* movie picture that was depicted on the movie posters displayed at the theaters at that time. I bought a second T-shirt that simply said "Universal Studios" and they both fit really well.

"Let's put them on now," Tony suggested.

"That's cool," I said. Dana and Hector agreed.

We went to the closest bathroom and put on our new *Star Wars* T-shirts. We were about to embark on that 1000-mile journey and the T-shirts became the "uniform de rigueur" for the trip back to El Paso. We pretended that by wearing them we were somehow protected by The Force, and nothing could stop us on our journey home.

When we left Universal Studios we went out to the car, got in and prepared for our trek back to El Paso. We had spent a long day at Universal Studios and had a great time. I felt bad about having to cut the trip short and miss being on *Family Feud,* but we had to go.

We stopped at a gas station to fill up and get snacks and drinks for our long trip home. After we got back in, I pointed the nose of the Trans Am to the east and we started the voyage home.

"What's the best way back?" I asked Dana. I sounded like

Dorothy telling the Good Witch "there's no place like home." I just wanted to figure out the quickest, least expensive way back to El Paso.

"Since we're in LA, the quickest way is to just take I-10 and keep straight east until we get there."

"Are we going through Phoenix this time?" I asked.

"Yeah, Phoenix, then Tucson again." Dana replied.

"Approximately how far?" Hector asked.

"The map says 801miles," Dana said.

"How long will that take us?" Tony asked.

"Hmm, ground speed at approximately 60 mph, with breaks and stops, actual speed of about 55 miles per hour, about, um, fourteen and a half hours." I calculated, "That should put us in El Paso at about eight tomorrow morning with the time change."

"Ouch. That's a long time," Hector said, "But I guess we have plenty to talk about to occupy the time."

"Yeah, we're going to be in here together for a while," Tony observed.

"Yep," I said as I looked for the signs for I-10 East.

"How do we get to I-10?" I asked Dana.

"Turn up here for Highway 101, take it west and it will run right into I-10," he said as he consulted the Trip Tik.

"Okay." I complied with his direction. I drove onto the on ramp for 101 West and immediately saw signs for I-10.

"Alright, we're rolling. You can take over when I get tired, okay?" I nodded at Dana.

"No problem. I'll keep you awake with my scintillating conversation."

"Yeah, right." I said.

We drove in silence for the next several minutes, listening to the tunes that had sustained us through this entire trip. The sounds of EWF, Parliament, Slave, the Fatback Band, and Mass Production flowed through the car, buoying our spirits as we set our faces to the east.

We came up on the signs for Riverside as we continued our journey out of the Los Angeles megapolis.

"Isn't that the exit for the Blanchards?" Hector commented.

"Yeah, that's it." I said contemplating the possibilities. It must have shown on my face.

"You still thinking about that night?" Tony asked.

"Aren't you?" I shot back.

"Uh huh, I was thinking about how I could have hit that shit if it weren't for Ralph and Buick here." Tony laughed touching Dana on the shoulder.

"I agree. The sounds of vomiting tends to turn off the amorous feelings of most young women." I said.

"Don't forget the smell." Dana smiled getting into the conversation.

"And in Hector's case, the tossing of cookies in front of his cheerleader just fucked it all up, for all of us," Tony said elbowing Hector.

"At least Dana waited until we left, then barfed." I chuckled. Hector was silent during all this.

"Cat got your tongue Hector?" I said.

"Nothin' to say," Hector replied.

"I'll bet." I looked back at Tony, "I don't know if I could have hit either Debbie or Lisa, or both, but it would have been nice to have had the chance."

296

"How exactly would you have done that in the house with all those people around?" Dana asked.

"I don't know," I said with some exasperation. ""With you as a diversion, maybe I could have found a back bedroom for a quickie, or set it up for later. I don't know. But we'll never know, will we?"

About that time I saw signs showing San Bernardino within a few miles, and the exit for Cal State at San Bernardino.

Dana looked wistfully towards the exit for Cal State at San Bernardino, where we met Aurianna.

"I should have gone to Disneyland," Dana said. "I wanted to spend more time with her, and you talked me out of it." He accused me.

"I'm sorry," I said, "I didn't want to break us up and I didn't want something to happen to you."

"Nothing would have happened to me," Dana enunciated. "You were just being selfish and didn't want anybody separated, especially for a girl."

"Again, I'm sorry. I thought you'd have another chance to see her and I was wrong." I felt bad for Dana; and I felt that I was partly responsible for his misery.

"Oh the great Big Brother was wrong." Dana laughed, derision in his voice, "News flash – Chris was w-r-o-n-g, wrong."

"What do you want me to do, apologize for the rest of my life?" I asked. "I said I was sorry. You need to get over it. I've never seen you like this over some girl. What is it about Aurianna?

"Love at first sight?" Hector chided Dana from the back.

"No. I mean, I don't know. Damn." Dana stammered. "I just know she was beautiful, smart, and I could talk to her about anything. She was..."

"Was what?" Hector cut him off.

"I don't know, different from any other girl I've met." Dana struggled to explain.

"Well, at least you all can write each other," I offered. "Who knows, maybe you can come back here at some point, or maybe she can visit you in New York."

"Yeah, maybe," Dana said dejectedly.

"Welcome to our world," I said. "I've felt that way about too many girls over the years, and you always seemed to avoid all that, until now. You were always so careful – above it all – to get hurt. Huh, maybe it's a good thing." I rationalized.

"Maybe you're right," Dana said in a low voice. "I will

definitely learn from this experience in dealing with other women. I'm not going to let any of them get on top of me like that, *ever* again. Damn."

I could hear the hurt in his voice. "Okay," I said. "You still going to keep in contact with Aurianna?"

"Yeah," he said looking out the window, "I miss her already."

We drove in silence for another several minutes, everyone lost in their thoughts about the trip.

"Now, I'm craving your body, is this real? Temperatures rising, I don't want to feel I'm in the wrong place to be real... Reasons, the reasons that we hear, the reasons that we fear our feelings a-won't disappear. And, after the love game has been played, all our illusions are just a parade and all our reasons start to fade... " slithered out of the speakers.

Reasons by EWF, my favorite slow jam. "We should have played this at the Party," I said. "Maybe we all would have got some pussy with this in their heads." I grinned into the rearview mirror, catching Hector's eye.

"I don't need some weak-assed song to get some pussy," Tony declared.

Oh here we go, I thought. "You have no fucking clue. Women love this shit. And when you can sing it to them and hit the right notes, that shit is powerful."

"How the fuck would you know, 'Mr. Didn't Hit it at UT?'" Tony cackled.

"Yeah okay, 'Mr. Experience,'" I shot back, "What about you at the Party? How would you have hit that pussy?"

"Well," Tony began, "you know, she was all over me."

This was Tony's revisionist history of the Party.

"I could have had the pick of any woman at the Party, but I chose her." He continued to brag. "I could have hit any of that pussy, even your precious Debbie," Tony snickered.

"Oh, I don't think so," I countered.

"Bull shit. She and her sisters were happy to have me at their party, so I'm pretty sure I could have hit that shit, even with Dana doing his 'take that shit to bed' routine and you running around trying to hit on some other woman." Tony continued to brag.

I was tired of hearing this shit. *It's time to bring him down a peg*, I thought.

"You weren't even supposed to be at the Party," I started.

"What the fuck are you talking about?" Tony asked.

I looked at Hector in the rearview, "You remember when Audrey came and got me before we went to the Party?"

Hector nodded, "Yeah, I asked you what was going on."

"Well, the sisters called and said they didn't want Tony to come to the Party because he wasn't uh…good looking enough." I looked at Tony in the rearview mirror.

"Bull shit!" Tony exclaimed, "That's total bullshit!"

"No bull shit," I said. "But I told them that if you didn't go, then none of us were going. We're the Transmanauts and we go everywhere together. They said okay, and so you went to the Party."

"You really told them that?" Tony asked.

"Yeah, that's what I told them."

Hector laughed, "So Tony almost didn't go." He looked over at Tony, "Maybe that will put a little pin prick in that big head of yours. It was getting really crowded in here with the four of us and your big head."

"Maybe Hector and I weren't the only ones drunk, and maybe that's why Tyanekwa talked to you, she was drunk and couldn't see straight." Dana joined in.

299

"Yeah, it was pretty dark in there. Maybe she didn't get a good look at you," Hector guffawed.

We all laughed at that – well, except Tony.

"Fuck all y'all." Tony grumped, "I still could have hit that shit, and I got her address, so maybe I'll hit that some other time."

"But she'll have seen you in the light of day and sober, that can't be good for you." Hector really was having a good time at Tony's expense.

I was almost sorry I'd brought it up, but I was getting tired of Tony's bragging, and now it was time to shut it down.

"At least Tony got some play and didn't barf all over his girl, Hector." I smiled at Hector in the rearview.

That shut Hector up. Dana didn't participate much in this conversation, maybe because his night at the Party ended in a pool of vomit on the side of the road.

As the night wore on, Tony and Hector fell asleep while Dana kept me awake by chattering incessantly about Aurianna. Aurianna this, and Aurianna that – on…and…on…and…on.

After a while, I said, "Is she all you're going to talk about?"

"What do you mean?"

"That's all you've talked about for the past few hours. I mean from the time it got dark, and even through the filling up of the gas tank at our last stop, that's all you've talked about."

"Sorry if I'm boring you, but I thought you'd understand."

"I do. You know I do. From Becky to Joan, back to Becky, and to Melanie, you know I understand, but dog Dana, that's all you've talked about. Please, just change the subject."

"Okay." He smiled. "I guess I've got it bad don't I?"

"Yeah, you do." I smiled back. "But it's good to know you're human."

"You need me to drive?" Dana asked changing the subject.

"Nah, I'm good," I assured him. "I feel fine, and we'll be stopping in about an hour and I'll be able to get out and stretch and get a coke or something."

"Okay, just let me know if you need me to drive," Dana said as he leaned over to his window and closed his eyes.

I drove to the music flowing out of the speakers bobbing my head, and swaying in the seat. This gave me a chance to just genuflect over the trip, my arrest, and what lay ahead in the future as we continued to drive east.

We passed through Phoenix, and as we came upon Tucson I pulled off the highway.

"Hey guys, wake up, we're in Tucson." I announced.

"Huh, what?" Hector was slow waking up.

"We're stopping for gas and if you need to go, go now," I said.

"Okay," Tony said groggily.

I spotted an Exxon and drove up to the pump. I got out and went inside the store and gave the attendant a fifty to fill up the tank. That was the last of the money. I came back out and began filling up the tank.

Dana had finally opened his door. "C'mon, let's go inside," he said to Hector and Tony. The three of them went inside while I continued to pump the gas.

As I closed the little panel over the gas cap, Dana came out with an armful of snacks. "You need to go? The bathroom is pretty clean."

"Okay, thanks," I walked to the store as Tony and Hector came out with their hands full of snacks and drinks.

I threw Hector the keys, "Tell Dana to move the car up here."

"Gotcha." He snatched them out of the air.

When I came back out with my change from the fifty, the car was parked by the store, and the engine was running.

"Everybody ready to roll?" I asked, getting back in the car.

"Yep, let's go," Dana said.

Almost immediately after pulling out of the gas station, we saw a traffic stop where the police had pulled over a young black man and had him in handcuffs.

"Déjà vu Chris?" Tony laughed.

I had to let him have his fun after I had made fun of him. "Yeah, looks sort of familiar. Think he has anyone in the car crying like a baby?" Well, I could only let his fun go so far.

"Shut up Chris," Tony fired back.

"Yep, I guess you do have a reason to go back to Cali and see Debbie don't you when you go back to court." Hector jumped in.

"I'm not going back for court; they can just issue a warrant for my arrest. Fuck 'em if they can't take a joke." I laughed.

"Hey man, that might affect your military career with an arrest warrant on your record," Dana added.

"Yeah, that's a consideration, but it's only for reckless driving. Maybe it won't be so bad," I said.

"I don't know, I think you're taking a big chance," Dana continued.

"I'll think about it." I ended the conversation.

We continued rolling east, and within an hour the sun began to rise to our front, illuminating the sky with roses, oranges and yellows in bright contrast to the night sky behind us.

"Getting closer," Dana said.

"Yeah, about three hours," I said.

We drove through the same interminable New Mexico desert, as we had the first day of the road trip. The desert didn't look any better this time around, but it signaled our closing in on El Paso.

Within the hour, the huge "WELCOME TO TEXAS" sign with the Texas flag loomed before us. We were now back in the great state of Texas.

"Yay, we made it," we all cheered. All except Hector.

I looked back in the rearview mirror, "Hey Hector, not happy to be back?" I asked.

"I just feel we're not going to be together like this again, and it just makes me a little sad thinking about it." Hector replied.

"Aw c'mon, Hector, we'll get together again," Dana said.

"Well, Chris is going back to Austin, to go to law school, then the Army. Dana, you're going off to West Point; Tony's going off to Tech and I'm staying right here in Las Cruces. It's just not going to be the same, that's all." Hector lamented.

I understood how he felt, and none of us made fun of his somewhat emotional outburst.

"Let's make a pledge that we'll make a road trip to New York – on the east coast instead of the left coast. How's that?"

"Yeah, yeah, we can make a pledge, but you know it'll never happen." Hector said.

"We're the Transmanauts, we can make it happen. You'll see," I said.

Somewhat appeased, Hector agreed with that plan. "Okay, I'll keep you to that."

We drove to Tony's house first and executed half of our Transmanautic exit to let Tony out of the car. I got out to open the trunk to get his bags. Tony walked to the back of the car.

"Anybody home?" I asked unlocking the trunk.

"Don't see any cars, probably not," Tony replied grabbing his bag. He pulled it out then put it on the ground.

"Hey man, gonna miss you," he said, a little quiver in his voice.

"Yeah, me too. Good luck at Tech this year. I'll be in touch."

"Okay."

We did a little soul hand shake, a brief hug, and he turned to Dana.

"See you bro'."

"I'll get you my address when I get up there," Dana promised.

They hugged and Tony picked up his bag and walked to his front door. We watched him until he opened the door and waved back at us.

Dana and I got back in the car and I drove over to Hector's house. I pulled into Hector's driveway; no cars there either.

"Nobody home?" I asked as I opened my door to let him out.

"Nah, probably at work or something," he said as he slid out of the back seat.

I walked back to the trunk and got out his bag.

"This is it my man," I said.

"You promised we'd get back together," Hector said.

"We'll do this again, some way or another." I promised again.

"Okay."

We did a little hug and Hector turned to Dana.

"Good luck at West Point. You and Mom drive safely."

"Hey, we're not leaving for a couple of days, so maybe you and Tony can come by the house before we leave." Dana said looking at me.

"Good idea, we'll have everybody over as a kind of 'bon voyage' party for Dana, maybe tomorrow night," I said.

"Okay, I'll be there for sure." Hector promised.

Dana and he briefly hugged and we watched Hector walk to his front door. When he opened his door and waved, Dana and I got back into the Trans Am to drive back to our house. We drove home in silence, weary, but happy.

That was our Road Trip. The adventure of a lifetime for the Transmanauts. No one else is a Transmanaut, only the four of us. We have tried to be there for each other for all of our lives, through crises, and the good times as well. The bond goes beyond friendship and beyond fraternity. We are a unique and very exclusive brotherhood, with no further initiation. There are no "honorary" or "fifth" Transmanauts. Either you were or you weren't – no in between. Only the one time could you become a true Transmanaut – you had to be on the Road Trip, or not at all.

The Chronicles of the Transmanauts are not over- Life has no road map, and Fate can take you where you least expect...

Fort Irwin

Black History Month, 2007, and the whole post was abuzz about the news that the new commanding general was African-American. How apropos. For the first time, Fort Irwin, California, nestled in the heart of the Mojave Desert, in Southern California, and home to the National Training Center – the premier training facility for our Army mechanized, armored, and motorized units before they deploy to Iraq and Afghanistan – was to be commanded by a Black one-star general, and things would never be the same.

No one had heard of this general, well, except maybe one person on post. I thought I might know him. But it had been thirty years, and I wasn't sure which brother it might be, Chris or Dana? All I knew was that a Brigadier General Pittard was going to take command of Fort Irwin and the NTC in July. No, it couldn't be, after thirty long years.

What happened to him? What happened to us? Not a day went by over the past thirty years that I didn't think about those guys. I had to find out. I had to know what could have been, and why it never was.

As the date approached, I was offered a job elsewhere, a promotion, but I turned it down. I had to know, and I wanted to be there when he took command of Fort Irwin and the NTC. In April, I found out his name — Brigadier General Dana J.H. Pittard, the one and only. My heart beat faster! Wow! He had really done it! He was a general, just like he said he would be thirty years ago.

I couldn't believe it! I had to see him in person and make sure for myself it was really him, and not some other guy with the same name. But I knew in my heart, it could be no other. And even though the post was excited about the possibility of its first African-American commanding general, I was the one person who was super excited by the pending arrival of the new CG, and looked forward more than anyone else to seeing him, again.

On that fateful day in July, the sun was shining bright, the sky was a clear and beautiful blue, which just seemed closer because of the 4,000 foot elevation — a typical day at the NTC and Fort Irwin. The change of command ceremony was to take place in the morning before it got too hot in the high desert. I sat with the other civilian directors in a reserved area that gave me a great view of the festivities. The new CG was seated with his wife Lucille, and two sons, Taylor and Jordan, in the covered area reserved for him and other VIPs who had come to the ceremony. There was the Iraqi general in the audience who commanded all of the Iraqi ground forces. He was there because he had served with General Pittard in Iraq. There were several other dignitaries in attendance for this most historic of occasions.

A four-star general presided over the change of command and introduced Brigadier General Pittard as one of the premier armor officers in the United States Army and one of its finest leaders and commanders. Then Brigadier General Dana J.H. Pittard stepped up to the podium to speak to his new post, and his first words gave me goose bumps.

"Rest!" he shouted to the assembled troops on the parade grounds. They didn't know what to do; no one had ever told them to "rest" during a change of command. But that was the first indication to the populace at Fort Irwin that this was a different kind of general, who had a different way of doing things, and confirmed to me – this was really him.

A reception followed the change of command ceremony. It was being held at the Officer's Club and was by invitation only. I didn't have an invitation and was unsure if I should even try to go. I talked to a friend of mine, John, with whom

I had shared my thirty-year long saga, and asked him what I should do.

John, a big, tall, light-skinned older man, said, "You need to go to the reception. I normally don't go to these things, but for you, I'll make an exception."

"You'll go with me, just in case he doesn't remember me? I don't want to feel foolish." I said.

John looked at me with a critical eye. "I don't think he'll have forgotten you. You're a strikingly beautiful woman and the toast of Fort Irwin. I'm pretty sure he'll remember you."

"Okay, I'll go, but only if you escort me in."

"No problem. I'll go get the car and we can drive over there."

John and I drove to the reception in his car. We were quiet as I contemplated this impending face-to-face meeting with excitement and a feeling of dread. *I don't care what John thinks, what if he doesn't remember me? I don't know if I can handle the embarrassment.*

John parked the car in the rapidly filling parking lot and we walked together to the club. I saw the long line which was quickly getting longer. Everyone who was invited looked to be here to meet the new CG. John and I got in the line and waited our turn. With each step, I became more nervous.

I don't know if I can stand this. I thought. *I'm so nervous I feel lightheaded. I just don't want to pass out and really embarrass myself.* Luckily John remained by my side, and gave me the strength to keep moving forward. As we got closer, I could see that the new CG was right inside the door with his new aide and his family to each side of him in the receiving line. The aide, who was closest to the door, got the name of the person in line and whispered it to the new CG so he could greet that person by name. As we went through the door, John let me precede him, and I decided not to give my name to the aide. Instead, I planned to surprise the new CG by asking him if he remembered me. This was my first time seeing him up close, and he still looked as good as he had thirty years ago. The same smooth milk-chocolate complexion, the pretty eyes and expressive face with the quick smile and laughing personality. One difference, I noted, was that he was really built – even in the Army Combat Uniform you could tell he was in great shape, which was a big change from the slender teenager I remembered. He was still handsome and I looked forward to seeing if he remembered me.

As I approached him, I said, "Sir, I don't know if you remember me, I'm…"

"Aurianna!? Is it really you? After all these years? It's really you!"

I didn't expect this response and outburst from Dana. His wife Lucille looked sharply at him. She was apparently surprised at his reaction to this woman in the receiving line. There had to be a story behind all this. And of course there was.

At this outburst, the reception line stopped as he gave me a long hug. John stood behind me just staring.

"What are you doing here?" he asked.

"I'm your Director of Auditing."

"Here? At Fort Irwin?"

"Yes," I replied. "I've been here almost ten years."

In the next several minutes we caught up a little on what had occurred in the past thirty years, the fact I had two grown sons, and that I had a master's degree in accounting.

Dana turned to his wife, "Lucille, this is Aurianna. I met her thirty years ago almost to the month when Chris, Tony, Hector and I took that trip to California."

"Nice to meet you Aurianna," Lucille said, "These are our sons, Taylor and Jordan."

"Hi guys," I said.

Dana's aide interrupted. "Sir, we still have a lot of people in the receiving line. Maybe we can get Miss Aurianna by the office if you'd like."

"Great idea. Aurianna, my aide will give you a call and set something up."

"Sounds great," I said. I was singing inside. *He remembered me and seemed to be as excited at seeing me as I was at seeing him.*

As we walked away from the receiving line, John said, "That was some reaction. I guess he did remember you. I told you not to worry."

"You were right," I said. Yep, we had some catching up to do, and I wondered what had happened…and what could have been.

Later that day, Dana's aide called me at my office to set up an appointment to have lunch with Dana the next day at his office. Of course I accepted. I was looking forward to catching up on old times and finding out what happened to us.

The next day, I went to his office for the catered lunch and we had a chance to talk and figure out how we had lost touch. I tried to look my best that day, and judging by his expression when I walked into his office, I think I succeeded.

He invited me to sit down, and once we got comfortable with our lunches, one of the first things I said was, "What happened with the other Transmanauts?" Yeah, I remembered the name they had given themselves back in 1977, and the names of the other Transmanauts, Chris, Tony and Hector.

"Well let's see," he started, "Hector attended New Mexico State University in Las Cruces, New Mexico, on a track scholarship, where he had a pretty good career. He pledged the same fraternity as Chris and his father, Kappa Alpha Psi, and eventually left NMSU and graduated from the University of Texas at El Paso with a degree in History. He worked for a few years in El Paso, and then moved out here to Los Angeles. The Road Trip had awakened in him a hunger to come back out to the West coast and establish a life out here. Sadly, Aunt Rose had died of leukemia in 1980, and didn't live to see Hector's return to Los Angeles. She was like a second mother to Hector; we all missed her tremendously."

"I'm surprised, I don't think he ever tried to contact me all this time," I said.

"No, I guess he didn't, maybe because he was so involved in training inner city youth in computer technology and computer literacy he never found the time. Several years ago he moved to Washington, D.C., where Tony lives, and got involved in mentoring inner city children through his fraternity, and his expertise in computer literacy. So he may have been gone by the time you moved back to California."

"What's he doing now?"

"He's working in the field of IT security, where he creates and develops curriculum for security awareness programs for major defense firms, and the government. I could tell you which agencies, but then I'd have to kill you." Dana laughed.

"Okay," I laughed along, "What about his social life, did he ever get married?"

"Yep, actually just last year. He married Pam on a romantic Caribbean island, and they reside in the Washington D.C. area."

"How's Tony? What happened to him?"

"Tony traveled a different path than Hector. He went on to attend Texas Tech University in Lubbock, Texas, and went through their Army ROTC program and was commissioned a second lieutenant in Air Defense Artillery, in 1981. While he was at Tech, Tony pledged the same fraternity as Hector and Chris, Kappa Alpha Psi."

"Did you ever pledge?"

"No, there wasn't a chapter at West Point, and I just haven't had the time to pledge since then, but if I ever were to pledge, it would be Kappa."

"Did Tony ever get married?"

"Yes, a few times. His first wife was his college sweetheart, Beverly. Coincidentally, Beverly, was crowned Miss Black Mt. Pleasant, Texas, in 1978, and competed against Melanie, Chris' girlfriend, in the Miss Black Texas pageant, in which Melanie was the first or second runner up. Tony and Beverly had two children, Bobbie and Becky. I'm Becky's godfather. Tony eventually got out of the Army around 1985, and moved to the Washington, D.C. area, where he works for a major defense contractor as an air defense systems engineer. Unfortunately, he and Beverly split up along the way; but he remarried for the second time in 2000, to Donna this time, and they also reside in the Washington, D.C. area."

"Remarried for the second time? That sounds like he's been married three times."

"Yeah, but his second marriage didn't last very long. Tony has a pretty funny story about that."

"I'll have to ask him about that some time. It sounds like Tony and Hector have done pretty well for themselves."

"Yeah, they have; interestingly, both of them attribute much of their success in life to their association and life-long friendship and support with the other Transmanauts. Hector believes our adventure in California and our friendship helped make all of us what we are today. He also remembers that there were times when he was on his own, and he would think about what the rest of us might say to him in certain situations, and he says that sometimes helped." Dana explained.

"That's really interesting. I have a similar experience along those lines, but right now I'd rather hear about you and Chris." I continued, "What happened to Chris? I know he was an Army officer and was going to law school to eventually get into politics, so what happened?"

"Chris' career path took some unexpected twists and turns. Sometimes plans don't always work out do they?"

That got my attention, "Now I'm dying to know what happened with Chris."

"Well, okay," he said. "If you're *that* interested, I'll give you the blow by blow of *Chris'* life after we left California."

I wondered if I said something wrong.

"As expected Chris did go to UT Law School in the fall of 1977, and met his eventual wife, Karen, during his second year of law school. Unfortunately, he underwent emergency surgery during his second year which kept him out for almost a month. He got so far behind in his studies that he decided to forego the rest of law school to pursue his Army career." Dana shifted in his seat before continuing his recitation, and took another bite of his lunch.

"He never became a lawyer?"

"Not then. In 1979 Chris went on active duty as an Infantry officer and went through jump school to become an Army parachutist; and Ranger School to become Ranger-qualified, and emerged as one of those fabled Airborne Rangers. He was initially stationed at Ft. Hood, Texas, not too far from where his fiancée, Karen, also a former beauty queen, was still attending school at UT. They were married in 1982, and have been happily married ever since. They have two beautiful redheaded daughters, Dani and Alanna, who have both graduated college. Hopefully, you'll get to meet all of them."

"I look forward to it; what happened to his law career?"

"Chris got out of the Army in 1992 as a major. When the Army was giving out money to get out, Chris decided to get out and go back to law school. This time he studied law at St. Mary's University, in San Antonio, where he graduated with honors. He's a civil rights and employment discrimination attorney with his own firm. He's been recognized as one of Texas' Best Lawyers in employment law."

"So what's he like now?"

"Well, he's been active in his community, he was a card-carrying member of the Professional Bowlers Association;

and studied and trained in the Korean martial arts, and holds a 1st Degree black belt in Tae Kwon Do Chung Do Kwan. Politically, he unsuccessfully ran for office on two occasions but he may try it again, who knows?"

Dana ended his recitation about Chris, "You know, he never did return to California to appear in court for the arrest. There's probably still a warrant out for him, so he may not want to come back here, even after thirty years." He laughed.

"What arrest? He got arrested while you all were here? I didn't know that."

"Yeah, we were drag racing in Van Nuys and got caught by the Van Nuys police, and Chris, since he was the driver, got arrested. That was one scary night." Dana laughed. "But we survived, and all of us went on to continue our lives as planned, for the most part."

"That's really interesting; it sounds like he's done well, but what about you? I know you don't like talking about yourself, but indulge me. Give me all the details of your life for the past thirty years." I implored.

If you insist," he said. "I was voted "Most Successful" at my 30th high school class reunion. That was kind of fun. As you know, I went off to West Point, but that first year was definitely the toughest. Sometimes I got a little down during that first year because I missed the Transmanauts, you, and our adventures. But, you know, I found a way to resurrect some of that Transmanautic magic."

"How's that?"

"During my career at West Point, I availed myself of the long-time tradition of West Pointers getting a fast car during their senior year. But in my case, I got my car during my junior year and hid it at my mom's house. I ordered what I called, 'The Texas Turbo Cockpit Transmajam-Am,' a 1980 Special Edition black and gold Trans Am with a 'cockpit' T-top and upgraded stereo system in the T-top cockpit above the driver's head, with a beautiful black velour interior. My car was the flashiest on campus. The final touch was my

313

specialized license plates 'Dana P,' known to collegiate women up and down the East Coast. It was the ultimate 'chick magnet.' And yeah, after my African-American Fifth Regiment classmates saw that car, it became 'The Texas Turbo Cockpit Transmajam-Am – And It's Bad Too!'"

"I wish I could have seen that car, it sounds beautiful." I laughed.

"Yeah, we had a good time with it."

"So Dana, tell me about the rest of your career."

"In 1979, as a cadet, I actually went through jump school before Chris did, and I also traveled to Fort Campbell, went through the Air Assault School and became an Air Assault Master. I graduated West Point in 1981, went to Fort Knox, for Armor Officer Basic Course, then on to Ft. Benning, Georgia, for Ranger School in 1982. Chris went through Ranger School first, but was recycled because of pneumonia, and I didn't want that to happen to me. But thanks to a classmate of mine, I suffered a broken wrist during a two-party climb in the mountains of Dahlonega, in northern Georgia, but I didn't let anyone know."

"What?!" I exclaimed. "Back up, how did it happen and why didn't anyone know?"

"During the two-party climb, I began to fall, and my classmate, who was on 'belay' was supposed to pull the rope taut to stop my fall."

Dana must have noticed the quizzical expression on my face.

"You know what belay is?"

314

"I didn't want to interrupt your story."

"That's okay. A guy 'on belay' is the guy who holds the rope for the guy climbing the mountain. Both guys have the rope tied to them so that if the guy climbing begins to fall, the guy on belay is supposed to stop his fall by pulling the rope tight against his body and that suspends the climber in the air so he can get his bearings and continue the climb." Dana continued, "Unfortunately, in my case, he didn't tighten up on the rope and I fell about 30 feet to the ground. I tried to brace myself with my free hand and that's when I broke my wrist. When they sent me to the clinic for x-rays, I gave them my unhurt hand. I didn't want to be recycled like Chris, and I wanted Chris to pin my Ranger Tab on me on my birthday." He explained.

"Wow! You were pretty tough." I said in wonderment.

Dana lowered his eyes, as if he was embarrassed by the compliment.

"Yeah, I survived Ranger School with a broken wrist. But I was also motivated by a message left for me two years earlier by Chris in one of the hooches in Dahlonega."

"What's a hooch?" I asked.

"That's what we called our little squad-sized barracks at the Mountain Ranger Camp."

"I'm sorry, go on," I said.

He continued his story, "I was sitting in my hooch reading or something, when one of the other Ranger students from a different hooch came in looking for me. He called out my name, and when I identified myself he came over and told me, 'We found the strangest thing in our hooch on one of the walls.'

"I asked, kind of bewildered, 'What sort of thing and what's it got to do with me?' He said, 'It's a message for you.' I said, 'On the wall?' He replied, 'Yeah, you want to see it?' I said, 'Sure, but how do you know it's for me?' 'Well, it's written for a Ranger Pittard, USMA Class of '81, so we figured it had to be for you,' he said."

Dana paused to collect his thoughts, "Then it dawned on me, Chris told me before I went to Ranger School that he had left me a message, and apparently it really existed. I had forgotten all about it. The other Ranger student led me to his hooch and on the right hand wall about halfway up, in indelible ink, Chris had written in two lines, *'Drive on Ranger Pittard, USMA Class '81/ from Ranger Pittard, Class 8-80'* on the wall of that hooch. Those other Ranger students, many of whom were my classmates from West Point, were impressed. So, when that accident happened, I made sure I didn't get recycled; I knew I was not going to fail. So, yeah, I also became one of those fabled Airborne Rangers in 1982, and, yes, Chris was there to pin my Ranger Tab on my shoulder, on my birthday. That was pretty special."

"Yeah, that was very cool." I nodded in agreement.

Dana continued his career description, "My first assignment was at Ft. Riley, Kansas, where I first met Lucille. She was from Junction City, a school teacher, and Army brat like me. We dated for about a year, got married in December 1985 in Philadelphia, and she joined me in Germany when the school year was over. Taylor was born in 1993 at Fort Leavenworth, and Jordan followed in 1995 at Fort Hood."

"What about the rest of your career?" I said as I finished my sandwich.

Dana continued, "Not that I want to brag…but I worked really hard to become what I believed was the consummate soldier/scholar. I've been published in *Military Review* and I've written chapters in a few compilation books on leadership in combat. It's sort of funny how things work out. I came through the NTC in 1983 as a scout platoon leader with my battalion out of Fort Riley, and as a squadron commander, and never thought I would come back here, and yet, here I am. I was a troop commander in the 11th Armored Cavalry Regiment, and commanded F Company, 40th Armored in the Berlin Brigade, the largest armored company in the free world. I was awarded the Douglas McArthur Leadership award for US Army Europe in 1990, and later that year, I took command of Delta, 1/37 Armor, one of only three American Canadian Army Trophy team companies. We had all the records for tank gunnery for Europe in 1990, and then Iraq invaded Kuwait in August, so we transitioned from training to prepare for war. We deployed to the 'Sand Box' to prepare for our role in Desert Storm"

316

"I knew that was you I saw on CNN during Desert Storm! That was you, wasn't it?" I interrupted him at that point.

He looked embarrassed, "Yeah that was me. They interviewed me as I was getting my tank company ready before we fought in the largest armored/tank battle in the history of modern warfare. There was even a book written about it, *Iron Soldiers,* where I'm featured as well as Lucille, 'my inscrutable wife.' A nod to the Japanese half of her heritage. Oh boy, she hated that description, and to add insult to injury, the author got her name wrong, called her Louise, her sister's name." Dana laughed. "But through it all – the deployments, advocating for families of Fallen Heroes, Wounded Warriors; uprooting our family every three years, chairing officers wives committees, holding down the home front, and supporting the Army mission – Lucille's been a real trooper and we've become a good Army team."

"Dana, it sounds like you've sacrificed a lot and experienced so much hardship and pain. What kept you going, and what happened after Desert Storm?"

"Well, my faith kept me going. Prayer and the belief that I was in the right place at the right time. Following Desert Storm I went to Command and General Staff College at Fort Leavenworth, and became a 'Jedi Knight' in the School of Advanced Military Studies course. In kind of a strange turn of events, I went to Fort Hood, as the G-3 Operations guy, and worked for Chris' first company commander who was the Division G-3."

"That was pretty cool, did you work for him long?"

"No, not really. While I was at Hood, I got an amazing opportunity when I was nominated to serve as a military aide for President Clinton. I guess my interview went well because I served as a senior military aide and reported to President Bill Clinton for two years."

"Really! You worked for President Clinton? I loved Clinton. You worked in the White House?" I asked.

"Yep, in the WHAMO."

"WHAMO? What's that?"

"I'm sorry, the White House Military Office, WHMO."

He laughed. Dana had a nice laugh.

"So you really did make it to the White House. Just like you said thirty years ago, incredible. So just between you and me, what was Hillary like?"

"She was a really nice person. An amazing woman. Who knows, she might be our next president."

"That would be great. So, it seems like you really enjoyed yourself in that job. Wow, all the people you must have met, and the places you've gone with the President. You've traveled the world!"

"Yep, it was an amazing experience."

"Okay, so where did you go next?"

"After the White House I went on to command the first Reconnaissance, Surveillance and Target Acquisition Squadron at Fort Lewis; was promoted to 0-6 in 2002, and in 2003 commanded a combat brigade in Kosovo, as a part of the peacekeeping mission. I took that same brigade to Iraq for Operation Iraqi Freedom."

"When did you make general?" I asked.

"Let's see, I was promoted to brigadier general last year, and as the Assistant Division Commander-Maneuver for the 1st Infantry Division, I commanded the U.S. Army forces that trained the Iraqi military and security forces for a year. And now, I'm here."

"Wow. You've had quite a career so far, with no end in sight. Your future looks so bright Dana, and I can't tell you how proud I am to have known you and seen how you've made your dreams come true. Your career in the Army is the stuff of legend."

"Well, thank you," Dana said a little embarrassed, "but I want to know what you've been doing over the last thirty years. I was so surprised to see you. Where've you been? Did you ever leave California? Where did you go to college? And, how did you get to be the Director of Auditing at Fort Irwin?"

"So many questions; where do I start?" I mused. "First, I was surprised you recognized me after all this time."

He looked a little embarrassed, "I would've recognized you anywhere. I had your picture on my shelf at West Point for almost two years."

Wow, I thought, *he sounds like he was as affected by our meeting thirty years ago as I was.*

"Okay, I'll start at the beginning, during the best three days of my life – those three days when I met the Transmanauts."

"The best three days of your life?" He seemed incredulous.

"Yeah. Before you guys showed up, I was pretty well resigned to possibly going to college at Cal State San Bernardino, where I first met you all, or some other local college, close to home, like Momma wanted. Momma wanted me to stay home and help her with her job, cleaning other people's houses. But when I met you guys, a whole new perspective on life was presented to me."

"What do you mean?"

"Well," I continued, "you all were different from any local guys I knew in Fontana. You guys were full of life, you were confident, and you had such a different perspective on your place in the world. You guys actually dared to believe that you would have some impact, even on the world stage. I wondered, 'Are all the guys in Texas like these four, or were you four just very special?' I never thought the last time I would see you was from the back of that bus, on the way to Disneyland on graduation night. But just the idea that you all were out there, and that I just knew you were moving forward with your lives gave me the courage to defy my mother and move to Texas."

"You lived in Texas? When? Where?" Dana exclaimed.

"I initially lived in Dallas where I did some modeling, then Texarkana, where I earned an accounting degree from the Texas A&M University system after working as a paralegal."

"A paralegal in Texarkana?" Dana interrupted me. "One of Chris' best friends, Mike, another Kappa, is an assistant DA in Texarkana. Did you know him?"

"I knew of Mike," I said. "He's the first and only African-American ADA in Bowie County – a tough prosecutor."

"Sorry to interrupt you. Please continue."

"Well, I always wanted to get into accounting, so I applied for and eventually earned my MBA."

"That's great Aurianna, I didn't realize you had your MBA."

"Well, that's not all. I applied for and was accepted to law school at Tulane University."

"Wow, did you go?"

"Nope, didn't have the chance to go, but it was nice knowing I could have gone to law school."

"Wow," Dana said. "That's amazing. And all that was because of us? That's wild. I never knew we had such a profound effect on you. You've really done well for yourself Aurianna."

"Thank you. And yes, you did have a profound effect on my life, all four of you," I replied. "I never saw you all again, but I did see you on television every once in a while and knew you were still moving forward with your career."

"What about your personal life Aurianna? I know you had two boys."

"Yes, I have two wonderful sons, Cornelius, Jr., and Calvin, both a little older than Taylor and Jordan. I got married in 1986 to a nice guy named Cornelius in Texarkana. I got married after I wasn't able to find you."

"What do you mean find me?" He inquired.

"Well, the first time was when I asked a friend of mine who was in the Army if he could locate you, and he found you at Fort Riley. I gathered up the courage to call you at your unit and when the soldier went to go get you, I hung up. I was too embarrassed and didn't want to get my face broken. I didn't think you'd remember a simple farm girl from Fontana." I explained.

"Oh, Aurianna," Dana looked thoughtful, "I remember that incident. I got to the phone and there was no one there. The soldier had told me it was a woman, but she didn't identify herself. That was you?"

"Yes," I said. "There was a second time. You know the reason I traveled to Texas in the first place was because of you guys. In 1985 I drove eighteen hours to El Paso with a girlfriend of mine to try to find you one last time before I got married. I couldn't find your old house; I guess you all had moved by then. I called 411 but no Pittards were listed. I even went to your old high school, I remembered the name – Eastwood – hoping someone there might have some information about you, but classes were out and no one was there. I was so disappointed and I felt foolish. I resigned myself to the idea I would never find you, so I went ahead and got married."

"Speaking of looking for one another," Dana said, "you know I did the same thing before I got married."

"What do you mean?" I asked.

"While I was an admissions officer with West Point, in 1984, I was assigned to recruit in California and tried to find you one last time. In fact, I found your house, and no one was home. So I searched late that night until I finally found Latisha's house and left a card and a note with her mother, who assured me she would get it to you. Since I never heard from you, I figured you really weren't interested. So I went ahead and got married the next year."

"I never heard about you coming by in 1984." I said with some emotion, "Had I known, I would have called or something. Well, at least you're still married." I continued, "I got divorced in 1995, and came back to California and got a job in civil service as an auditor here at Fort Irwin, and eventually was promoted to the position of Director of

Auditing."

"That's great," Dana said. "Congratulations! By the way, how's Cee Cee?"

"Cee Cee died several years ago." I still get emotional when I think of Cee Cee dying so young.

"I'm really sorry to hear that. I really liked Cee Cee, and I know you two were extremely close. What about Latisha, what happened to her?"

"After high school, Latisha settled down in Fontana with her high school sweetheart and she's had four kids. She's happy with being a mother and wife, but that just wasn't enough for me."

As I finished my recitation of my career, I know a pained look crossed my face. I was thinking about how different our lives might have been if either of us had been successful in finding the other. I needed to ask him an important question, but wasn't sure how to broach the subject.

"Dana," I began hesitantly, "when you left California, I was under the impression we had a pretty special connection. I wrote you several times, and waited for several months … and I only got one letter from you. What happened? Why didn't you continue to write me?"

"What do you mean?" Now it was Dana's turn to be uncomfortable, "I wrote several letters to you, but you didn't respond. I think I got one letter from you … and then none after that. I just thought you had moved on and forgotten about me."

I was stunned, "I never received more than one letter from you and I sent you several letters. You mean you never got them?"

"Nope," he said. "And you never got mine?"

"No, I didn't get any more than the first one."

"You lived on Oleander right?"

"That's right." I was surprised. "You remembered."

"Of course. I remember everything about you."

We sat there for a moment, silent. I found myself holding my breath; a wave of emotion washing over me.

"Each time I wrote a letter," I exhaled, "I would give it to Momma to mail as I rushed off to work every morning, and then I would check the mail every day for a return letter …but I never got another one after the first letter. I don't know what could have happened to our letters, Dana?"

He looked at me for a moment, various emotions playing across his face. He started to speak, and then a strange calmness came over him.

"You know, I'm a combat veteran; I've led men into battle, felt the flames of war, and seen death and destruction … and known that but for the Grace of God, it would have been me lying dead on the battlefield. Faith and prayer helped sustain me. I prayed that I would bravely lead my soldiers into battle, decimate our enemy, and return my warriors safely home; and I prayed for blessings for my sons, Taylor and Jordan, and that I would have the opportunity to see them grow up. Being in combat gives you a different perspective on life, and makes you appreciate the small things. God does answer prayers Aurianna. I don't know what happened to the letters, and it really doesn't matter. What really matters is that I've had a chance to see you again after all these years."

It took me a moment to answer. " Maybe you're right, it doesn't matter what happened to the letters. I don't know what the future holds, but at least we can be friends ... and we'll always have those three days in '77." A flicker of anger darted through my mind, *Momma, I don't know if you had anything to do with those letters, but if I ever find out you did, I'll never forgive you.*

"Dana, thank you for lunch." I took a deep breath, gathered my things, and slowly pushed myself up from the chair. "This has been the surprise of my life, meeting you again like this. I can't wait to tell Momma about you and the other guys. I know she'll be shocked."

"I'm sure she will." Dana laughed as he stood up. "I'll

bet she never thought she'd hear from us again. It looks like Fate had a different plan."

"You're right about that, she never thought you guys would amount to much. I can't wait to see the expression on her face when I tell her." I smiled at the thought. "Well, I need to get back to work. This has been great." I looked around the office at all his awards and plaques, and all the accoutrements of a general officer.

"It's hard to believe, we stood on my porch thirty years ago not knowing our futures, but you guys had a plan and you succeeded," I said as I turned towards the door.

"Aww, you're successful too Aurianna," Dana protested.

"I know Dana, but *you* guys…" I shook my head and chuckled.

He came around the desk and gave me a brief hug. "I look forward to working with you as my Director of Auditing."

"Thank you," I said, and walked towards the door.

Dana's aide was at the door to escort me out. With one last look around, I left Dana's office. *What if…?* I wondered … *After all this time.*

I left Dana's office thinking about what he said about the letters. I just couldn't let it go. I had to go home and find out what happened to them. Only one person could have sabotaged me like that--Momma!

324

The next day I made the two-hour drive to Momma's house to find out what happened. As I pulled up to the front of the house, I envisioned how the five of us stood on that porch thirty years ago and how those guys talked about their plans for the future. Now I was going to find out what happened to my past. I got out of the car, walked up to the porch and swung the front door open.

Walking inside, I could hear Momma in the kitchen. I

headed straight through the house and surprised her.

"Auriana, baby. What are you doing here?"

"We need to talk," I said.

"Sure baby, what's wrong?'

"In the living room," I demanded, turned and walked out of the kitchen and sat down on the sofa; coincidentally, the same sofa Dana sat on thirty years ago. Momma sat in a chair facing me. I continued, "You know the post I work on, Fort Irwin, has a one-star commanding general now."

"Yes, I read about that somewhere," she replied, not really knowing where this was going.

"He happens to be African-American."

"That's nice, but what's that got to do with me?" Momma had a quizzical expression on her face.

I dropped the bombshell. "His name is Brigadier General Dana James Hillian Pittard, the same guy who sat right here in this room, on this sofa, thirty years ago."

"Oh my God," Momma exclaimed. "You're kidding. What a coincidence. But I still don't know why you had to come home to tell me. You could have just phoned and told me that."

"You're right, I could've just called, but I wanted to see the expression on your face when I told you those four guys from Texas made it."

She looked stunned by the news. "What do you mean?"

"His brother Chris is a successful attorney in Texas. And the other two, Hector and Tony, have also done well. They all finished college, and are successful in their chosen careers. That's why I came home, Momma, just to let you know what happened to those guys."

"Wow, that's pretty amazing," she murmured to herself.

I took a deep breath. "I had a real long conversation with Dana yesterday, and asked him why he stopped sending me letters after his very first one from West Point. He asked

325

me the same question, because he only got my first letter and he didn't receive any more of the several that I sent him." I paused and glared at Momma for emphasis. "I figured that the only way my mail to him could have been stopped was by you; and the only way his mail to me could've been intercepted was by you. That's why I'm home Momma. I need to know the truth." I was practically yelling. "Is that what you did to me? Kept me from communicating with Dana? Tell me the truth!"

Momma didn't say a word as she got up from her chair and walked out of the room. I got up to follow her as she headed out to the garage. She opened the door without a word and went to the very back in the corner and moved a couple of storage boxes out of the way until she found what she was looking for-a shoe box. I stood there at the garage door stupefied...what was this?

She walked back over to me and said, "I'd hoped this day would never come. These are the letters between you and Dana. You're right, when you gave me your letters to mail to him, I never sent them; and whenever he sent you a letter I grabbed it and put it in this shoebox."

I was dumbstruck, "What were you thinking?" Strangely, the first thought that came to my mind was that she had violated federal law by interfering with the U.S. Mail, but more important, WHY?

She answered my question, "I saw how you two acted when you were together. I saw how you looked at each other, like no one else existed. I was afraid he was going to take you away from me, away from your family. So I did everything I could to stop your relationship after he went back to Texas."

326

I couldn't believe what she had just told me. I asked her, "Do you remember a note Dana left for me back in 1984 with Latisha's mother asking me to get in touch with him while he was out here in California?"

"Yes," she said coldly. "It's in there with the letters along with the note he left you in 1977," she continued. "I'm sorry baby, but I thought I was doing the right thing for you."

"You mean for you! You were only thinking about yourself. How could you be so selfish and screw with my life like that?"

Momma repeated, "I'm sorry baby, I really am. But he was ambitious. He was gonna 'be somebody' and men like that don't stay around. They use you and leave you and I didn't want that for you."

"You couldn't know that!" I yelled and snatched the box out of her hands. "Please leave me alone."

Momma turned and without saying another word, walked back out of the garage.

I read each and every one of those letters, remembering the emotions that caused me to write them, the promise of the future in every one of those words written on the page. As I sat there on the garage floor surrounded by all those letters between us, I cried even harder thinking about what could have been, but never was.

After a long while, I eventually gathered up the letters, wiped my face, labored to my feet, and walked disconsolately back in the house. Momma was waiting for me in the sitting room, resting on that same sofa.

I looked at Momma. "I don't know if I'll ever speak to you again. This was despicable and I don't know if I can ever forgive you. You stole my chance at happiness." Without a backward glance, I stormed out of the house and slammed the door behind me. She didn't say a word as I left.

I got into my car and spun out of the yard. Through my tears I looked in my rearview mirror as Momma came out on the porch and watched me drive off.

With my home behind me, I was alone with my thoughts of those three days in 1977 and the whirlwind of events for the past two days, seeing Dana again, finding out what happened to the other guys, and the revelation from Momma. Unbelievable.

I still wasn't sure what to think about Momma, but one thing was sure, she hadn't stopped the Transmanauts from reentering my life, even after thirty years. Fate had prevailed after all that time.

I had to smile through the tears as I drove down I-15 on my way back to Fort Irwin.

The Transmanauts...again...Wow.

Epilogue

On July 10, 2010, the headlines in the *El Paso Times* blared, "Pittard Takes Charge of Post," chronicling the first time an African-American had taken command of Fort Bliss, Texas, and the first time that a commanding general who called El Paso home, took command of Fort Bliss. Thousands were in attendance.

I was there, along with Hector and Tony, and about a hundred of their high school classmates, to watch our fellow Transmanaut, Major General Dana J.H. Pittard, take command of Fort Bliss, and to watch history in the making.

This was also a reunion with Aurianna, the girl we had met on our Road Trip. Aurianna was now an auditor for the U.S. Army at Fort Sam Houston, in the heart of San Antonio, where my family resides; and, in an interesting twist of fate, was conducting an audit at Fort Bliss when Dana took command.

The convergence of our lives at this point in time was the work of Destiny, and a wholly unexpected development from over thirty years before. Who knew?

The five of us had a great reunion following the change of command ceremony. The Transmanauts and Aurianna reminiscing about the Road Trip and the intervening thirty-odd years since those carefree days in California – each of us telling our stories.

The one story that was not told was that of the Trans Am. The magnificent black and gold chariot that was the inspiration for the Road Trip. That car had a personality of its own. It was fast, it was sleek, and it was bad. When I sat in the cockpit, surrounded by the black and gold interior, and staring at the instrument panel, I could almost hear it whispering to me, *Go fast... run the race.* And of course, I did – all the time. I never lost a race.

The Trans Am was also the ultimate chick magnet. Whenever I showed up in that car, it attracted the attention of the fairer sex. I drove the Trans Am for two years across this great country with the main objective to visit women – from Atlanta, to Connecticut, to Virginia, Maryland, Philadelphia, New York, Texas, and everywhere in between. I really loved that car. Unfortunately, it was repoed as a casualty of my parent's divorce, and ended up in the boneyard of fast cars--a sad end to a great car.

I eventually got another sports car, a beautiful 1982 Toyota Supra, that was wrecked on my wedding day…but that's another story. Make no mistake, it was not a Special Edition Trans Am – for me there'll never be another car like the Trans Am or another year like 1977.

This is an end to the Road Trip that could not have been written in 1977. The Transmanauts – Chris, Dana, Hector and Tony – survived this coming of age experience, and grew up to be responsible men, husbands, and fathers – successful in their chosen fields.

Bonds that were forged so long ago had a deeper resonance than we ever suspected. These bonds – though stressed and strained at times – were forged for a lifetime.

But life still holds surprises, and the *full* story of the Transmanauts is yet to be told.